Popper

For Karen

POPPER

Philosophy, Politics and Scientific Method

Geoffrey Stokes

Polity Press

First published in 1998 by Polity Press
in association with Blackwell Publishers Ltd.

Editorial office:
Polity Press
65 Bridge Street
Cambridge CB2 1UR, UK

Marketing and production:
Blackwell Publishers Ltd
108 Cowley Road
Oxford OX4 1JF, UK

Published in the USA by:
Blackwell Publishers Inc.
Commerce Place
350 Main Street
Malden, MA 02148, USA

ISBN 0-7456-0321-1
ISBN 0-7456-0322-X (pbk)

A catalogue record for this book is available from the British Library and has been applied for from the Library of Congress.

Typeset in 10½ on 12 pt Palatino
by Ace Filmsetting Ltd, Frome, Somerset
Printed in Great Britain by T J International, Padstow, Cornwall

This book is printed on acid-free paper.

Key Contemporary Thinkers

Published

Forthcoming

Contents

Acknowledgements

Various parts of this work were completed for different purposes in a number of universities. I must therefore acknowledge the support of the Department of Politics at Flinders University, the School of Social Inquiry at Murdoch University, the Center for the History and Philosophy of Science at Boston University, the Division of Humanities at Griffith University and the Department of Government in the University of Queensland. This book draws on portions of material published in three papers: 'Karl Popper's Political Philosophy of Science', *Philosophy of the Social Sciences* 27(1) 1997; 'Politics, Epistemology and Method: Karl Popper's Conception of Human Nature', *Political Studies* 43(1) 1995; and 'From Physics to Biology: Rationality in Popper's Conception of Evolutionary Epistemology', in K. Hahlweg and C. A. Hooker (eds), *Issues in Evolutionary Epistemology* (SUNY, 1989). I would also like to thank Mr and Mrs Mew and the estate of Karl Popper for permission to quote from his published works.

I must express my appreciation to Rodney Allen, Bill Brugger, April Carter, Robert S. Cohen, John Forge, Toby Huff, Tatsuo Inoue, John Kane, Martin Leet, Jeremy Shearmur, Matti Sintonen, Bas van Fraassen, Tom Wilson and Richard Yeo, who each took the time to comment upon different drafts of chapters of this book. Unfortunately, I could not accommodate all their criticisms and I remain responsible for any errors or misinterpretations. Thanks are due to Anthony Giddens, who encouraged me to write the book and who was patient enough to accept the seemingly endless delays in submitting the manuscript. I am also grateful to Rob Imre and Jeremy

Chenoweth for their invaluable research assistance. I owe a special debt to my wife Karen Gillen for keeping me to the task and also for editing and proofreading the manuscript and preparing the index.

Abbreviations

From the Postscript to The Logic of Scientific Discovery. Ed. W. W. Bartley III. London: Hutchinson.

SB   K. R. Popper and J. C. Eccles. 1981 [1977]. *The Self and its Brain.* Corrected. Berlin: Springer International.

UQ   K. R. Popper. 1976. *Unended Quest: An Intellectual Autobiography.* London: Fontana / Collins.

Preface

This work aims to broaden our understanding of the philosophy of Karl Popper (1902–94). It is one of the few studies to present Popper's work as an evolving 'system of ideas', and to take account of the wider range of his writings. The book also offers a critical analysis of the achievements and shortcomings of Popper's philosophy.

Popper's ideas have won acceptance and provoked controversy among an academic as well as a more general audience. For this reason, his work has received much critical attention in, for example, books by Magee (1973), Ackermann (1976), O'Hear (1980), Burke (1983), Williams (1989) and Shearmur (1996). Given the prominence of Popper's arguments about knowledge, there is a tendency among critics to regard his social and political thought as primarily founded upon epistemology (e.g. see Burke 1983: ix). It is claimed, for example, that Popper's political prescriptions are drawn from analysis of the ideal behaviour of scientists and the operation of the best kinds of scientific community. Certainly there is something to be said for this interpretation, but it offers only a partial insight into the conceptual relations between the various components of Popper's philosophy. Furthermore, such an interpretation encourages us to neglect the vital role that non-epistemic values play in the formation of Popper's epistemology and methodology. Analysis of the broader doctrine of 'critical rationalism' – a title applied retrospectively by Popper and others – aims to demonstrate how his social and political values establish the character and limits of his epistemological project as well as those for much of the rest of his philosophy.

Popper's philosophy offers a series of responses to a number of interrelated problem situations in modern epistemology, methodology and politics. Accordingly, I have tried to organize this examination of his work into chapters on problems as they arise in his writings. Along the way reference will be made to key debates and criticisms of his work. It should be noted also that Popper's arguments usually begin with critiques of doctrines, such as historicism, that he wants to refute and reject. Because of constraints on space, this study does not examine these critiques in detail, focusing primarily on his more substantive proposals.

The first chapter deals with the conceptual relationship between politics, epistemology and methodology. Chapter 2 indicates the political origins of Popper's early concern for epistemology. The third chapter analyses his epistemological investigations of the 1920s and 1930s. The main focus is upon the doctrine of falsificationism set out in *The Logic of Scientific Discovery* (originally *Logik der Forschung*), but it also considers later elaborations and criticism of those arguments. Chapter 4 enquires into Popper's social and political theory, and chapter 5 examines his early philosophy of social science. Most of the sources for these studies are writings that Popper completed in the 1930s and 1940s as a response to the political problems of the time. Based on works published since the early 1950s, chapter 6 outlines Popper's attempted solutions to the metaphysical questions partially arising from tensions between his epistemology and the priority given to freedom in his political philosophy. A key source is his *Postscript to The Logic of Scientific Discovery*. Chapter 7 explores how these metaphysical conjectures influenced a distinctive, 'evolutionary' reformulation of Popper's epistemology and theory of rationality. Chapter 8 considers the problems of rationality, politics and ethics in the context of debates between the Frankfurt School of critical theory and critical rationalism.

Geoffrey Stokes
Brisbane

1

Introduction: Politics, Epistemology and Methodology

It is a disturbing fact that even an abstract study like pure epistemology is not as pure as one might think . . . but that its ideas may, to a large extent, be motivated and unconsciously inspired by political hopes and Utopian dreams . . . As an epistemologist I have only one interest – to find out the truth about the problems of epistemology, whether or not this truth fits in with my political ideas. But am I not liable to be influenced, unconsciously, by my political hopes and dreams? (*CR*: 6)

Karl Popper is a philosopher of knowledge and politics, of rationality and freedom. In his work we find theories of scientific rationality and principles for the conduct of politics. Popper's methodological doctrines provide an influential normative programme for the scientific study of nature and society. He also offers compelling arguments against political authoritarianism and in support of liberal democracy. Popper is a pivotal philosopher of modernity and the Enlightenment. This is especially evident in his aim to provide a general theory of critical reason and his advocacy of personal moral responsibility in the 'open society'. In his later work Popper provides a metaphysical account of the place of mind and self in an 'open universe', a world characterized by indeterminism. This later philosophy is set within an evolutionary account of human nature and the growth of knowledge.

A constant theme in Popper's work is the importance of philosophy for understanding and solving the practical problems of the world. Of particular concern have been the links between philosophy and politics. Popper considers that even theories of knowledge are intertwined with political hopes and dreams. Accordingly, his epistemology has express political import. It is part of a project to examine critically the theoretical underpinnings of political ideologies and movements. This chapter sets out the interpretative method to be adopted. It then offers an overview of the interrelationships between politics, epistemology and methodology, and indicates their place in Popper's work.

Aims and Method

The major aim of this study is to present Popper's philosophy as a 'system of ideas' whose progressive unfolding reveals a more general philosophy of life and cosmology. A further goal is to analyse his philosophy with reference to its coherence, persuasiveness and suitability to its own avowed goals. Popper has provided the general interpretative method whereby we may examine his work. On his account, any serious theory is an attempt to solve a particular theoretical or practical problem. He proposes that any rational analysis should proceed from an investigation of both the nature of the problem and the particular problem situation in which thinkers locate themselves (*CR*: 197; *QTSP*: 200). A problem situation may be regarded as the intellectual context – philosophical, scientific or historical – within which we locate a problem. Our point of departure, therefore, is an interpretation of the problems and problem situations which engaged Popper's intellectual energy. Such an approach is possible because he has often pointed out the coherence, continuities and changes in his ideas.

Investigating a thinker's intention and context is not an uncontroversial strategy in the history of ideas.[1] Taking this path, however, allows for an immanent critique which focuses primarily upon internal coherence, consistency and appropriateness to theoretical or practical goals. An external critique based upon different assumptions would complement this strategy but is not essential to it. Such a critique could conceivably be undertaken through a materialist history of ideas which demonstrated how Popper's philosophy itself was a form of 'ideology', understood in the Marxian sense as illusion that disguises oppressive social and economic realities. Foucault's analysis of 'regimes of truth' as discourses of power could also contribute resources for another kind of external critique. But these are projects that lie more within the sociology of knowledge and are different from what is attempted here. My argument, however, owes a debt to critical theory and the work of Jürgen Habermas, who articulates the idea of epistemology as social theory. For reasons that are set out in chapter 8, however, I do not regard critical theory as supplying an external critique of Popper's work.

Key Concepts

Given the centrality of politics, epistemology and methodology to this study, a brief discussion of these terms is necessary. I take the term politics in its broadest classical sense to refer to those theories and practices oriented towards pursuit of the good life. In contemporary usage the word 'politics' generally refers to those activities concerned with the exercise of political power and strategies for achieving political goals. An argument may also be called political which aims at the clarification of values and principles guiding the conduct of government, or which provides an account of an ideal society and polity.

I take epistemology to mean the philosophical study of the definitions, foundations and validity of knowledge. This project is normative and prescriptive. Its goal is to devise a set of epistemic values to guide the creation and acquisition of knowledge. Such values constitute a cognitive ethic or 'code of intellectual deportment' which shapes human practices for acquiring knowledge (Gellner 1976: 165). Epistemologists propose criteria such as accuracy, coherence or consistency, for what counts as good or bad, true or false, rational or irrational, forms of knowledge. An empiricist epistemology, for example, requires good knowledge to be based primarily on experience, that is, evidence derived from observation or other senses. By comparison, a rationalist would argue for the importance of a priori reason, formal logic or theory, in advancing knowledge. A rationalist epistemology would rely on the use of logically consistent or coherent knowledge founded primarily upon philosophical reason or, in the case of science, the theoretical ordering of experience. Most epistemologies, including Popper's, incorporate varying degrees of commitment to both empiricism and rationalism. Epistemology may also prescribe ideal forms of explanation or the types of relations to be sought after between theory and evidence.

Methodology refers to the study of the forms of reasoning in substantive disciplinary fields of enquiry, and their application in formulating *general* rules of practical procedure. The most common models are those drawn from analysis of scientific practice, and may include, for example, the experimental method, or, in Popper's case, the method of conjecture and refutation. Selecting a methodology will depend in part on the epistemological or practical goal (Caws 1967: 339). It will also depend upon its appropriateness to the discipline, such as natural or social science and sub-fields within them.

Debate can occur over the kinds of methodologies, such as induction and deduction, best suited to meeting specified epistemological criteria. Studies in methodology, therefore, can be both descriptive and prescriptive. Methodology must, however, be distinguished from 'method' in the sense of specific research techniques – such as those of sampling, statistical analysis, participant observation – used to collect and analyse evidence in a particular discipline.[2]

As we shall see in chapter 2, Popper's early work takes epistemology to be virtually synonymous with methodology, which in turn is held to be equivalent to the 'logic of scientific method'. Research into epistemology and methodology is part of a larger philosophical project which aims to provide an account of rationality, in the sense of rules for rational enquiry and rational action. In the twentieth century, Popper's work is arguably the most highly developed and systematic form of this tradition of rational criticism. Most commentators have also stressed the unity, if not the coherence, of Popper's thought, and the indissoluble tie between his epistemology, methodology and politics.[3]

Epistemology and Politics

The normative conceptions of epistemology and methodology constitute the intellectual core of Popper's work. He aimed to provide an objectivist theory of knowledge and methodology which provided non-arbitrary, theoretical criteria for choosing between competing hypotheses in natural and social science. As a consequence, much attention has been devoted to analysing his recommendations for the philosophy of natural science. But the application of his doctrines to social and political questions has also attracted controversy. Popper's epistemology has become a key intellectual resource in struggles between different political ideologies such as liberalism and Marxism.

The political appeal of Popper's political arguments may be attributed to their foundations in epistemology and science. Epistemology appears to offer a higher set of standards for appraising the quality of arguments based upon empirical theories and facts, or upon moral or interpretive argument, *and* for adjudicating between them. At its simplest, the better the underlying epistemology, the more rational an argument is deemed to be.

Herein lies the attraction of Popper's proposal that scientific theories ought to be empirically falsifiable. This is not simply a guide to the scientific study of the physical or natural world. To the extent that it helps clarify competing epistemological, empirical and metaphysical claims, falsifiability is also an instrument for resolving social and political problems which rely upon those claims. The intellectual authority of falsificationism derives from its apparent capacity to unmask the claims of 'ideologies', conceived pejoratively as systems of thought or political doctrines which are dogmatic or closed to criticism. In these instrumentalist terms, Popper's epistemology has explicit political intentions and consequences.

One of the problems with this instrumentalist interpretation, however, is that it assumes a conception of epistemology which is value-free or neutral between conflicting political goals. The focus upon the purely instrumental role of theories of knowledge obscures our understanding of the recursive and evolving relations between politics, epistemology and methodology in the work of any thinker.[4] Epistemology may set norms for the rational appraisal of theories, but these are embedded in a wider set of values guiding social interaction and communication. As the analysis in this book aims to demonstrate, epistemology comprises, and, indeed, requires, certain non-epistemic ethical norms, such as honesty and toleration, without which the epistemic norms would be unworkable. Theories of knowledge may therefore be both instrumentally and inherently political.

Argument

Examples of the ways in which politics pervades epistemology may be found through study of Popper's philosophy. Yet, he suggests that, in searching out the 'truth' of his epistemology, he is not interested in whether it 'fits in with' his political ideas (*CR*: 6). But, if this 'truth' (which for Popper would always be provisional) did not fit in with his political ideas, a decision would have to be made about whether to modify or reject either his political ideas or the epistemology. It is my argument that Popper's commitment to certain political values such as freedom and toleration are conceptually prior to any epistemological commitments. Evidence for this claim may be found within the larger doctrine of critical rationalism which articulates meta-philosophical arguments for choosing between competing epistemologies. Such arguments are generally of a moral and political nature, and are based upon the possible consequences that epistemologies may have for society and politics. Although epistemology and methodology are key components in Popper's thought, their character is determined by their role and relevance within a political philosophy.

For these reasons an epistemology cannot be regarded as a neutral instrument, but rather one which more or less reflects political values and commitments. This interpretation receives support from analysis of the evolution of Popper's philosophy, where it is evident that his earliest and most enduring concerns were moral and political. In accord with Popper, I am not arguing that the historical or psychological origins of his philosophy have any direct bearing upon their truth, falsity or utility. Nor do I want to reduce Popper's epistemology to politics or social theory. The aim is to indicate the key intellectual components and priorities in his thought, to show how they form a complex whole, and how they lead to certain problems and inconsistencies.[5]

It should be stressed at the outset that the conceptual relationship between epistemology and other political values and assumptions is rarely formal or deductive. Such ideas often operate more as a set of presuppositions or premises which set the limits or possibilities for epistemology. Depending upon the line of argument, for example, certain metaphysical doctrines about the character of the world and its knowable objects represent key a priori assumptions required for epistemology or methodology. Just as a metaphysical doctrine may be said to 'endorse' or 'sanction' a political doctrine (Watkins 1958: 81), so also may the latter endorse epistemological and methodological doctrines.

It will be argued that Popper's politics are constitutive of, or contained within, his more technical epistemological project. Not only does his epistemology contribute instrumentally to the achievement of political values such as freedom, but it also embodies certain political values such as the ethics of criticism, self-criticism and toleration. Just as important, the epistemology presupposes the existence of liberal democratic political institutions which guarantee freedom of thought and expression. Popper's theory of knowledge is also predicated upon a particular view of human weaknesses and capacities, as well as a theory of history and politics. Accordingly, it is necessary to devote more attention to his substantive moral and political theory than is usually the case.

Despite his qualms about political contamination, Popper allows that epistemology does not exist in any pure form, even in his own work (*CR*: 30). The structure and evolution of his philosophy is permeated by his political intent to promote the values of the 'open society'. We may also explain important shifts of intellectual interest and direction in Popper's work as resulting from his conscious and unconscious awareness of key ethical and political concerns. Such modifications are not just the result of narrowly epistemological investigations; they arise from attempts both to refine his epistemology *and* reconcile it with his political principles. By building upon what was often only implicit in his early work, Popper develops a theory of rationality and freedom which attempts to maintain a coherence between the political and the epistemological.

2

Popper's Project: Problem and Method

The major epistemological goal of Karl Popper's early intellectual work was to construct a criterion for distinguishing between science and pseudo-science. In carrying out this task he also formulated standards for choosing between competing scientific theories. Popper's search for a criterion of demarcation became a larger project to develop a normative theory of scientific rationality. By providing objective and universal standards for progress in knowledge, scientific rationality precluded appeals to subjective preference, intellectual intuition or personal faith. In so doing, scientific rationality appeared to avoid the problems of dogmatism and relativism, and provide better reasons for its conclusions and practical successes. With his analysis of the rational growth of scientific knowledge, Popper hoped to solve the problem of the rational evaluation of other forms of knowledge. This project also had the political objective to overcome those forms of dogmatism that led to violence. Popper was therefore attempting to solve a number of different problems at the same time. This chapter outlines Popper's initial problem situation and discusses various critiques of the method he uses to establish his project.

Historical and Intellectual Background

The problems that originally prompted Popper to his philosophical vocation arose out of the political and intellectual ferment surrounding World War I and its aftermath. His encounters with

Marxian socialism, the psychological theories of Sigmund Freud and Alfred Adler, and the scientific discoveries of Albert Einstein each left a deep impression upon him. In formulating solutions to questions surrounding epistemology, Popper also drew upon the philosophy of Kant, and notions about philosophy, science and politics that were dominant within the Vienna Circle. Marxism and Freudianism posed formidable critiques of the core liberal values of human rationality, free individual choice and personal moral responsibility. Because both theories were also buttressed by their claims to scientific status they attracted wider intellectual support. Although European philosophers had long been concerned with determining the correct method of science, the question had acquired new significance before and after the war in Europe. On the resolution of this issue hinged a number of other vital political decisions.

Popper (*UQ*: 33) claims that a particularly disturbing series of events prompted him to develop a politically responsible epistemology. For several months in 1919 he considered himself to be a Marxist and a communist. He understood Marxist theory as demanding the intensification of the class struggle in order to bring about the stage of socialism more rapidly. This meant accepting that the revolution would inevitably claim some victims, but that they would be fewer than those claimed by capitalism. Popper's theoretical acceptance of such violent possibilities dissolved after he witnessed a demonstration by young socialists and communists in which several of the participants were shot and killed. Although shocked by the actions of the police, he was even more horrified at what he considered to be his own personal moral responsibility for the tragic event. The problem for Popper lay in the Marxist claim that its social and economic theory was based upon scientific principles, and its presumed knowledge of 'the laws of historical development' (*UQ*: 33). Popper had accepted these theories uncritically, partly out of loyalty to his friends and 'the cause' (*UQ*: 34). As he saw it, his dogmatism had unwittingly helped to promote violence and the loss of life. Popper immediately repudiated Marxism, although he remained a socialist for many years (*UQ*: 34). His awareness of the link between a 'dogmatic' approach to knowledge and politically inspired violence was a major catalyst in his intellectual development. Although ideas are always important, it appeared that ideas about knowledge had a far more crucial role in politics. Epistemologies could either encourage or discourage personal moral responsibility, or promote peaceful or violent social change.

Popper dates his formal concern with epistemology from autumn 1919, when he became interested in how to determine the scientific character of a theory. He wanted to discover the differences between the seemingly scientific theories of Einstein and the allegedly 'pseudo-scientific' theories of Karl Marx, Freud and Adler (*CR*: 33–4). The latter were impressive because of their apparent explanatory power and their psychological impact (*CR*: 34–5). Yet, Einstein's theory had just as powerful a psychological and intellectual influence upon Popper. The core epistemological and methodological principles of Popper's philosophy were derived from analysis of the implications of Einstein's revolutionary discoveries in theoretical physics (*UQ*: 37).

The important insight that Popper (*UQ*: 38) gained from Einstein was his apparent willingness to consider his theory untenable if it did not withstand certain tests.[1] Popper saw this attitude as quite different from the alleged dogmatism of Marx, Freud and Adler, who, on Popper's account, did not attempt to investigate the conditions under which their theories might be false.[2] Popper concluded that the correct scientific attitude was one that risked the theory, as distinct from the dogmatic or pseudo-scientific attitude that looked for confirmations. At first sight, this 'critical attitude' appears more akin to a psychological characteristic. It is, however, a form of cognitive ethic which Popper adapted into the specific methodological precept that one must seek crucial tests that could refute a theory (*UQ*: 41). Such was the ethical insight that became the foundation of Popper's fallibilist epistemology and his falsificationist philosophy of scientific method.

The question of what distinguished science from pseudo-science was for Popper a 'genuine' philosophical problem and not simply a matter for abstract theoretical speculation. In his deliberations, he was guided by his understanding of the Prussian philosopher, Immanuel Kant.[3] Popper remarks that the problem of demarcation, or the limits of scientific knowledge, was also Kant's problem (*LScD*: 34, 313). Like Kant, Popper thought that its solution had serious ramifications for both scientific method and politics. Kant's idea of enlightenment – understood as a process of self-emancipation through knowledge – was decidedly political. Improved powers of reason were vital for overcoming the human propensities for error, superstition and prejudice, and thereby promoting social progress (Reiss 1970: 5).

These common political concerns of Kant and Popper arose from their responses to the political and intellectual turmoil of their respective eras. In Popper's account, inspiration for their theories came from similar sources, namely, the revolutionary scientific achievements of their day. Just as Kant had effectively criticized Baconian philosophy of science by drawing out the implications of Newton's theories, so also Popper based his conception of scientific method upon the achievements and approach of Einstein, which, in turn, had effectively revised the Newtonian schema. By extending the Kantian ethic of self-criticism to epistemology, Popper (*CR*: 26–7) saw his own philosophy of critical rationalism as putting 'the finishing touches to Kant's own critical philosophy'.

The Philosophy of the Vienna Circle

By the time Popper began discussing his ideas with members of the predominant philosophical school of his day, the Vienna Circle, he saw himself as an unorthodox Kantian and a realist (*UQ*: 82). As a result, he found himself in conflict with several major tenets of the Vienna Circle, but the differences were not as wide as is usually thought. His efforts to make sense of science and scientific method clearly reflected the philosophical assumptions of that group. Those in the Vienna Circle also shared a concern for the damaging political consequences of dogmatic thinking. Its members stressed the social function of philosophy for overcoming irrationality and ideological fanaticism. Of particular importance was the idea that 'ideological claims should be tested by scientific methods' (Kolakowski 1972: 208). In a world of bitter and violent political conflict, the scientific attitude and its method for arriving at knowledge offered an effective antidote to the claims of contemporary ideologies such as Marxism and fascism (Kolakowski 1972: 237). The rationality of empirical science also had a vital role to play in combating the dogma and metaphysics of reactionary forms of theology (Ravetz 1984: 6). For this doctrine, known as logical positivism, science was the model for all human knowledge.

In accord with the members of the Vienna Circle, Popper accepted the premise that philosophical problems existed at three main levels of analysis. First, there were questions of empirical fact whose solutions were the province of the special or empirical sciences. Second, there was the problem of the representation of those empirical questions, that is, the question of the language to be used in understanding the empirical problems. Such issues could only be settled by clarifying concepts and propositions, and this was the task of philosophy. Finally, there were metaphysical questions that could neither be put into the language of science nor rendered into scientific problems (Kraft 1953: 191–2).

The members of the Vienna Circle were concerned to demarcate between positive science and speculative metaphysics. In this project, epistemology was the enquiry into the logical structure of scientific knowledge with the objective of distinguishing meaningful from meaningless discourse (Kraft 1953: 26). Philosophy became synonymous with epistemology, which in turn became synonymous with the logical analysis of scientific knowledge. The central task of philosophy was to engage in the logical analysis of 'concepts, propositions, proofs, hypotheses, [and] theories of science' (Kraft 1953: 26). The empiricism of the Vienna Circle lay in the proposition: 'Statements about reality can be valid only on the basis of experience' (Kraft 1953: 16). Members of the Vienna Circle attempted to solve their demarcation problem by proposing that empirical verifiability be the necessary condition of both the meaningfulness of a statement and its scientific status (Quinton 1967: 398).

Popper differed from the Vienna Circle in that he was not interested in distinguishing between sense and nonsense, science and metaphysics. He was aware that metaphysical speculation could lead to scientific hypotheses, and that certain sorts of knowledge made sense and had meaning although they were not scientific (*LScD*: 38). Popper's achievement in this regard was to shift the emphasis in demarcation from the logical or linguistic clarification of statements to the analysis of the *methods* used in confronting them with empirical evidence. While generally accepting that how one represented empirical questions was central, he thought that linguistic analysis was no more than one of the tools to be used in assessing how one chose between competing theories (*LScD*: 15–16).

From Popper's perspective, knowledge was rational and 'objective' primarily according to whether it could be formulated in certain kinds of statements that were also open to public scrutiny and discussion. Subjective knowledge, exemplified as 'feelings of conviction' about a theory or possible evidence in support of it, was only of interest to science if it could be formulated into public statements, and, preferably, testable ones (*LScD*: 99). Neither the intensity of such feelings nor their accumulative weight could be called upon to support or reject a scientific statement. Popper also shared with the Vienna Circle the belief that little of epistemological significance could be gained by enquiry into the behaviour and procedures of scientists, as this would have constituted an unacceptable naturalism or 'appeal to experience' (*LScD*: 50–3). Regarding the question of empiricism and the importance given to the construction of scientific statements, Popper remained close to the Vienna Circle's philosophy of logical positivism (Kraft 1974: 187).

Certainty and Induction

Part of the process of demarcating science from pseudo-science required reappraisal of the principles that had guided past scientific practice. Einstein's discoveries had thrown the problem into sharper relief. His theoretical achievements did not appear to fit the previously dominant model of scientific rationality, and the growth of scientific knowledge no longer appeared to be an orderly process. Einstein's theory amounted to a virtual revolution in which many of the old concepts such as time, mass and length had to be radically reinterpreted. More significantly, it undermined two key philosophical assumptions of scientific method: that science should aim at certainty and that it should proceed by the logic of induction. If such an established and technologically useful set of scientific theories as Newton's could be overthrown, then any other apparently hegemonic scientific world-view could suffer a similar fate. Popper considered science could no longer have as its prime goal the certainty of its knowledge. On the historical evidence, scientific knowledge was always open to revision and refutation.

Just as important, the principle of induction no longer seemed a secure foundation upon which to base scientific method. Previous quests for greater certainty had rested upon the inductive or accumulative character of scientific knowledge. Induction is the inference of universal statements or propositions from a set of singular or particular statements such as the accounts of results of observations or experiments (*LScD*: 27). Scientific laws seemed to be based upon inductive methods where the accumulation of past experiences allowed one to make predictions of the future. Popper found that many scientists and philosophers of science accepted induction as providing the criterion of demarcation for the empirical sciences (*CR*: 52). For such thinkers, the logic of scientific discovery was identical to the 'logical analysis' of inductive methods (*LScD*: 27).

Following David Hume, Popper argued that, from a strictly logical point of view, we are not justified in inferring universal statements from singular ones. Any conclusion drawn by this method may always turn out to be false: 'no matter how many instances of white swans we may have observed, this does not justify the conclusion that *all* swans are white' (*LScD*: 27).[4] Accordingly, whatever its alleged practical indispensability for science, the principle of induction does not have any logical validity. Popper also rejected its reformulation in terms of providing a degree of probability for scientific statements. In place of the traditional core epistemological principles of induction and verifiability, Popper proposed testability or falsifiability. He argued that whereas universal theories are not deducible from singular statements, 'they may be refuted by singular statements, since they may clash with descriptions of observable facts' (*UQ*: 86). He would only admit a system as empirical and scientific if it was capable of being tested or refuted by experience (*LScD*: 41–2). In effect, Popper dissolved the old problem of induction, or at least reformulated it in such a way that his solution was appropriate.

Epistemological Goals and Method

Although primarily concerned with the specific problem of demarcation, Popper argued that his solutions could be extended to the wider philosophical problems of epistemology which 'should be identified with the theory of scientific method' (*LScD*: 49). As he later testified, the problem of the growth of knowledge was 'the central problem of epistemology', and this could best be studied '*by studying the growth of scientific knowledge*' (*LScD*: 15).[5] Popper's specific goal was, 'to establish the rules, or . . . the norms, by which the scientist is guided when he is engaged in research or in discovery' (*LScD*: 50). Yet, the standards for ascertaining the growth of scientific knowledge were to be formulated largely in terms of logic (*LScD*: 52). Popper's project therefore was primarily normative and prescriptive rather than empirical and descriptive. By drawing out the standards of rationality in science, his goal was to provide a 'logic' of scientific discovery, that is, to give a 'logical analysis' of the procedure whereby a scientist 'constructs hypotheses, or systems of theories, and tests them against experience by observation and experiment' (*LScD*: 27).

Following the Vienna Circle, Popper was concerned with what may be called the 'reconstructed logic' of a scientific research programme. His task was to extract and refine the essence of scientific method, and so construct an idealization of it. Scientific practice could then be measured against this ideal model. Given his objectivism, Popper explicitly dissociated himself from reconstructing the psychology of discovery, whose focus was the subjective processes involved in the stimulation and release of an inspiration (*LScD*: 31). His prescriptions for scientific method are derived from a rational reconstruction of the objective results of scientific practice. In an important sense, the English title of Popper's first book is therefore a misnomer. It is not about the logic of 'discovery' in its more commonly accepted psychological meaning, but about the logic and context of 'justification', a term that Popper would repudiate because of its overtones of certainty.

Popper was not interested in reconstructing everyday scientific practice. Instead, he focused upon the 'heroic' science of Galileo, Kepler, Einstein and Bohr (Popper 1974b: 977). With Einstein as the outstanding example, Popper's task was to reconstruct one of the most formidable scientific achievements of twentieth-century physical science, and present its 'logic' as the epitome of science and scientific rationality. He aimed to elaborate a conception of scientific rationality that was objectivist and based primarily upon the logical analysis of the statements of science. To this extent, Popper's methodology may be characterized as strongly, but not exclusively, 'formalist' or 'logicist'.[6] That is, although he relied upon applied logic, he was also concerned with 'decisions about the way in which scientific statements are to be dealt with' (*LScD*: 49). This approach rejected the use of any external or 'informal' criteria taken from the psychology, history or sociology of science, for assessing the growth of scientific knowledge. Popper's model of scientific rationality is therefore not concerned with the whole range of reasons why scientists accept or reject theories; rather, it prescribes how scientists ought to behave if they are to remain scientists.

In the priority he gave to theory in science, and the primacy of logic in formulating prescriptions for scientific rationality, Popper was a rationalist. He rejected the assumption of naive empiricism that all knowledge arose from sense data and its reliance upon crude appeals to experience. Yet, he still wanted his epistemology and theory of method to be classified as empirical:

> My empiricism consisted in the view that, though all experience was theory-impregnated, it was experience which in the end could decide the fate of a theory, by knocking it out; and also in the view that only such theories which in principle were capable of being thus refuted merited to be counted among the theories of 'empirical science'. (1974b: 971)

Popper's epistemology aimed to dispense with induction, subjectivism and the quest for certainty, while remaining empirical. The methodology was to be normative in that it set a series of standards, not only for the appraisal of already formulated theories, but also for the construction of such theories. Central among these was the requirement that scientific statements be constructed in such a way that they were falsifiable.

Falsifiability derives its methodological virtue from the logical principle of *modus tollens* and provides the core of Popper's epistemology and methodology (*LScD*: 41). Whereas it is impossible to verify universal statements on the basis of past singular statements, the deductive inference of *modus tollens* allows universal statements to be refuted by the acceptance of a basic or singular statement. There is therefore an essential asymmetry between verifiability and falsifiability. Similar to the logical positivism of the Vienna Circle, Popper's epistemology is based upon a distinction between 'analytic' statements, like the rules of logic that are true by definition and independent of matters of fact, and 'synthetic' statements whose truths are grounded in fact. Once a statement has been put into falsifiable form, it can only be rejected if its empirical or 'synthetic' claims are shown to be false. Where application of other methodological rules (to be discussed in the next chapter) may be open to discussion and interpretation, the rules of deductive logic are held to be unassailable (*LScD*: 42).

Meta-epistemological Critique

This account of Popper's initial project raises the issue of how we may criticize and choose between competing epistemologies and methodologies. In the terms outlined in the previous chapter, one could generally appeal to epistemology as the arbiter. For example, a methodology would be preferred which had greater epistemological virtue, such as greater promise of providing coherent or consistent knowledge. But given the virtual equivalence of epistemology and methodology in Popper's early work, we must ask whether there are any meta-epistemological (or perhaps meta-methodological) criteria available. In this regard, Popper's criteria are less definitive. The statements outlining them are neither formal (analytic) nor empirical (synthetic), and could be called philosophical or metaphysical. For Popper, they have the character of 'conventions' or proposals for agreement: 'As to the suitability of any such convention opinions may differ; and a reasonable discussion of these questions is only possible between parties having some purpose in common. The choice of that purpose must, of course, be ultimately a matter of decision, going beyond rational argument' (*LScD*: 37). Popper readily grants that his choice has been guided by his value judgements:

> But I hope that my proposals may be acceptable to those who value not only logical rigour but also freedom from dogmatism; who seek practical applicability, but are even more attracted by the adventure of science, and by discoveries which again and again confront us with new and unexpected questions, challenging us to try out new and hitherto un-dreamed-of answers. (*LScD*: 38)

The choice of norms or methods will depend, he notes, 'upon the *aim* which we choose from among a number of possible aims' (*LScD*: 49). However such goals and values are selected, meta-epistemological or meta-methodological argument is required to appraise whether the substantive epistemology or methodology contributes to promoting them.

The account above indicates some of the varied theoretical and practical criteria by which Popper's epistemological and methodological proposals may be evaluated. His prescriptions can be appraised in terms of internal logical consistency; epistemic consequences, namely their capacity to illuminate and resolve problems in epistemology (*LScD*: 38, 55); and their contribution to understanding the rationality of past scientific achievements. Finally, Popper encourages us to appraise his proposals against the dual values of practical utility for science *and* promoting 'freedom from dogmatism'. All these criteria are essential to Popper's problem situation.

Contrary to the view of one critic (Nola 1987: 450), the values Popper writes about are not solely methodological or epistemic. As we have seen from the outline of his intellectual biography, the value 'freedom from dogmatism' is expressly political, although substantial content needs to be given to the phrase. Popper's first published book, *The Logic of Scientific Discovery* (1934; first English translation, 1959), provides only a bare indication of what a sophisticated theory of science and politics might look like. In later works, however, he expands upon such issues (*PH*; *OSE I*; *OSE II*; *CR*). For example, he argues clearly for the rejection of the 'authoritarian' epistemologies of Bacon and Descartes because of their potentially violent political consequences (*CR*: 3–30). A criterion for appraisal would be whether such rules promoted authoritarian values or those of freedom and toleration.

A first critical task is to appraise the general method and argument Popper used to come to his more technical recommendations, and then to assess whether his substantive proposals meet their avowed objectives. Since Popper acknowledges that methodological principles must have some utility for the procedures and progress of science, one could presumably appraise them according to their actual or possible consequences for scientific work. Where a methodology impeded the growth of scientific knowledge, or failed to provide a satisfactory explanation of the rationality of past scientific practice, the rules would be thrown into doubt and possibly have to be modified or rejected. Accordingly, we would evaluate epistemology and methodology in terms of their instrumental value in achieving both epistemic and non-epistemic goals.

The Problem of Epistemic Norms and Naturalism

One central issue in evaluating Popper's epistemic programme is that since it is philosophical and normative, it is not easily criticized or empirically 'tested' with reference to the actual behaviour of scientists. To do so is to risk that circularity of argument which also characterizes criticisms of a naturalist epistemology (Brown 1988; Giere 1989) and a naturalist, even evolutionary, ethics (Ruse 1986b). It would be impossible to investigate the rationality of science without holding some prior conception of rationality that would influence one's choice of examples of rationality in science (Papineau 1989: 435). On the other hand, to accept as rational all that scientists do would be to forgo the normative task of providing standards prescribing what scientists ought to do, and thereby relinquish the possibility of criticizing scientific practice (Siegel 1989). Nevertheless, the circularities involved are not vicious. Persuasive conclusions depend on argument in which both normative and empirical strategies play a part. The main point here is that there can be no strict formula or algorithm for determining any kind of rationality.

Over the years many critics have taken up similar issues surrounding the conceptual relationship between philosophy and history of science.[7] Imre Lakatos, for example, attempted to clarify such dilemmas regarding science by arguing that although the methodologist is primarily concerned with the 'internal history' of science, which elucidates the logical relations between propositions and their confrontations with experience, this process must be supplemented with 'an empirical (socio-psychological) "external" history' (Lakatos 1970: 91). Since all methodologies operate as historiographical theories, they can be criticized with reference to the adequacy of their rational reconstructions (Lakatos 1970: 109). The implication accepted for this study is that although Popper's philosophical propositions are indeed normative, empirical factors must enter into their appraisal. His reconstructions function as hypotheses to be tested against the facts contained in competing interpretations of the history of science. A key problem then becomes that of deciding whether an historical or empirical example that appears to contravene contemporary standards of rationality is indeed irrational (or of an inferior rationality), or is a valid (or superior) example of rationality that requires us to revise our original standards. Some critics (e.g. Hooker 1981; Laudan and Laudan 1989; Stump 1992) have demonstrated a variety of historically evolving forms of rational procedure in science, and queried whether there can be a universal and timeless form of scientific rationality.

The Problem of Rational Reconstruction

A next step therefore is to enquire into the adequacy of Popper's particular reconstruction of science and query why a general model of scientific rationality should be derived solely from the discipline of theoretical physics. Kneale (1974: 208), for example, has pointed out that Popper has focused upon scientific discoveries about the 'frame of nature' whose statements have the character of universal laws concerning all possible worlds. Much of science, however, is concerned with the 'content' of nature, whose statements are limited generalizations about the actual historical world. Where theoretical physicists are often intent upon the frame of nature, biologists, geologists and astronomers study the content of nature (Kneale 1974: 211). Accordingly, we should be wary of prescribing that all scientific theories have the form of 'unverifiable propositions of unrestricted universality' (Kneale 1974: 217).

Popper's (1974b: 987–9) reply to this criticism reaffirms the importance of singular statements in science, but it does not overcome the original objection that one can accord high scientific status to discoveries that are of an historical and non-repeatable kind.[8] A second related criticism queries the particular events in scientific history which Popper has chosen rationally to reconstruct. Such choices can only be made with an informed historical hindsight and remain fraught with interpretative difficulties. Although Popper later acknowledges these problems, he contends that there are 'a number of important falsifications which are as "definitive" as general human fallibility permits' (*RAS*: xxiii).

Popper's focus upon the logic and context of justification raises another difficulty. Although he recognizes that scientific theories have their origins in metaphysics, myth and even psychological intuition, in his earliest work he disclaims that these are amenable to logical or rational analysis (*LScD*: 31, 38). He denies that the psychological, sociological or historical context can exhibit a useful model of rationality. Such claims have also fuelled much criticism. Hanson (1970: 620–2), among others, has questioned whether one can distinguish easily between the sorts of reason given for accepting a hypothesis, and those for initially suggesting it. As Nickles (1980: 31) reminds us: 'Setting out the completed, tested, theory is but the last stage of a sophisticated process of reasoned activity, and to ignore the rest would give (and has given) a very distorted conception of scientific learning.' The 'good reasons' with which science operates are rarely based upon purely formal criteria.

Such criticisms receive support from Popper's own work on the methodology of social science where he advocates a form of rational reconstruction as the basis of theoretical explanation (see chapter 5). If one applied situational analysis to scientific discoveries, then one would have to take into account the whole range of ascertainable influences upon a scientist's decision. To deny this approach Popper would have to exclude a priori that such influences have any rational pattern (as he does in *LScD*: 31 and *PH*: 157), or to argue empirically that scientific work was an exceptional kind of social activity that transcends, eliminates or overrides psychological factors.

The Problem of Logic

As we have seen, the principles of formal logic appear to provide a 'hard core' of epistemological certainty amid the shifting sands of philosophical and empirical investigation. Popper's reliance upon *modus tollens* rests upon a firm distinction between synthetic and analytic statements – a distinction that has come under strong criticism. The work of W. V. O. Quine, for example, casts serious doubt on whether there exist statements, of the kind termed analytic, which are devoid of any factual component. With reference to the first of what he calls 'two dogmas of empiricism', Quine argues that the truth of any statement, even those apparently analytical truths of formal logic, depends upon both linguistic and extra-linguistic fact. Quine (1963: 41) contends that the truth of a statement cannot be analysed into discrete linguistic and factual components. That is, its truth may be ascertained only by a combination of semantic (definitional) *and* empirical criteria. By implication, the truth of scientific statements formulated in the deductive terms advocated by Popper would also depend upon both logic and empirical fact, and the boundary between them would be difficult to determine.

The significance of this problem may be seen more clearly with reference to the associated, if not identical, 'dogma' of reductionism. By this, Quine means the notion that one can confirm or refute a statement on its own without reference to its place in a larger theoretical context. Contrary to this 'dogma', Quine (1963: 41) argues for the holistic claim that 'our statements about the external world face the tribunal of sense experience not individually but only as a corporate body'. Our knowledge, scientific or otherwise, is a 'man-made [*sic*] fabric which impinges on experience only along the edges' (Quine 1963: 42). On this view there is no automatic link between a refutation by experience and a particular theory. An empirical refutation may entail re-evaluation of any one of a range of theories within a system. Quine's critique is all the more powerful because it still maintains that scientific systems must be 'kept squared with experience' (1963: 45). Popper's later reply to such arguments acknowledges the importance of 'background knowledge' and the difficulties involved in ascertaining refutation, but claims that the problem is not insuperable. He simply counters that in many cases one can isolate the hypothesis needed to refute a theory or theoretical system (*CR*: 238–9). Such a reply, however, concedes a larger role for pragmatic interpretation in science, and a corresponding diminishing role for formal criteria.

The Politics of Scientific Rationality

From the discussion above several conclusions can be drawn about Popper's project. His general aim was to formulate universal, epistemological criteria that were free of any subjective or psychological consideration. This theory of knowledge was to be, as far as possible, an ethically neutral instrument that served scientific, philosophical and political goals. More specifically it was intended to encourage the growth of science, to enable the philosophical demarcation between science and metaphysics, and also to assist in curtailing our human propensity for dogmatism. Indeed, it can be said that Popper's rules for rational choice between theories function to maintain particular epistemic or cognitive controls on individuals as knowing subjects, preventing them from exercising their subjective and irrational preferences. Nonetheless, some reservations must be expressed about the character of this particular cognitive ethic, the means by which it has been derived, and its possible consequences. Popper has engaged in a process of methodological reduction whereby rationality is deduced from epistemology, which is equated with the method of a particular form of physical science. The epistemic consequence is unduly formal, and limits the range of sources upon which we might draw to understand and prescribe for scientific rationality.

The reasons for such a reduction are both epistemic and non-epistemic. Theoretical physics offers a spectacular example of the growth of knowledge in terms of consistency, increasing generality and content. It is also a highly abstract discipline seemingly quarantined from non-epistemic or ideological influences, and whose methods do not rely upon psychological factors. Such a reduction, however, lies firmly within the philosophical tradition of positivism, and certain scientific and political consequences are evident. At its most extreme the political goal of such an epistemology is to minimize the subjective and 'irrational' element of human behaviour and to reduce the status of human beings to that of rule followers.[9]

It must be conceded, however, that subjectivism – defined simply as 'feelings of conviction' that are unable to be expressed clearly in the form of public statements – may be a dangerous source of epistemological and political dogmatism. Whoever expresses the greatest level of emotional conviction may win the day and encourage the indiscriminate use of physical force against opponents. Yet, Popper requires more of science than to put intellectual intuition into public statements. By demanding that science render such statements into a particular logical form he risks reproducing another form of dogmatism, that of excessive formalism. The quest for scientific rationality may have to take account of 'good reasons' which lie somewhere between the extremes of intuitionism and formalism.

In one important respect, however, the knowing subject retains an important role for Popper in choosing between the diverse values or the ends of life. Here, the younger Popper appears to accept the prevailing view, popularized by Weber (1978: 24–6), that values were essentially matters of personal preference and decision, and that one could not adjudicate rationally between them. It was presumed, however, that one could appraise objectively the means to those ends. In a world of competing political ideologies and apparent ethical relativism, scientific knowledge and its method gave a more secure foundation for rational thought and action of an instrumental kind. A problem for Popper becomes that of whether he can provide any rational and objective arguments for his own values.

Whether Popper's epistemological, methodological and political goals may be attained by the means he proposes is one of the central questions treated in this book. If we regard Popper's philosophy as a system of ideas, it can be shown that as his political concerns crystallize so his philosophy of science evolves beyond the constraints set by his early formalist model of scientific rationality. The reservations noted above about the founding assumptions of Popper's rational reconstruction also indicate potential problems not only for the universal applicability of his proposed model of rationality, but also its utility for science itself. The interplay between objective, subjective and pragmatic criteria can be discerned in the elaboration and critique of the methodological doctrine of falsificationism in the next chapter.

3

Methodological Falsificationism and its Critics

This chapter offers a critical analysis of Popper's early prescriptions for scientific rationality. We shall examine the doctrine of methodological falsificationism, its concept of explanation and underlying metaphysics. A major aim of this critique will be to appraise Popper's proposals in terms of their utility for science, their ability to shed light on the history of science, and their coherence with the goals of his broader epistemology. Finally, we shall consider the incipient political values contained in Popper's early methodology.

Falsificationism

Popper's earliest concern was with the conditions under which a theory could be judged untenable (*UQ*: 41). This 'dogmatic' falsificationism, which required a theory to be rejected on discovery of a falsifying instance, was soon superseded.[1] Among the problems in this version are its assumptions that there is both a clear distinction between theoretical and factual propositions, and a firm empirical base of facts which could conclusively disprove a theory. In addition, dogmatic falsificationism dealt with single theories and not with comparison of competing theories. By 1920, however, Popper had concluded that *'the criterion of the scientific status of a theory is its falsifiability, or refutability, or testability'* (*CR*: 37). He conceives of the 'testing' of a theory along four main lines:

First, there is the logical comparison of the conclusions among themselves, by which the internal consistency of the system is tested. Secondly, there is the investigation of the logical form of the theory, with the object of determining whether it has the character of an empirical or scientific theory, or whether it is, for example, tautological. Thirdly, there is the comparison with other theories, chiefly with the aim of determining whether the theory would constitute a scientific advance should it survive our various tests. And finally, there is the testing of the theory by way of empirical application of the conclusions which can be derived from it. (*LScD*: 32–3)

A large part of the 'testing' of a theory, therefore, is a theoretical enterprise in which logic is the main tool of analysis. Only after the initial logical work is completed does experimental practice become possible. Popper's model of scientific rationality thus comprises two major types of methodological rules, the formal and the non-formal. Scientific rationality first consists in applying the rules of deductive logic, to ascertain (a) the scientific status of a theory, (b) its merits relative to other theories, and (c) the logical structure of those 'basic' empirical statements used to confirm or reject the theory. The broader methodological rules come into play in appraising whether to test a theory, and deciding whether a theory has been confirmed or refuted. We must also distinguish therefore between *falsifiability* as a criterion of demarcation and a methodology, and the rules to be used in finally deciding on the *falsification* of a theory.

Falsifiability

To be falsifiable, single scientific theories or hypotheses should have the logical form of 'strictly universal statements', which could be expressed in the form of *prohibitions* or 'negations of strictly existential statements' (*LScD*: 69). Any hypothesis must be able to generate singular empirical statements which would, if confirmed or corroborated, refute the theory.[2] Once a theory is accepted as scientific, then the more falsifiable theory is to be preferred to the less falsifiable one. The more 'basic statements' or predictions a theory generates, the greater the empirical claims, and the more falsifiable the theory (*LScD*: 113). A scientific theory also needs to be *consistent* as well as falsifiable (*LScD*: 92). For Popper, *simplicity* was also a virtue, and could be equated with a degree of falsifiability, and increasing empirical content (*LScD*: 142).

The demand for simplicity and increasing empirical content provides the foundation for a methodological rule which stipulates that any new theory is acceptable only if it can incorporate or explain the content of a previous theory (*LScD*: 157–8). The requirements for simplicity and generality lead to the supplementary norm that scientists must put forward 'imaginative and bold conjectures' or *risky predictions*, which require systematic tests and experiments in an attempt to refute them (*LScD*: 279). The call for severe testing requires Popper to exclude *ad hoc* auxiliary hypotheses that aim to save the theory from falsification (*LScD*: 42). To this end, he will only accept auxiliary hypotheses which increase the falsifiability or empirical content of the system of theories (*LScD*: 82–3).

For each of these rules, however, historians and philosophers of science have demonstrated convincingly that there are cases where their strict application would not have been fruitful for science. For example, at certain times it may be in the scientist's interests to accept a theory which may appear to have less empirical content than previous or competing theories (Feyerabend 1975: 176). In addition, Thomas Kuhn (1970: 157–8) has argued that a new theory is more often supported because it shows fertility or future promise of solving more problems than previous theories. That is, a proposed theory may not be able to explain fully its predecessors. Both Kuhn (1974: 266–7) and Paul Feyerabend (1974a: 218–22) argue further that new theories may be incommensurable with their predecessors. By this they mean that it is often extremely difficult, if not impossible, to compare successive theories which contain different assumptions, consequences and conceptual structures.

Regarding the seemingly incontestable requirement of consistency, other critics (e.g. Maxwell 1972: 136–7) have suggested that there must be provision for exceptions. A working scientist may wish to accept for the time being an apparently inconsistent theory, anticipating that further theoretical work might remove the inconsistency. Furthermore, it could well be the aim of severe testing not to overthrow the theory, but to extend it and develop more auxiliary hypotheses.

One difficulty with the idea of a bold conjecture or a novel prediction is that neither can be determined simply by reference to their logical structure. A theory is 'bold' or a prediction is 'novel' when assessed against a particular kind of historical context, which includes the background knowledge, or established framework, of scientific theories (Chalmers 1982: 56; Cleveland and Sagal 1989). Popper (*CR*: 238–9) acknowledges this problem, but argues that we must temporarily accept our background knowledge as unproblematic. The methodological point, however, is that a scientist will need to exercise some of the interpretative skills of an historian in deciding between theories.

Applying Popper's falsifiability criterion without qualification may impose premature closure on a scientific project. Whatever its improvement upon the verificationism of the logical positivists, the falsifiability criterion alone fails to supply all the standards needed for judging the scientific status of a theory. A sufficiently comprehensive conception of scientific rationality would require articulating the 'good reasons' that scientists may sometimes have for ignoring the usual procedures. Where Popper's initial prescriptions offer a useful point of departure for science, logical analysis needs to be supplemented by other kinds of methodological norms. Some of these more pragmatic standards are evident in Popper's rules for falsification and corroboration, and in the critiques offered by historians of science.

Falsification

Falsifiability and its associated methodological rules provide the initial criteria for determining the scientific character and strength of a theory. Further criteria are needed to guide practical appraisals of how a logically satisfactory theory may be either *empirically* refuted or confirmed. For this purpose, singular statements need to be available which could 'serve as premises in an empirical falsification' (*LScD*: 43). Consequently, Popper proposed rules, not only for the appraisal and construction of universal theories, but also for the treatment of singular 'basic' statements, which operate as *either* falsifications *or* confirmations of those theories.

Such sentences supply the link between the theory and the perceptual experiences embodied in the practice of research. In essence, a basic statement or basic proposition is a statement of a singular fact (*LScD*: 43). Yet, Popper is keen to criticize the early positivist distinction between theory and fact on the grounds that no definite assertion can be made which would express a definite datum of experience. Popper (*LScD*: 94–5) writes: 'Every description uses *universal* names (or symbols, or ideas); every statement has the character of a theory, of a hypothesis.' Whether basic statements are true or false is virtually impossible to determine. It is possible, however, to test such assertions intersubjectively and so confirm or disconfirm them.

For Popper, basic statements must have the logical form of singular existential statements which can contradict a universal statement. Since no such basic statement can be derived from a strictly universal statement alone – that is, from a 'non-existence statement' or prohibition – they must be derived from a universal statement accompanied by initial conditions (*LScD*: 102). Basic statements must contain a 'material requirement' concerning the event which the statement tells us is occurring at a particular place and time. The event must also be *observable*, that is, able to be tested by observation. More precisely, a basic statement must, Popper stresses (*LScD*: 103), 'either be itself a statement about relative positions of physical bodies, or that it must be equivalent to some basic statement of a "mechanistic" or "materialistic" kind'. These basic sentences are the ultimate test-basis of science and the means for maintaining Popper's empiricism.

Such basic statements must be subjected to tests, but sooner or later scientists have to stop at a basic statement which they *'decide to accept'* (*LScD*: 104). There is, however, no defined place at which to cease testing, and scientists must at some time or other decide to be satisfied 'for the time being' (*LScD*: 104). According to Popper (*LScD*: 104) this also means that scientists will usually stop with a basic statement that is easy to test, and for which 'the various investigators are likely to reach agreement'. A disagreement will entail further tests. If further testing leads to no results or agreement, we could conclude that the statements were not intersubjectively testable, or perhaps were not dealing with observable events.

Popper's relatively straightforward proposals become more problematic when it is understood that testing in practice is a complex procedure. Scientists rely upon supplementary laws and theories used to construct instruments such as microscopes or telescopes. The test situation will also require a number of other initial conditions to be met in setting up the experiment (Chalmers 1982: 64). Popper (*LScD*: 50) also acknowledges that no conclusive refutations are available, but he does not consider this to be a serious problem.[3]

There is a further reason why falsification can never be conclusive. Perceptual experiences are presumed to be psychological events, and no logical relations hold between them and the statements describing them. Yet, Popper (*LScD*: 105) explains: 'Experiences can *motivate a decision*, and hence an acceptance or rejection of a statement, but a basic statement cannot be *justified* by them.' The link between experience and a basic statement is therefore psychological or subjective. Scientific rationality as described by Popper does not rely solely upon the application of logical rules, but also upon pragmatic decisions, for which there are no obvious decision procedures.

Popper considers a theory to be falsified only if we have accepted basic statements which contradict it, and only if this result is *reproducible* and corroborated (*LScD*: 86). A falsifying hypothesis is simply a basic statement asserting the existence of a particular fact, thing or event (*LScD*: 87). This in turn is open to falsification, since the non-appearance of the 'fact' is always a possibility. The rules for accepting a theory are very similar to those for rejecting it. The theory chosen will be that which is 'the fittest to survive', that is, it will be the one which has 'stood up to the severest tests' and 'which is also testable in the most rigorous way' (*LScD*: 108). Thus a scientist may decide to accept a theory for *two* reasons; first, because it is the most falsifiable and, second, because it has survived rigorous testing.

Popper's treatment of basic statements provides several important difficulties for his general methodological aim. Brown (1977: 74–5) has pointed out the paradox that occurs when one treats a basic statement as a falsifiable conjecture. In cases where a low level hypothesis contradicts a theory, there is no clear indication as to whether one's prime duty is to reject the theory, or to defend it by attempting to refute the low level falsifying hypothesis. Thus Popper's methodology does not provide a simple or uncontroversial guide to scientific practice regarding basic statements and falsification of scientific theories.

Corroboration

In his early work, Popper thought that the concept of corroboration allowed him to dispense with the terms 'true' or 'false'. He used the term corroboration to describe how well a theory has stood up to tests, usually by comparison with competing theories. If a theory is refuted by a novel set of events, then Popper proposes that the new or revised theory must not only account for those, but also explain the phenomena covered by the older theory, which would survive as 'a kind of limiting case of the new theory' (*LScD*: 252, 276). Corroboration also does not so much depend upon the number of corroborating instances as upon the severity of the different tests to which the hypothesis can be or has been subjected (*LScD*: 267). In a later work, Popper (*CR*: 242) extends this empirical criterion to require that 'the theory should pass some new, and severe, tests'. He suggests that even though a theory may not be falsified, it may be superseded by a more testable or falsifiable theory.

Once a simple falsifying hypothesis has been corroborated, however, the theory has to be rejected. 'In general', Popper writes (*LScD*: 268), 'we regard an inter-subjectively testable falsification as final (provided it is well tested).' To maintain his falsifiability norm, Popper will allow a positive corroboration to be overthrown by a negative one, but he will not allow the reverse. After a theory has been decisively falsified it may not be resurrected at a later date. It appears from this and other statements that falsification entails its rejection, whether or not an alternative theory is available.

In a footnote designed to clarify his original idea Popper (*LScD*: 87) suggests: 'In most cases we have, before falsifying a hypothesis, another one up our sleeves; for the falsifying experiment is usually a *crucial experiment* designed to decide between the two.' Imre Lakatos (1974: 119, 122) has argued, however, that a sophisticated falsificationism requires a theory to be accepted as falsified only if one has an alternative theory available whose claims are corroborated by the falsifying instances of the old theory. Unless there was a better one available it would not be rational to cease working with a theory. At times, it would also be plausible and rational to suspend judgement on alleged falsifications until one had allowed for the greatest development of a theory. Popper (*CR*: 312 fn) provides for such a contingency when he advocates the 'dogmatic attitude' of holding on to a theory for as long as possible so that we can determine its strength. Later on he advises that we should not give in to criticism too easily (Popper 1974a: 55).

It is difficult to deny that corroboration involves a trace of induction, in which one accepts a statement as confirmed because of the number of severe tests that it has survived in the past (O'Hear 1980: 62–7; Warnock 1960: 100–1; Watkins 1984: 254). Once a theory has withstood certain tests, it is accepted and used in the belief that it will continue to withstand them in the future. Its past successes and corroborations are reasons for supporting it in future practice, despite the fact that it is still to be regarded as tentative. Popper's theory of scientific rationality would appear to require some residual inductivism.[4]

The testing of a theory depends upon basic statements whose acceptance or rejection 'depends upon our *decisions*', which are also in part determined by 'considerations of utility' (*LScD*: 108). Theory choice is not based upon some ultimate proof or justification, but upon the decision to accept a basic statement. A decision to accept a basic statement therefore becomes a form of convention. Although Popper agrees that theory choice is a 'practical matter', he distinguishes himself from traditional conventionalists who use a convention such as simplicity to choose between universal statements (*LScD*: 109). Popper's conventionalism only applies to basic statements. This conventional element also enables Popper to distinguish himself from positivists who accept basic statements as justifiable by immediate experience.

Popper is adamant that agreement on basic statements must always remain possible. 'If some day', he (*LScD*: 104) explains, 'it should no longer be possible for scientific observers to reach agreement about basic statements this would amount to a failure of language as a means of universal communication.' Here it is important to note that vital methodological decisions become dependent upon social criteria such as transparent communication, honesty and good faith in argument. Popper likens the process whereby decisions are made to accept basic statements to that of a 'trial by jury', in which there are rules governing the procedure, and certain reasons and 'justifications' are required (*LScD*: 109–10). Nevertheless, the whole process remains open to revision and challenge. As Popper is well aware, neither juries nor scientists always obey the rules, nor are they immune from prior subjective convictions which may influence their judgements. Ultimately, the selection and acceptance of these basic statements are the province of scientists and the scientific community. Such judgements become conventions, or agreed-upon decisions, founded upon epistemic and non-epistemic considerations.

On the evidence presented so far it would be more plausible to suggest that rational decisions regarding both the falsifiability and falsification of a theory cannot escape some broader historical and interpretative judgements. Scientists would decide on a particular course of action depending upon their logical *and* historical assessment of the promise or utility of a theory. A scientist would appraise the scientific status of a theory, its value in comparison to competing theories, whether or not to test it, and whether or not to regard it as confirmed or refuted. That is, at each stage of appraisal decisions would have to be made according to an interpretation of where the theory stands with respect to the 'background knowledge' of the time.[5] Such procedures would, however, limit the prospects for developing purely theoretical criteria for scientific rationality, and allow the use of more pragmatic criteria.

Falsification and the History of Science

Since the early 1960s, historians of science have taken issue with Popper's falsificationist account of scientific progress and also advanced their own alternative methodological programmes. Kuhn, Lakatos, Feyerabend, Chalmers and others have demonstrated how many of the great scientists continued to persevere with their theories despite apparent and unambiguous early refutations. Newton's theory of gravitation seemed to be falsified by particular observations of the orbit of the moon. Despite what appeared to be unequivocal falsifying instances, Bohr developed and retained his theory of the atom. Maxwell's kinetic theory of gases was first introduced in the knowledge that it seemed to be refuted by measurements of the specific heats of gases (Chalmers 1982: 66–7).

The Copernican Revolution in astronomy provides one of the most striking examples of the problems with a falsificationist history of science (Chalmers 1982: 67–75). When Copernicus proposed that, instead of the earth being the stationary centre of a finite universe, it was merely one of a number of planets orbiting around the sun, the theory could not be defended in terms of the scientific knowledge of the time. Only a few of its mathematical features seemed to be an advance over its main rival the Ptolemaic system. Furthermore, Copernicus' theory was only accepted after one and a half centuries of scientific progress in a number of related disciplines such as mechanics and optics. The Copernican theory required a new cosmology whose formulation took place over several hundred years. For Feyerabend (1975: 66–7), the Copernican hypothesis is a case where its 'invention, defence and partial vindication runs counter to almost every methodological rule one might care to think of today'.[6]

Kuhn generalized many of the above insights into an original critique of dominant assumptions about scientific progress. He aimed to show that scientific research is usually guided by what he calls 'paradigms' which are initially defined as 'universally recognized scientific achievements that for a time provide model problems and solutions to a community of practitioners' (Kuhn 1970: viii). Kuhn not only describes how paradigms operate, but also how they come to be overthrown and replaced in the historical process of 'scientific revolution'. On this account, the history of science is characterized by typical patterns in which periods of 'normal science' are followed by times of 'revolution'. During the period of normal science major theoretical achievements remain unquestioned. Normal science primarily consists in rounding out the paradigm, realizing its promise to provide solutions to the problems that the scientific community considers important. According to Kuhn (1970: 35), most scientists practise normal science, which means that they engage in 'puzzle-solving' and do not search for unexpected novelty. Puzzles are defined as those problems that the scientific community considers both important and to be capable of solution. Because normal science only focuses upon solvable problems it appears to progress quickly in comparison to other fields of study.

Kuhn points out that although puzzle-solving is often highly successful in extending the scope and precision of scientific knowledge, new and unexpected results do occur. At first, such difficulties are not regarded as falsifications, but simply as further puzzles which will in time be solved by research within the paradigm. What may in fact be radical challenges to the paradigm are rarely perceived as such (Kuhn 1970: 64). It is not until a number of novel phenomena appear which cannot be explained or predicted that scientists see them as anomalies. Awareness of anomalies within a particular field usually precipitates a deep crisis, in which 'formerly standard solutions of solved problems are called into question' (Kuhn 1970: 83). Thus comes about a period of 'extraordinary science', in which scientists undertake a search for new theories and new paradigms and many theories proliferate and compete with each other (Kuhn 1970: 84–91). This process of 'scientific revolution' occurs when scientists begin those innovative investigations that lead them to a new set of theoretical and practical commitments (Kuhn 1970: 6).

For Kuhn, scientific revolutions are similar to political revolutions in that the choice between paradigms is akin to a choice between incompatible modes of community life. The choice cannot be decided simply by the traditional evaluative procedures of normal science, 'for these depend in part upon a particular paradigm, and that paradigm is at issue' (Kuhn 1970: 94). Since paradigms are essentially different and even incommensurable ways of seeing the world, the process of adopting a new one is similar to that of a gestalt switch in perception. For this reason, the principles of falsificationism are insufficient for theory selection. Because no paradigm ever accounts for all the facts or solves all its problems, anomalies can always be found and theories falsified. Kuhn argues that falsification is really just another form of verification and, further, that acceptance of a falsification depends upon what the paradigm will regard as a falsifying instance.

On this interpretation science is non-cumulative and paradigm change will ultimately occur because of a mixture of both scientific, and 'non-scientific' reasons. Among the most important scientific claims made by the proponents of a new paradigm is that it can solve the problems that led the old one into crisis (Kuhn 1970: 153). These claims are often based upon evidence of greater quantitative precision, and are themselves bolstered if a new paradigm predicts phenomena that had not been known to exist previously. In addition, arguments for paradigm change may be based upon the apparently non-scientific standards, such as aesthetic criteria. Important in this process is intuitive or tacit knowledge, arising from personal hunches that the new paradigm promises to solve more problems than its predecessors or competitors.

Kuhn claims that no single argument or factor is predominant in this process of persuasion and conversion. The final choice is a communal one made by the scientists who, by writing papers, textbooks and lectures, gradually come to embrace the new paradigm (Kuhn 1970: 159). Contrary to the view of many of Kuhn's critics, this does not mean that science is irrational, for a scientist may use many sorts of good epistemic reasons for choosing one theory rather than another. These include logic as well as the values of 'accuracy, scope, simplicity, fruitfulness and the like' (Kuhn 1974: 261).[7]

Kuhn's analysis further contributed to a blurring of the lines between the context of discovery and the context of justification. In this he expanded upon themes in the work of Michael Polanyi (1958; 1966) who had argued for a radical transformation of epistemology to include the concept of 'personal knowledge'. Polanyi considered that tacit and intuitive knowledge was the source of conjectures about the world and was as much a part of the scientific enterprise as the more objective criteria for verifiability and falsifiability. In fact, Polanyi is the subject of Popper's (1974b: 1067) sharp rebuke in the 1959 Preface to *The Logic of Scientific Discovery* where he objected to the 'obscurantist faith in the expert's special skill, and in his personal knowledge and authority' (*LScD*: 23).

Nonetheless, the critics of Kuhn and Polanyi have not demonstrated that subjective influences are unimportant in the evaluation of competing paradigms. Indeed, Kuhn's analysis has drawn further support from other historians of science. Ravetz, for example, has demonstrated how the fallibilism of science derives in part from its reliance upon tacit knowledge and craft skills:

Since no argument in science can be formally valid, and hence no conclusions necessarily true, the acceptance of conclusions must be governed by criteria of adequacy. . . . They belong to the body of craft knowledge of the methods of the field, with particular techniques of using tools and with other controlling judgements such as those of value. The methods are informal and even tacit, and are transmitted interpersonally rather than publicly; they are incapable of being tested scientifically themselves, but arise out of the collective craft experiences of the field. (Ravetz 1973: 406)

Part of the process of deciding between scientific conclusions will entail an interplay of objective and subjective factors. It is evident from the account above, however, that the term 'subjective' denotes a form of intersubjective knowledge that is discussable, but not usually testable, and whose weight and place in the overall context of decision is variable.

Popperian philosophers of science have criticized Kuhn for presenting his model of the history of science as a foundation for normative prescription. He has been charged with advocating irrationalism, relativism, psychologism and 'mob rule' in science.[8] Yet, on many fundamentals Kuhn's prescriptions do not differ significantly from those of most of his Popperian critics. Apart from drawing attention to the role of 'subjective' factors in science, Kuhn's major departure from Popper seems to lie in his proposal that it is beneficial for scientists to engage in the activities of 'normal science'. For Kuhn, such activities are the necessary base from which revolutionary science can proceed.

As a response to the apparent failings of both Popper and Kuhn, Lakatos formulated his normative 'methodology of scientific research programmes'. Despite his anti-Kuhnian rhetoric, Lakatos shares Kuhn's view of the limited role of falsification in science. Lakatos (1970: 113) is also scathing in his assessment of Popper's history of science, which he considers 'distorts history to fit his rationality theory'. Yet, Lakatos argues against Kuhn that whatever the accuracy of his history of science his normative prescriptions for the scientific method are inadequate if not irrational.

In a way that is surprisingly similar to Kuhn's analysis, however, Lakatos (1974: 177) stressed the importance of larger research programmes in the history of science rather than the success or failure of individual theories. He argued normatively that a research programme must not be jettisoned too soon in case it had not had a chance to prove itself. The scientist must maintain a 'hard core' or 'negative heuristic' which outlines the basic assumptions of the programme and which should not be subject to criticism, falsification or modification early in its scientific life. Research programmes also delineate a 'positive heuristic' which constitutes those auxiliary hypotheses and arguments needed to supplement and confirm the 'negative heuristic'. The 'positive heuristic' indicates the lines of possible future development of a research programme and is the focus of ongoing scientific work (Lakatos 1974: 133–6).

For Lakatos, deciding between theories within a particular research programme is a relatively simple task based upon the results of experimental testing. Any move in the game of science is possible provided the scientist does not resort to *ad hoc* hypotheses or attempt to refute the hard core. One chooses between scientific programmes according to whether they are either progressive or degenerating, which in turn is assessed according to whether their theories are successful or not in predicting new facts (Lakatos 1974: 156–7). Where in practice Popper's methodology ultimately relied upon the acceptance or rejection of basic statements, Lakatos depends more on judgements about universal theories. Nevertheless, similar problems to those encountered with Popper's decisions on basic statements apply. There are no firm criteria for knowing when progress has been made, or when to abandon a research programme. Such decisions cannot be made by simple recourse to methodological norms.

One of the most original critics in this field is Feyerabend, who comes to conclusions similar to those of Kuhn about the history of science and the role of method in achieving scientific progress, but makes more unsettling methodological prescriptions. He argues that because scientific change often requires choice between incommensurable theories, paradigms, or conceptual systems, scientists have rarely been constrained by strict epistemological and methodological rules. In historical fact, the opposite has more often occurred and for good reasons. Indeed, Feyerabend (1975: 23) regards them as 'necessary for progress'.

On the grounds that 'anything goes' in the practice of science, Feyerabend makes this his methodological prescription and thus argues, somewhat mischievously, 'against method'. He proposes an 'anarchist' epistemology in which freedom of the individual is a prime political and intellectual value. Such a strategy was intended to overcome the difficulties faced by Lakatos's attempt to formulate an objective and non-relativist Popperian methodology. Nevertheless, it is important to see that Feyerabend was not arguing for absolute 'anarchy', disorder or pure whim in science, but simply for the freedom of researchers to pursue their work unconstrained by the prevailing methodological fashions (Feyerabend 1978: 39–40; 1987: 36). He also questions whether science ought to be regarded as the highest form of rationality.

A number of conclusions emerge from these critical accounts of the history of science which cast doubts over the adequacy of Popper's early description of and prescriptions for science. First, most scientific theories were soon refuted, but they were maintained nonetheless. Even when accepted by the scientific community, they were embedded in anomalies or possible refutations. Second, an accepted refutation never decided the fate of a single theory, but a whole theoretical system. Third, intuition, or tacit knowledge, played a significant role in the growth of scientific knowledge. Fourth, no purely formal or theoretical criteria have been decisive in the history of science. These conclusions suggest that an epistemology based upon scientific rationality must incorporate non-epistemic or social values and goals. Some of these issues arise again in Popper's prescriptions for scientific explanation.

The Logic of Scientific Explanation

As well as serving to demarcate science from pseudo-science, falsifiability and falsification were integral to the scientific goal of providing *complete*, causal explanations. Popper (*LScD*: 61) advocated the methodological rule that 'we are not to abandon the search for universal laws and for a coherent system, nor ever give up our attempts to explain causally any kind of event we can describe'. Scientific understanding, therefore, is to be gained by revealing the causes of events and by showing how they are merely part of a set of more general phenomena. Although Popper's original schema was superseded by his propensity theory of explanation, a brief outline of the hypothetico-deductive (H-D) model will serve to indicate further the formalist character of his early philosophy of science and problems within it.

Popper formulated his prescriptions for the H-D model of explanation in terms of the logical relationship between propositions.

To give a *causal explanation* of an event means to deduce a statement which describes it, using as premises of the deduction one or more *universal laws*, together with certain singular statements, the *initial condi-*

tions. For example, we can say that we have given a causal explanation of the breaking of a certain piece of thread if we have found that the thread had a tensile strength of 1 *lb.* and that a weight of 2 *lbs.* was put on it. (*LScD*: 59–60)

From (a) universal statements (laws, or hypotheses) and (b) singular statements describing initial conditions, one deduces (c) a specific singular statement or prediction. The initial conditions are called the *cause* of an event, and the prediction called an *effect* (*PH*: 123). That which is to be either explained or predicted may be termed the *explicandum*, while statements outlining the causes (laws and/or initial conditions) constituting the explanation may be called the *explicans*. Depending upon our problem, the H-D model may be used for either explanation, prediction or testing. The original H-D model comprised the following three main components: a deductive thesis which requires that the *explicandum* be logically deduced from the *explicans*; a covering law thesis which requires the *explicans* to contain one or more universal laws as well as a statement of initial conditions; and a symmetry thesis which claims that, from the standpoint of their logical structure, there is an identity or symmetry between the logic of explanation and prediction. These theses have attracted considerable philosophical criticism, and none of their supporting arguments has withstood scrutiny. Although most of the attention was directed towards Carl Hempel's (1965) more sophisticated defences of the deductive-nomological model, the same criticisms are applicable to Popper's analysis. Since Popper eventually abandoned the main features of this model of explanation we shall only consider here the more pragmatic problems with his argument.

Following the pattern set earlier in thinking about falsifiability and falsification, we may distinguish between *evaluating* the logic of explanation, and the other methodological task of deciding whether to *accept* an explanation. For the latter, logic may be only one criteria amongst many – subjective or pragmatic – which are not easily assimilated into a single methodological formula. By itself formalism does not allow us to know when we have achieved a satisfactory explanation. Ultimately, intelligibility is the irreducible requirement of the logic of explanation. On this view, an explanation may be intelligible or not in the light of background knowledge and context (Tuchanska 1992). For example, we may explain why a particular man is not pregnant by reference to the fact that he has regularly taken birth control pills, and that every man who takes such pills avoids pregnancy. Although the explanation fits the H-D model, we do not accept it as an explanation because we already know that men do not become pregnant. We would reject it as an explanation because of our elementary knowledge of the human body (Gärdenfors 1980: 418). That is, the explanation is basically unintelligible. Similarly, even though an explanation may not fit the H-D model, we may accept it in part because of its intelligibility, intuitive appeal and even its practical applicability, in the hope that further research may uncover theories and facts which fit the prescribed logical form.

All this points to the importance of pragmatic criteria in both the decision to test and accept an explanation. Where Popper argues for his criteria as the most rational guide to theoretical choice and practical action, in some contexts an exclusive reliance upon them could be called irrational. For example, in constructing the first atomic pile at the University of Chicago, scientists had to make predictions as to whether the nuclear reaction they would initiate could be controlled, or whether it would spread through the surrounding buildings and city, or even further (Salmon 1981: 125). Where there is no best-tested or corroborated theory upon which to base future tests, the decision to test may be influenced by the possible practical results. In such cases, unless one subscribes to the value of truth at any cost, moral factors become critically relevant. On this argument, accepting an explanation may be based upon an appraisal of how far it meets a broader non-epistemic ethic as well as epistemic ones. Conceivably, a satisfactory explanation may be one which not only makes our world more intelligible and predictable, but one which also furthers values such as social justice or ecological balance.

Popper's early account of a satisfactory explanation creates a further problem when we note that accepting an explanation because it appears to be corroborated may be interpreted in inductive and instrumentalist terms as accepting it because of its past practical successes. Nevertheless, Popper denies that theories and explanations are just instruments for making predictions and supplying us with useful knowledge of the world. In his early work he holds to a relatively undeveloped form of scientific realism which claims that our theories *do* give us knowledge of reality. There is under Popper's early formulation, however, no way of ascertaining that this is the case. Indeed, there is no reason why instrumentalists could not embrace Popper's methodological norms. The search for more general theories and the best corroborated explanations could equally serve instrumentalist as well as realist purposes. Generality, corroboration, and severity of testing would enable the creation of better instruments or help in ascertaining how far theories could be applied (O'Hear 1980: 92–3).

Popper's original aim was to provide a set of standards for the appraisal of scientific explanation, in which the logical structure of statements and the logical relations between them were paramount. As we have seen, however, formal criteria are not unproblematic guides to the analysis of the statements and propositions comprising an explanation. Notions of explanatory adequacy cannot avoid recourse to pragmatic criteria and context.[9] These are not extraneous matters, but of ineradicable methodological significance (Putnam 1978: 42, 47). Popper's later writings on the issue of explanation, the aim of science and the moral responsibility of the scientist hint at just such a broader conception of rationality.[10]

Early Metaphysics

Although the strength of Popper's early epistemology lay in his more formal methodological prescriptions, he also made a number of metaphysical assumptions. Because the latter were regarded as untestable, in his early work Popper preferred to direct attention to the methodological rule or convention which a particular assumption seemed to imply. Popper's earliest published work reflects a number of relatively undeveloped ontological assumptions concerning realism, the nature of physical laws and causality. His realism, which simply consisted in the conviction that there existed an external world independent of our knowledge of it, was accompanied by a belief that this world was of a determinist character. Natural laws were represented by theories that were understood as revisable universal statements describing the structural properties of the world. Popper accepted Hume's view that law statements described actual regularities, or patterns of events in nature, and that these were not subject to change. Scientific method, as he saw it (*LScD*: 252), presupposed '*the immutability of natural processes*, or the "principle of uniformity of nature"'. Popper thought that without this determinist metaphysical faith practical action was almost inconceivable.

Nevertheless, Popper's realism did not extend to a thoroughgoing realist analysis of causality. He thought that cause and effect were sufficiently described by explanations based upon the H-D model.

Although the avowed aim was for a complete causal explanation, his early notion of necessity was far from that of realism. The only necessity Popper recognized was logical necessity. That is, an unrestricted statement of regularity combined with statements about initial conditions will *logically* necessitate that a particular effect will occur. This conception of necessity, however, is of a formal rather than a natural or physical character, and simply allows us to make a causal inference (see Mackie 1980). A common criticism is that the discovery of a regularity is insufficient grounds for postulating a causal connection. Further descriptions of causal mechanisms are required.

The most we can say about Popper's realism is that it understood the physical world as a somewhat ordered cosmos comprising regularities and uniformities, and not as essentially chaotic (*UQ*: 21). He later described this view of nature as *metaphysical determinism*, a doctrine which holds that every aspect of every event is precisely causally determined (Popper 1950: 120–1). In the 1930s, Popper considered there to be no empirical evidence or other arguments which could support the opposite view of metaphysical indeterminism (*UQ*: 94; *LScD*: 216). He complemented his early metaphysical determinism with what could be called *scientific indeterminism*, a doctrine which held that the complexity of the processes in the natural world was such as to render it impossible to discover or predict all the relevant causal determinations of events (Watkins 1974: 374–5). The scientist's task was to keep searching for underlying determinist causal laws, and so aim to improve one's theories about the world. But beneath these tentative and conjectural hypotheses was a physical world ruled by powerful causal and determinist forces. The logical, methodological and political dilemmas created by these arguments later pressed Popper to revise his metaphysical views (see chapter 6). He came to think that a totally determined universe would make moral responsibility a pointless notion (Popper 1948: 150–2).

Social Foundations of Scientific Rationality

The general conclusions Popper draws from his early work about the empirical base of science are striking:

> The empirical basis of objective science has thus nothing 'absolute' about it. Science does not rest upon solid bedrock. The bold structure of its

theories rises, as it were, above a swamp. It is like a building erected on piles. The piles are driven down from above into the swamp, but not down to any natural or 'given' base; and if we stop driving the piles deeper, it is not because we have reached firm ground. We simply stop when we are satisfied that the piles are firm enough to carry the structure, at least for the time being. (*LScD*: 111)

The methodological implications of this picture of science are simple, but radically disturbing. The ideal of science can no longer be absolutely certain knowledge (*LScD*: 278). Science itself can only hope to discover new and more general problems, and to proceed by rigorously criticizing those tentative solutions it may find in the process (*LScD*: 281). Scientific knowledge will always be uncertain, hypothetical and corrigible. The insight that all knowledge is fallible constitutes Popper's most formidable contribution to the understanding of science and epistemology.

The sources of such a thoroughgoing fallibilism, however, can be traced to the non-formal requirements of scientific method. As we have seen, deductive logic could only be used in conjunction with other methodological criteria for falsification and corroboration. Criticism must proceed by means of discussion and informed argument about not only the actual results of investigation, but also the application of the methodological rules. Accordingly, scientists always have to take into account two sorts of considerations: their relations both to their objects of study, and to their fellow scientists. Because of the pragmatic, contextual and even tacit influences upon the kinds of decisions that scientists have to make, scientific rationality assumes a less definitive character. To admit the relevance of contextual factors is to challenge the notion that there can be a purely theoretical and objective criteria for theory evaluation and choice. It may be ventured that such foundations are available neither for scientific rationality nor for rationality in general.

This conclusion does not imply that the scientific rationality is impervious to understanding, analysis or criticism. If sense is to be made of this contextual rationality, then we must consider how scientists use interpretative skills which are embedded in methodological assumptions appropriate to their various disciplinary fields. Such interpretative issues are largely taken as unproblematic in Popper's early philosophy of science. His theory of scientific rationality is primarily concerned with those statements which can be put into logical form, and which are also open to objective or public scrutiny. Public assessment, however, is only a precondition of science and does not in itself overcome those problems of interpretation which occur in times of scientific crisis. The shared values necessary for the resolution of scientific disputes, such as those which occur during a scientific revolution, are not just of a technical or epistemic nature.

When Popper speaks of the 'critical attitude' as the only proper one for the scientist, he alludes to the social values necessary for science to flourish. The critical attitude constitutes not only an ethic but also a subjective psychological state in which one is open to new ideas.[11] Both may be either encouraged or suppressed by particular social conditions and styles of human community. Popper makes explicit these social and political foundations of science in *The Poverty of Historicism*, first written in 1935 but only published in 1944 and 1945:

> Science, and more especially scientific progress, are the results not of isolated efforts but of the *free competition of thought*. For science needs ever more competition between hypotheses and ever more rigorous tests. And the competing hypotheses need personal representation, as it were: they need advocates, they need a jury, and even a public. This personal representation must be institutionally organized if we wish to ensure that it works. And these institutions have to be paid for, and protected by law. Ultimately, progress depends very largely on political factors; on political institutions that safeguard the freedom of thought: on democracy. (*PH*: 154–5)

Progress in science does not just depend upon its internal capacity to accumulate knowledge, but also upon the free competition of thought encouraged by a society in which there are substantial political freedoms (*PH*: 90 fn. 3; *LScD*: 279 fn. 2).

Appraisal

Do Popper's methodological proposals provide a satisfactory criterion of demarcation and also promote the growth of scientific knowledge? On the argument above, without rules of a less formal and less definitive kind, the requirement that scientific statements be falsifiable may well bring investigation to an end before the scientific promise of a theory has been demonstrated. A less restrictive and more fruitful approach might be to require science to have as an ultimate objective the falsifiability of its statements. Such a rule would then allow for the rationality of suspending judgement upon theories which might initially appear to be unfalsifiable.[12] For those who would reject this more limited proposal, one would have to query the empirical value of a *science* founded on theories which no conceivable experience could show to be false. Such theories would be thoroughly metaphysical. Although they may offer significant contributions to our knowledge, we need not call them scientific.

We may also conclude that if the falsifiability criterion is used with due regard to the history and context of theories under examination, it may provide a valuable initial rule of thumb for scientific practice. Without the skills of interpretation and practical judgement, however, Popper's proposals for the falsification and corroboration of scientific theories are also of limited value. His formalist conception of scientific explanation takes no account of pragmatic criteria, which are primarily dependent upon an understanding of context. At the individual level subjective preferences and intuitions are also important. Nonetheless, such influences have to be balanced by concern for the objective standards of the scientific community, and also the values of the wider society. Scientific rationality must contain norms that are both narrowly epistemic with their concern for accuracy, simplicity and so on, but they must also be more broadly social in the respect for truth, open communication and toleration. Scientific rationality therefore does, and must, comprise both formal and informal types of rationality (Tianji 1985).

Detailed case studies in the history of science also challenge Popper's claim (*RAS*: xxxi) that his methodology throws 'much light' on the past growth of scientific knowledge. Such studies reveal that the major scientific discoveries of the past could not always be reconstructed along the lines suggested by methodological falsificationism. Furthermore, it must be concluded that there is a dual role for history in devising methodological norms. One must initially take into account the history of science when choosing which scientific events to reconstruct. And any resultant methodology drawn from them must also allow a place for historical appraisal of the context of a theory. Given that scientists must reach an informed consensus on the status and quality of scientific theories, Popper's proposals do not overcome the problems of relativism. Nor does he appear to have achieved his objective of banishing induction from science.

Finally, we must ask whether the methodology meets Popper's meta-epistemological criteria of evaluation. In this regard, it is clear that Popper cannot avoid advocating dogmatism at certain stages in science. His fallibilism exhibits a paradox in that its main formal component is not open to challenge. The deductive logic of *modus tollens*, which enables the determination of the scientific status and strength of a theory, is itself a form of dogmatism. Furthermore, scientific rationality, of either the formal or the broader interpretative kind, cannot simply be an instrument for achieving political goals such as freedom from dogmatism, if only because dogmatism of one kind or another is, at times, essential to successful scientific practice (*LScD*: 105; *CR*: 312). The decision to remain dogmatic or not must include appraisal of background knowledge, and is not easily guided by strict methodological rules.

In summary, the successful operation of Popper's model of rationality in science already *presumes* the existence of a particular form of community and society characterized by free critical discussion. Where there is contention in science, agreements and conventions still need to be made and their effectiveness is only secured by the strength of the non-epistemic social values and practices. Popper's theory of the growth of scientific knowledge is embedded in a world-view that implicitly values particular social arrangements and particular human capacities. To complete his theory of scientific rationality, Popper's task becomes that of developing and refining his underlying social and political theory. Such work, however, heralds the decline of a strict demarcation between science and non-science, and a less formal approach to the question of method. With it, Popper's epistemology takes on more of the character of a social theory and comes to assume the title of critical rationalism.

4

The Politics of Critical Rationalism

Critical rationalism comprises a social and political theory as well as a philosophy and methodology of social science. This chapter sets out key tenets of Popper's social and political thought, as well as a few of the problems with them.[1] It examines his conception of human nature and shows how this provides a framework for his theory of history, his critique of historicism and his conception of the open society. After considering Popper's central political values of freedom and reason, the chapter analyses the related epistemic and political programmes of democracy and piecemeal social engineering. It is argued that a major political task of critical rationalism is to curb certain negative human needs and tendencies towards dogmatism, and to encourage more favourable capacities. This study concludes that Popper cannot sustain a thoroughgoing anti-dogmatism. A further conclusion is that, contrary to widespread belief and Popper's own declaration, his political ideas cannot be classified as liberal in any straightforward way.

Historical and Intellectual Background

Although Popper rejected Marxism in 1919, he claims that he remained a socialist until 1932. It was the socialist ethic and its idea of justice to which Popper (1972: 13) retained allegiance, not its political strategies. Awareness of the growth of authoritarianism in the Soviet Union and what he saw as deficiencies in the Marxist theory and practice of Austrian social democracy pressed him to revise further his political views. Both the idea and the experience of violence were catalytic. Popper (*UQ*: 107) later reflected that by holding to their threat of achieving their objectives by violent means, social democrats were implicitly provoking state authorities to a ruthless response. Concluding that the socialists were unable to achieve their goals, let alone resist their enemies, Popper adopted a more traditional, if somewhat qualified, liberal political stance. Deciding that freedom was more important than equality he re-affirmed his rejection of violence. His (1972: 13) growing realization that 'institutionalized socialism renders the state too unwieldy and bureaucrats too powerful vis-à-vis citizens' also brought him to conclude that socialism and freedom were incompatible. As he later described his position, a liberal was one 'who values individual freedom and who is alive to the dangers inherent in all forms of authority' (*CR*: viii). Popper's liberalism, however, was at that time primarily a defensive position. It upheld liberal democratic ideals and values against an apparently burgeoning tide of authoritarianism.

Popper (1972: 14) was also inspired by his first visit to England in 1935–6, where, away from the Austrian dictatorship, he felt that he could 'at last breathe freely'. His nine-month stay in England was a 'revelation and an inspiration' (*UQ*: 111), prompting him to deploy the term 'open society'. Because of his Jewish ancestry, National Socialism and its violent anti-Semitism became by 1936–7 a threat sufficient to force him to leave Austria. In 1937 he emigrated to take up a lecturing position in New Zealand at Canterbury University College, Christchurch. Popper's time in New Zealand, and later travels to the USA, strengthened his high regard for western liberal democracies (*UQ*: 112, 128).

The core of Popper's social and political theory resides in two books, *The Poverty of Historicism* and *The Open Society and its Enemies*, both written between 1935 and 1945. Popper regarded these enterprises as his 'war effort' (*UQ*: 115). Not only were they intended as a defence of freedom against the more obvious impulses towards totalitarianism and authoritarianism, but they were also directed against the tendencies towards 'large-scale "planning"' that Popper thought would appear after the war (*UQ*: 115). The major focus of both books is upon the justifying ideas, primarily theories of knowledge, behind these political forces. From this critique Popper elaborates principles for political action and prescriptions for historical and social science method.

Although the idealized practice of the scientific community provides some inspiration for Popper's political prescriptions, this broader project owes much to Kant's philosophy. The problems of dogmatism and violence, and Popper's espousal of the values of reason, toleration, peaceful discussion and respect for the individual all find their antecedents in Kant's moral and political philosophy (Popper 1992: 140). Popper's extension of Kant's ethical precept of criticism and self-criticism, as a guide to an understanding of both natural and social phenomena, provided a foundation for his philosophy of critical rationalism. An optimistic belief in the possibility of obtaining social reform and peaceful relations within and between nations was a common motivation in the work of both Kant and Popper. The following analysis of Popper's conception of human nature indicates the scope of his project.

Human Nature

Popper rightly rejects the utility of a general theory of human nature for explaining human behaviour and history. Nonetheless, he maintains a number of long-standing assumptions about human beings, their needs and capacities, that influence the shape of his political thought, as well as his understanding of the limits and possibilities of political action.[2] The origins of Popper's conception of human nature may be found in his knowledge of biology and psychology. For Popper, human beings are similar to any organism, in that they have inborn needs or expectations (*CR*: 47). He considers the major problems in social life and politics to be dogmatic thinking and behaviour, and these are held to result from our almost overwhelming biological and subjective need for regularities. Although Popper (*UQ*: 50–1) acknowledges the importance of other dispositions and needs, such as those to love, sympathize and communicate, reference to 'the need for regularity' recurs throughout his writings. He writes:

> It was first in animals and children, but later also in adults, that I observed the immensely powerful *need for regularity* – the need which makes them seek for regularities; which makes them sometimes experience regularities even where there are none; which makes them cling to their expectations dogmatically; and which makes them unhappy and may drive them to despair and to the verge of madness if certain assumed regularities break down. (*OK*: 23–4)

These observations contain the kernel of Popper's approach to human nature and social structure. The stress upon regularities brings a significant ambivalence into his social thought. Depending on how they are treated, regularities may be the source of either human creativity, social order and tranquillity, or personal despair and social chaos.

According to Popper (CR: 132), people tend to hold on to the uniformities they discover, become afraid of change and even wish to dominate others. Where this occurs, the failure of a regularity provokes social disorder, and also encourages people to create traditions and taboos. More important, this also 'partly explains the strongly emotional intolerance which is characteristic of traditionalism' (CR: 132). The attachment to regularities is a source of dogmatism and intolerance, attitudes which are anathema to Popper. Nevertheless, he views social regularities such as social traditions more favourably than would many liberals. Partly for logical reasons and partly in recognition that people cannot cope with the breakdown of regularities, Popper advocates the maintenance of tradition by arguing that it brings order and predictability into our lives and even provides the foundation of social structure. Tradition, by which he seems to mean culture or settled ways of thinking and acting, gives us 'something that we can criticize and change' (CR: 131). The important political task is to discriminate between valuable and harmful traditions. Popper suggests that we take up the tradition of critical thought or critical rationalism, which is based upon the higher moral and intellectual capacities of human beings. This tradition of reason is the key to grappling with all other more dangerous traditions (CR: 135). Epistemology and methodology therefore lie at the core of Popper's social philosophy because of their powerful impact upon human thought and behaviour.

Popper's conception of human nature also has direct implications for the sort of society he wants to promote and the methods and principles by which it is to be guided. His criticism and endorsement of various political programmes are largely founded upon how he thinks they will impinge upon key human strengths and weaknesses. Slow gradual reform is proposed because it will not suddenly remove the traditions to which people have become accustomed and thereby create anxiety, or worse, terror and violence. Popper's political ambiguity on the subject is expressed as follows:

> I am repelled by the idea of keeping men under tutelage and authority.
> But I must admit on the other hand, that the pessimists who feared the

decline of authority and tradition were wise men. The terrible experience
of the great religious wars, and of the French and Russian revolutions,
prove their wisdom and foresight. (*CR:* 374)

The oft-noted contradiction between Popper's advocacy of bold-
ness, novelty and revolution in intellectual but not in social life may
be explained more with reference to his theory of human nature
than to his epistemology. Although he (1976b: 291) justifies the
distinction in epistemological terms, it becomes clear that objective
knowledge is preferable because of the constraints it exercises over
subjective fears and impulses. In Popper's view, the disembodied
self, best exemplified in the scientist, has no personal attachment to
the theories it has created and willingly submits them to the critical
scrutiny of others. In the world of ideas, where such intellectuals
thrive on novelty, continual change is apparently unproblematic.
Among the mass of people, however, the expectation of regularity
and reliance upon tradition is so great that their breakdown is a
source of personal distress and, eventually, violence.

This account of Popper's conception of human nature demonstrates his concern not just for the search for truth and discovery of
error, but also for the practical impact of ideas upon the social life of
human beings. Here we may see a conservative tone to his political
thought. Popper's project may be interpreted as an attempt to supply more suitable epistemological controls upon human thought
and action. His conception of human nature also suggests a theory
of history in which epistemology plays a vital role.

Epistemology and History

Popper's social and political thought includes a more general, speculative philosophy of history which indicates the character of historical progress. His work depicts the evolution of human beings from
their lower animal nature to their higher intellectual capacities.
History may be conceived as a continual struggle between these two
sides of human nature.

For Popper, ideas are the main influences upon whether or not
human progress is maintained. All social change and conflict, wars
and revolutions can be viewed as the outcome of conflict between
opposing ideas and ideologies (Popper 1973a: 174). Despite such
conclusions, he shares with the historicists whom he so vehemently
attacks a belief that there exists a direction to human history given

by the growth of knowledge (1969: 182–4). He (1969: 186) claims that 'the growth of knowledge, and thus the history of science, is the heart of all history.' It is the continuation of our biological evolution and as such represents 'a kind of universal plot, the main plot of human history, perhaps of the evolution of life' (1969: 184).

Although the most crucial episodes in the evolutionary story are behind us, with the emergence of consciousness, language and science, the social dilemmas produced by them have remained. For Popper, these are best exemplified in the evolution of the different social arrangements that have arisen from the exercise of different human faculties. The 'closed' and the 'open' societies represent 'ideal types' of two different stages of social and cultural evolution. Where the lower biological needs are dominant, the social structure has the character of a closed society in which all social life is guided by myths and rigid taboos. A magical attitude prevails which prevents any distinction being made between the regularities of nature and social customs. In the closed society there is no scope for self-doubt and personal moral responsibility. Changes in such societies come about more by the introduction of new magical taboos than by rational attempts to improve social conditions (*OSE I*: 172).

Popper maintains that the breakdown of the closed society began in Greece around 600 BC, when new intellectual values and methods of acquiring knowledge arose together with an original style of politics. Popper locates this shift in the Ionian school that inaugurated the new tradition of critical thought. Its innovation was to question and discuss dogmas and traditions instead of merely accepting them. Within this historical and philosophical transition Popper discerned the emergence of scientific method. Thus, science is distinguished from other myths because it is accompanied by a second order tradition of criticizing myths (*CR*: 127). This 'momentous innovation' also came to be associated with new political values, 'a new faith in reason, freedom and the brotherhood of all men' (*OSE I*: 184).

Both the idea of criticism and democratic practice allowed human beings to commence their graduation into the open society, where they could become aware of the importance of personal decisions and individual moral responsibility. People were able to pursue new kinds of personal relationships that were not determined by the accident of birth and such practices became the source of a new individualism. Where biological and physical bonds became weaker, more abstract relations such as those of exchange and cooperation linked together people and groups. Because of the breakdown of the biological character of the closed society, Popper (*OSE I*: 175) regards the transition as 'one of the deepest revolutions through which mankind has passed'. It provided the foundation of modern civilization.

In Popper's history of ideas, Plato's uncritical epistemology and authoritarian political theory were responsible for suppressing the values of the open society and these were only revived during the Renaissance and Reformation.[3] Popper also perceives a vital link between the epistemologies of Bacon and Descartes and the movements for political and religious liberation. Popper calls their epistemologies 'optimistic' because of their 'optimistic view of man's power to discern truth and acquire knowledge' (*CR*: 5). He sees 'epistemological optimism' as responsible for producing '*Europe's industrialism, its science, and its political idea of freedom . . . every one of those characteristic and fundamental aspects of European civilization*' (Popper 1994a: 192–3). In their opposition to tradition and authority, such theories of knowledge were revolutionary and provided a foundation of liberalism.

Yet, Popper was critical of epistemological optimism. Since Bacon and Descartes thought that all knowledge derived ultimately from divine authority, Popper concluded that they had not dispensed with an appeal to authority (*CR*: 15–16). Failing to see that all knowledge amounted to guesswork or *doxa*, and was prone to error, left their epistemologies with a number of unacceptable political implications. For example, Popper claims that the theory that truth is manifest is 'the basis of almost every kind of fanaticism' (*CR*: 8). Such a theory leads to the view that, if truth is there for all to see, then 'only the most depraved wickedness' can refuse to see it (*CR*: 8). It also supports a 'conspiracy theory of ignorance' in which one must identify powers or individuals who conspire to conceal the truth. Since truth is not usually manifest, an authority is needed to interpret and propound it (*CR*: 8–9).

By promoting particular social values and political practices, epistemologies are powerful agents of historical change. Nonetheless, where Popper's explanation of the origin of critical thinking itself is presented in terms of material economic factors (*OSE I*: 177), its revival in the Renaissance was partly attributed to the rise of science. This kind of ambiguity in Popper's theory of history indicates an empirical weakness that is characteristic of his social and political theory, and suggests limits to the power of his prescriptions. If material factors are important, then epistemology can contribute to, but not determine, social progress.

For all Popper's rejection of historical stages, his comments mark out major steps in the cultural evolution of humankind. Indeed, his fallibilist epistemology exemplifies the highest stage so far of episte- mological development. Yet, Popper's political goal was to intro- duce authentic scientific method into both the study of society and democratic practice (*PH*: 87). This task required dispensing with alternative doctrines such as that of historicism. His exposition and criticism of the methodological and political doctrine of historicism extends his theory of history into the twentieth century.

Historicist Doctrine of Politics

For Popper, one of the most powerful manifestations of the per- petual drive to subvert social and epistemological progress is the doctrine of historicism (*OSE I*: 2), which he defines as 'an approach to the social sciences which assumes that *historical prediction* is their principal aim, and which assumes that this aim is attainable by discovering the "rhythms" or the "patterns", the "laws" or the "trends" that underlie the evolution of history' (*PH*: 3). Popper (*PH*: vii, 3) criticizes historicism not simply because of its intellectual errors, but because of its detrimental effect upon moral and political life. The broad political scope of his work is indicated where he states that his enterprise was intended as 'a defence against totali- tarianism and authoritarian ideas' (*UQ*: 115). He aimed to criticize tendencies within both epistemology and politics, especially those associated with fascism and communism.

Popper categorizes historicists as either 'anti-naturalist' or 'pro- naturalist', depending upon their views on the applicability of the methods of natural science to social science. Whereas pro- naturalists favour the application of the methods of physics to social science, anti-naturalists reject the use of such methods. Politically, anti-naturalist historicists are activists who aim to remodel the whole of society along the lines of a utopian plan. Their project usually requires the seizure of key positions and extends the power of the state further into the private sphere of society (*PH*: 67). Holistic plans may need to transform human beings so that they fit into the scheme for the new society. Protesting that human lives should never be used to satisfy the utopian artist's desire for self- expression, Popper (*OSE I*: 165) criticizes the Platonic aestheticism inherent in some holistic and utopian blueprints. The problem for Popper is that change attempted upon such a scale is easily misman- aged, and planners would have to fall back on a piecemeal approach.

Popper (*PH*: 89) argues further that it would be necessary to suppress the inevitable criticisms and objections to large-scale social planning and that, as a result, the changes could not be evaluated scientifically. Even worse, it could lead to the elimination of individual differences, the suppression of free and critical thought, and, ultimately, the creation of dictatorship (*PH*: 90). Because holistic social experiments take no account of the lessons learnt from small experiments and mistakes, the historicist's mistakes are likely to be substantial (*PH*: 92). Consequently, Popper (*CR*: 343) thinks it unreasonable to assume that a complete reconstruction of society would lead to a workable system. He is convinced that revolutionary methods would only increase unnecessary suffering, encourage violence and eventually destroy freedom.

Even the alternative pro-naturalist historicist strategy of simply attempting to adjust to historical prophecies can also become antiliberal and anti-democratic. In the face of relentless historical laws, the belief that people of good will may be persuaded to take planned action for social reconstruction is the equivalent of a 'fairy tale' (*PH*: 47). Since the task of this form of social science is to prophesy and not to engineer, there are limits to individual action. Only those actions which fit in with the predicted course of events can be regarded as reasonable (*PH*: 49). One danger is that those historicists who become disappointed in their social prophecies come to despair of reason and to advocate political irrationalism (*CR*: 340–1).

Finally, Popper thinks that the pro-naturalist form of historicism also implies a kind of moral theory called 'moral futurism', which asserts that what is morally good is morally progressive (*PH*: 54). The latter, in turn, is determined by the standards to be adopted in the period to come. On this view, social aims and ends are no longer matters of human choice or moral decision; they can only be discovered scientifically by determining the historical tendencies and diagnosing the needs of the time (*PH*: 74–5). Popper criticizes this moral theory because it may encourage people to give up personal responsibility for events in their society. If one knows that things are bound to happen, one may feel free to relinquish any struggle for controlling social evils (*OSE I*: 4–5).

Popper's arguments against the historicist doctrine of politics have the character of an explanatory and predictive historical theory about the causes of social harm. The main difficulty with this analysis is that, beyond personal observation, Popper supplies little empirical evidence to support the view that a belief in historicist methods brings about historicist social policies and that these always cause great human suffering. Certainly, revolutionary methods have, at various times and in different countries, brought great misfortune. Such consequences may be attributable to a range of causes, such as ruthless struggles for internal political control, in which historicist methods play a minor role. Popper's conjectures on these topics are never subjected to the searching empirical scrutiny that he would usually advocate. That revolutionary political change need not produce totalitarianism, and may in fact be essential to overthrow a dictatorship and establish democracy, is a possibility that he recognizes (*OSE II*: 151–2).

The moral futurism Popper associates with pro-naturalist historicism need not encourage moral relativism and the relinquishing of personal responsibility. A sophisticated moral futurism could easily justify the adaptation of moral principles to changing contexts. For example, it would be futile to maintain a moral code formed for one set of circumstances when substantially different historical conditions prevail. Apart from an extreme moral futurism which, in rejecting all moral principles except those to prevail in the distant future, virtually renounces the claim to morality, there is considerable scope for moral evolution *and* personal responsibility.[4]

One of Popper's main criticisms of holism is its attempt to remould human beings. Since his own arguments are intended both to inform people and persuade them away from harmful political stances, change itself is not at issue, only its scale and scope. The title of *The Open Society and its Enemies*, however, suggests a Manichaean conflict between 'the friends and foes of liberty and rationality', between liberalism and totalitarianism, democracy and tyranny (Freeman 1975: 27–8). Whatever their polemical force such stark dichotomies do little justice to the complexities of past or present political struggles. Somewhat similar difficulties arise with Popper's critique of utopianism (*CR*: 355–63).[5]

The Open Society

One of Popper's most striking contributions to contemporary political thought may be found in his conception of the open society. This image of a self-critical, democratic polity stands in sharp contrast to the political dark age of closed and tradition-bound pre-scientific tribal societies. Comparisons with the authoritarian societies founded upon the misguided scientistic assumptions of historicism overwhelmingly favour Popper's social vision. The concept of the open society operates both as a minimalist ideal to be sought after and as a celebration of the achievements of modern rationality and liberal democracy. Much of its appeal lies in its apparent capacity to limit the impact of our inevitable errors and to contain potentially harmful social tendencies.

The open society aims to promote criticism and diversity without succumbing either to violent repression or irreconcilable social division. Its citizens are aware that they alone are responsible for their philosophies, science or morality, and thus authority and tradition are constantly questioned. This adventure in creative and critical thought produces conflict, but such problems are resolved by peaceful means. The values of freedom of thought and speech, toleration and individualism operate as both a motivation for, and a constraint upon, individual behaviour. Those more substantial differences are to be channelled into the democratic process whereby governments can be replaced by free and regular elections.

Popper recognizes the possibility of certain dangers in the historical evolution of the open society. He suggests that it could become the 'abstract society' in which social relations might become so rational as to be devoid of any personal quality (*OSE I*: 174). Although Popper acknowledges that modern industrial societies exhibit many such features, he denies that the process of abstraction or rationalization will complete itself. Human beings, he affirms (*OSE I*: 175), will continue to have 'social needs which they cannot satisfy in an abstract society'. These emotional needs will still be catered for in various family and other social groups. In this formulation, however, we see the familiar function of the private sphere providing emotional and biological regeneration for authentic life in the public sphere. Popper's neglect of the problems of unequal power and authority within family and personal life places him clearly within the mainstream of patriarchal political thought.

Although Popper (*OSE I*: 173) admits that such democracies fall short of his ideal, he is optimistic about their potential. He believes that their members are coming to exercise greater rational reflection and increased personal responsibility for their actions. Nonetheless, his judgements overlook those social forces, such as commercial advertising and the mass media, whose manipulative power may be as great as those 'magical' forces and taboos of the closed society. Whereas he (*CR*: 370) acknowledges the problems of corruption, petty authority and 'pocket dictators', he considers that the 'free world' has 'very nearly, if not completely, succeeded in abolishing the greatest evils which have hitherto beset the social life of man'.

These evils are considered to be those of poverty, unemployment, sickness and pain, penal cruelty, slavery, religious and racial discrimination, lack of educational opportunities, rigid class differences and war. Whatever their alleviation, a problem that Popper himself addresses elsewhere, no critical thinker could claim that these evils had been abolished. Even if the material standard of living in nations of the first world has improved, there are many indications that the problems of alienation and widespread disenchantment with democratic government have increased.

Perhaps these problems simply confirm Popper's view that the transition to the open society remains incomplete and its achievements are always under threat. These come from at least two directions. On the one hand, biological needs, old traditions, but perhaps more important, the difficulties of living with rationality and personal responsibility all combine to challenge the new society. It is beset by a 'new uneasiness', the strain of civilization (*OSE I*: 176). In Popper's view we must not succumb to such pressures, for to return to the closed society would be to forgo our humanity and 'return to the beasts' (*OSE I*: 200–1). The passions of our lower nature are always liable to rise up and overthrow the controls instituted by self-critical scientific rationality. On the other hand, as Shearmur (1996: 136–7) points out, the open society may be inherently self-destructive because critical thought continually erodes those older 'closed' traditions that sustain social institutions. Nevertheless, with a widespread appreciation of democratic values and carefully constructed political institutions, Popper thinks that the open society can create new traditions and remain viable. For all its intuitive appeal, Popper's concept of the open society remains little more than a sketch. This is particularly evident in its guiding values of freedom, reason, toleration and non-violence.

Freedom and Individualism

Popper's antipathy towards historicism and totalitarianism extends beyond their responsibility for human suffering, to the substantial political costs it incurs. Although physical well-being is one criterion of improvement in the human condition, the advancement of political freedom through democratic practices has a higher priority (Popper 1972: 15). Indeed, Popper (1992: 215) has written that 'only liberty makes life worth living'. Given the prominence of the rhetoric of freedom in Popper's writings, it is surprising that there is no systematic or detailed treatment of the concept. Whereas there are numerous references to the practical necessity for protecting freedom of speech and thought, the philosophical underpinnings are implied rather than stated. Popper's conception of freedom becomes apparent through analysis of his emphasis upon individualism. Indeed, freedom, for him, has no meaning outside individualism. Conceiving oneself as a separate individual, recognizing one's individual capacities and utilizing them in a humane way is the essence of his conception of freedom. Yet, freedom of the individual must be tempered by altruism and concern for others. In this regard, he (e.g. *OSE I*: 102) often cites Kant's categorical imperative: 'always recognize that human individuals are ends, and do not use them as mere means to your ends'. Such concerns are also evident in Popper's (*OSE I*: 265) awareness of the 'paradox of freedom' in which 'freedom in the absence of any restraining control must lead to a very great restraint, since it makes the bully free to enslave the meek'. These conditions lay the grounds for distinctive Popperian arguments that encompass both positive and negative conceptions of freedom.

From Popper's critique of historicism and utopianism it would seem that he gives a high priority to *negative* liberty, that which is concerned to protect the individual from planned and ruthless incursions into one's privacy (Berlin 1969: 122–31). 'If the growth of reason is to continue,' Popper (*PH*: 159) has written, '. . . then the diversity of individuals and their opinions, aims, and purposes must never be interfered with (except in extreme cases where political freedom is endangered).' That is, freedom from political coercion appears to be the predominant value. An examination of the principles guiding the open society, however, reveals a somewhat different but complementary emphasis. In freeing themselves from the collectivist ethic of the closed society, human beings exercise individual initiative (*OSE I*: 173, 190), and make rational choices based upon conscious, critical reflection. Here we find characteristics associated with a *positive* conception of liberty that refers to autonomy and self-development. This sense is present in Popper's (*OSE I*: 1) observation that the open society 'sets free the critical powers of man'. Thus, freedom is given an epistemological emphasis associated with the fulfilment of particular human capacities, namely, those of rational, critical thought and the search for truth. In Popper's work there also appears a positive concept of freedom as 'self-mastery' that bears some affinity to Berlin's (1969: 134–40) and Kant's idea of self-abnegation as the ascetic self-denial of worldly attachments.

The recognition that knowledge, whether of a moral or scientific kind, is one's personal creation, allows for the notion of individual freedom as self-development. Popper's formulation, however, is more restrictive than that criticized by Berlin. For example, it does not extend to self-realization conceived as all-round fulfilment or expressivism.[6] According to the conception of human nature outlined above, individuals can only become themselves through critical and creative interaction with ideas. To acquire objective knowledge, one must suppress certain emotional and biological propensities. Failure to do so is to retreat from critical thought and to forfeit one's status both as a free individual and as a member of the open society. For Popper, therefore, there are a number of dangers inherent in adopting a comprehensive principle of self-realization, especially one that is expressivist. Indulging the latter could encourage the degenerate political ideology of romanticism.

Because of the more limited epistemological meaning he gives to this positive concept of freedom, Popper does not share all Berlin's fears of the dangerous consequences of pursuing positive liberty. Indeed, Popper gives freedom as 'self-mastery' his own particular meaning. He would argue that unless one recognizes one's lower animal drives and passions, and devises ways of curtailing them, one risks a worse political fate, namely the extinction of both rationality and political freedom. To allow such drives free rein at either the social or the political level is to abandon a vital conception of what it is to be human (*OSE I*: 190). Shearmur (1996: 32–3) confirms that, although Popper commended Berlin on his discussion of negative liberty, he enquired whether there was not a positive concept of liberty compatible with negative liberty. Popper had in mind the search for truth understood as an expression of 'self-liberation' and which was also anti-authoritarian. On the argument above, however, Popper's concept of liberty has two related dimensions. The first 'negative' dimension requires protection of the individual. But this is virtually a prerequisite for a second 'positive' concept of freedom understood as the self-realization of human capacities, with an emphasis upon critical and rational thought.

This discussion suggests that Popper maintains a clear distinction between the public and the private sphere of individual action. For example, he argues that there are several limited purposes for which state power ought to be used, namely to secure equal freedom for all and to overcome concrete and identifiable evils. Any intrusion upon individual freedom or privacy for such 'empirical' purposes may be regarded as the legitimate and proper role of government. Nonetheless, the pursuit of 'higher' metaphysical values such as happiness is to be left to private individual initiative (*OSE II*: 237). Intellectual self-development is a public activity.

With a notable qualification, Popper's dichotomy between public and private appears to reaffirm the traditional liberal appeal to an inviolable area in which the individual may be free from public interference. Mill (1962: 138) and others, for example Berlin, see this sphere as the repository for several different activities such as those concerning personal relationships, conscience and even the scientific, moral or theological liberty of expressing and publishing opinions. For Popper, however, science and any form of objective knowledge is necessarily of a *public* character. Its quality and existence is not guaranteed, but undermined by privacy, since this would not normally allow for extensive criticism. The capacity to pursue self-fulfilment privately or hold private opinions marks out a substantially weaker and subjective form of autonomy.

Popper's demarcation between the public sphere of self-realization through critical rational thought and the private sphere of emotional expression and self-fulfilment raises other issues. He implies that all emotional difficulties can be resolved by rational restraint, or even repression, and that the only obstacles to self-realization are external. The exercise of critical thought itself, however, may be impeded as much by internal psychological factors as by external ones. On Shearmur's (1996: 33) account, Popper discusses a somewhat similar theme in a letter to the liberal philosopher and economist Friedrich Hayek. Popper (cited in Shearmur 1996: 33) writes: 'with zero inner strength all kinds of action would be [coercive] which do not coerce a man of average inner strength; so that one way of increasing one's freedom [from] coercion is, clearly, the increase of one's inner strength.'

Charles Taylor's (1979a: 193) critique of negative liberty is pertinent here, as he draws attention to the problem of internal constraints upon freedom and the role of self-understanding in overcoming them. For Taylor, self-understanding is a vital precondition of autonomy or self-mastery. For Popper, however, this strategy would be futile. 'Self-analysis', he maintains (*OSE II*: 223), 'is no substitute for those practical actions which are necessary for establishing the democratic institutions which alone can guarantee the freedom of critical thought, and the progress of science.' Although Popper's notion of individual responsibility requires a concept of liberty as self-mastery, understood in epistemological terms, he does not indicate adequately how this may be attained.

Within Popper's defence of individualism is to be found a broad theory of freedom that incorporates both negative and positive dimensions. The core positive conception of liberty, understood as self-realization, however, is essentially of a public and social character, necessarily qualified by the equal claims of others. The curbing of individual freedom is demanded by the altruistic value of equal respect for individuals. Such 'controls' are achieved by various means. The most obvious are democratic institutions which protect freedom of expression, ensure equality of treatment before the law, and, where necessary, promote limited social reform. Thus Popper affirms the indissoluble tie between democracy, liberty and equality. Yet, there is evidence of a stronger social democratic project that requires firm intervention by the state to secure the conditions necessary for the exercise of freedom.[7] Essentially, he argues that the state ought to engage in more interventionist programmes of social and educational reform and protect individuals from economic exploitation. As we shall see below, however, Popper also imposes strict limits upon the pursuit of equality (*UQ*: 36). Nonetheless, because of his egalitarianism and his humanitarianism, Popper's concept of freedom cannot be limited to non-interference.

Popper's advocacy of negative and positive forms of freedom reinforces arguments about the difficulty of making sharp distinctions between the two concepts. Moreover, it is clear that there is no logical or necessary connection between the idea of rational self-mastery and political oppression. Popper has a classical liberal's distrust of government, a social liberal or social democratic concern for autonomy and self-development, and also their humanitarianism. Such a combination reflects his efforts to reconcile liberalism and democratic socialism (Shearmur 1996: 33). Although freedom may be expressed through human rationality, the latter also constrains the exercise of individual freedom. The open society imposes epistemological and ethical controls on its members, which include the values of rationalism, toleration and non-violence.

Reason, Toleration and Violence

Popper offers a number of different meanings for rationality. Depending upon the context, to be rational may mean being goal-oriented, falsifiable or engaging in problem-solving by trial and error; it may involve being reasonable, critical, self-critical or open to criticism, tolerant or intellectually humble, and it may be characterized by the use of argument rather than passion or violence. This section explores the affinities and relations between different meanings that are central in Popper's thought.

Rationalism is defined initially as the use of *evidence and argument* and is a method that 'seeks to solve as many problems as possible by an appeal to reason, i.e. to clear thought and experience, rather than by an appeal to emotions and passions' (*OSE II*: 224). Popper concedes that there is one form of argument, namely propaganda, which he considers very likely to produce violence. Popper's rationalism therefore requires a complementary notion of *reasonableness*, which is 'an attitude of readiness to listen to critical arguments and to learn from experience' (*OSE II*: 225). Here may be found the moral core of Popper's fallibilism, which lies not so much in the methodological technique of falsificationism which generates 'errors', but in an ethic which requires us to have doubts about our knowledge. We are urged to follow Socrates and espouse an intellectual humility that acknowledges how little we know (*OSE I*: 130).

The process of doubting, however, must be a conscious 'attitude' or policy of *openness to criticism* which has both a subjective and an objective character. The subjective or more psychologistic aspect requires one to be prepared to listen to criticism, to be able to accept criticism, to practise self-criticism, and to engage in mutual criticism with others. On the other hand, the objective or epistemic component comprises the particular method of argument to be used once the subjective attitude or moral stance has been adopted. This includes the application of principles of logic, experimental testing and the method of trial and error problem-solving.

Nevertheless, Popper recognizes a number of practical problems. Merely listening to arguments and criticism, for example, may encourage frustration or inaction. Severe criticism could simply provoke social division and violent conflict. Popper (*OSE II*: 225) therefore suggests that the critical attitude must be accompanied by a belief that by following rationalist procedures widespread social agreement may be attained. Rationalism implies the possibility of social cooperation and something like scientific objectivity. Reasoning must also be conceived as a *social process*. The results are social, not individual, products emanating from mutual discussion and argument.

Since to reason is to engage in social communication, this activity requires non-epistemic or moral rules of social conduct. Central among these is the moral imperative to take others and their arguments seriously. For this reason, rationalism 'establishes what may be described as the "rational unity of mankind"' (*OSE II*: 225; Popper 1992: 199). The attitude of reasonableness includes the moral constraints of *toleration*, mutual respect and the readiness to compromise (*OSE II*: 225). Popper (*OSE I*: 265 fn. 4) qualifies this principle with reference to the *paradox of tolerance*, and contends that we ought not tolerate those who practise intolerance.

Finally, Popper defines reason as peaceful discussion or *nonviolence*. Indeed, the major argument for critical rationalism is that it is the only alternative to violence (*CR*: 355; *OSE II*: 238). Rational critical discussion, he (1972: 17) explains, 'enables us to eliminate bad hypotheses and to dismiss them as erroneous without exterminating their authors or proponents'. Popper therefore chooses reason, or rationalism, primarily because of its beneficial social consequences. Rationalism comprises a set of principles that are both epistemological and ethical.

Despite their apparent plausibility there are a number of theoretical and practical difficulties in Popper's concepts of toleration, violence and reason. With regard to toleration it must first be noted that he focuses primarily upon free speech and thought in pursuit of knowledge. Outside his exclusion of physical violence Popper does not refer to action itself. That is, he neither refers to the more general field of morality nor to that area of action which Mill (1962: 206) called 'self-regarding'. Popper's concept of toleration does not, for example, extend explicitly to the fields of sexual morality, pornography, suicide and the like. Furthermore, what counts as intolerance often depends upon the ultimate consequence. Failing to tolerate fools gladly would hardly count as a threat to democratic order. To incarcerate all whom one perceived as a fool would.

As Popper's paradox of tolerance suggests, however, it may be defensible to put limits on toleration. In politics as well as science there are grounds for remaining dogmatic and intolerant of criticism, in order to attract stronger criticism, while holding to a general principle of tolerating diverse opinions (Popper 1974a: 55). On this account, therefore, intolerance may be entrenched or temporary. Such practical dogmatism in both social and scientific life would not appear to demand the censure of intolerance that Popper's precept would require. Both applying and withholding the principle of toleration requires complex forms of practical judgement. Popper's proposals need more elaboration before they can be a useful guide to social or scientific practice.

The difficulty in finding a satisfactory way of dealing with such issues is most evident in the problem of defining and distinguishing between reason and violence. If one is uncertain about whether an action is violent or not, one can hardly be certain about whether to tolerate or resist it. Practical judgement in such matters is unavoidable. The utility of such distinctions is also reduced by Popper's attachment to the value of *instrumental rationality*, which stresses the effectiveness of particular means to given ends. This is most evident in Popper's suggestion that it would not be entirely rational or reasonable merely to argue with someone who is an admirer of violence and who is threatening to shoot you. The only sensible response for Popper (*CR*: 359) is to control the person 'by the threat of counter-violence'. Once the rationality of counter-violence is admitted, however, then so is the use of violence for other means. Although he has numerous and strong reservations about the effectiveness of violence, Popper (1972: 18; Popper and Eccles 1974: 118) allows that it may be rational in the effort to establish an open, democratic society.

Such difficulties indicate that 'rationality', 'rationalism', 'reasonableness', 'criticism', 'non-violence' and 'toleration' are not all synonyms in Popper's work. The question must then be asked: Where one form of rationality appears to contradict another, which is to be allocated priority? Ultimately, it seems as if the choice necessarily involves a series of pragmatic moral judgements in which one explores the social consequences and chooses the least harmful. By arguing for the use or threat of violence in the fight against dictatorship, Popper both reaffirms the pre-eminence of rationality conceived as efficiency, and indicates its subordination to values such as democracy and freedom. This approach justifies the use of violence as force of law under liberal democratic regimes and the deterrent value of nuclear weapons to achieve world peace (Popper 1994a: 125). Despite his strong commitment to reason as non-violence, Popper is prepared to revoke it if it is considered rationally ineffective for the attainment of higher social goals or moral values. It is for such pragmatic reasons that he is not a pacifist.

If we accept, as Popper does, that argument and violence are both forms of action which may be means to particular goals, then we may characterize them either as rational or irrational depending upon their perceived effectiveness in promoting those ends (see Edgley 1973: 22). In his explicit discussions of argument and violence, Popper focuses primarily upon the physical harm or injury able to be inflicted upon people, and makes no reference to any notion of psychic or moral harm. Yet, his entire philosophy may be regarded as an argument against the moral harm perpetuated by particular ideologies and epistemologies. Such ideas are harmful not just because they lead to physical violence, but also because they predispose people to attitudes which may be considered both instrumentally and inherently violent, and curtail a person's freedom. More important for Popper, they may encourage individuals to relinquish personal moral responsibility for their actions.

Depending upon the context, the expression of emotion may also be deemed rational in many of Popper's senses. The promotion of a non-violent society could well be dependent upon the use of increased emotional self-expression as a means of dissolving the psychological blocks which prevent mutual acceptance and openness of communication. Popper's own passion for truth and hatred of violence appear to serve as motivations for creating an open society. For all their intuitive appeal, the dichotomies of reason and emotion and reason and violence are insufficient for the weight they have to bear in Popper's political thought.

The discussion above confirms that Popper's epistemology comprises a non-epistemic ethic which sets the social and political rules for the human cooperation necessary for the acquisition of knowledge. Yet, judgements about when to apply or suspend such rules as toleration or peaceful discussion become essentially pragmatic matters for which there are no firm guidelines. In politics, as in science, such decisions are dependent upon interpretations of the relevance of the principle for a given context. Democracy provides the overarching institutional context for Popper's social and political theory.

Democracy and Piecemeal Social Engineering

Democracy performs a vital function for both politics and epistemology. It provides a peaceful means for reform and change of government, while ensuring the freedom of thought and speech necessary for intellectual progress (*OSE I*: 4, 126; *CR*: 350; *PH*: 154–5). This process encourages a pluralism of ideas and groups (*PH*: 155). Such pluralism is the necessary precondition for the 'working out of political meanings and aims', and is vital for the processes of critical thought and the goal of emancipation through knowledge (Popper 1992: 148).

Popper's theory of democracy typically grows out of his criticism of other approaches to government, initially that of Plato and later of Marx. He denies (*OSE I*: 120; 1988: 24) that the guiding principles of politics should be determined by answers given to the question

'Who should rule?'. Instead, we should ask (*OSE I*: 121): '*How can we so organize political institutions that bad and incompetent rulers can be prevented from doing too much damage?*' Popper (1988: 24) also asks the complementary question: How can rulers be 'got rid of' without bloodshed and violence?

In response, Popper argues that democracy should be founded upon a '*theory of checks and balances*' (*OSE I*: 122). Assuming that even the best rulers have failings, this theory relies on institutional means for curbing their power. The major check is provided by periodic elections that enable people 'to oust their government without using violent means' (Popper 1972: 16). This points up the difference between democracy and its opposite, tyranny, which 'consists of governments which the ruled cannot get rid of except by way of a successful revolution' (*OSE I*: 124). Popper denies that there is any true meaning or essence of democracy. He is adamant, however, that it does not mean 'the rule of the people', or even that the majority should rule, if only because this is impossible in any concrete or practical way (*OSE I*: 124–5). Nor does his theory of democracy assume that 'we can ever develop institutions . . . which are faultless or foolproof' (*OSE I*: 125). In Popper's view (*OSE I*: 125), acceptance of a bad policy in a democracy is 'preferable to the submission to a tyranny, however wise or benevolent'.

Democracy relies upon the political methods of general elections and representative government, and Popper (*OSE I*: 125) considers these are always open to improvement. Democracy must allow individuals both to criticize majority decisions and, within the law, to attempt to revise them (*OSE I*: 125, 189; Popper 1972: 14). There is also an additional stimulus of organized public opinion. 'For in a democracy,' Popper (*CR*: 345) notes, 'the rulers will be compelled by threat of dismissal to do what public opinion wants them to do.' Accordingly, within a democracy opportunities ought to be available for ideas to replace force and violence as the determinants of political decision-making.

Except on the issue of proportional representation, Popper provides little detail on such practical matters as methods of representation, size and nature of electorates, and length of terms of office. He rejects proportional representation because of its origins in dubious theories of sovereignty, and also because of its propensity to produce unstable coalition governments. In Popper's (1988: 26) view, two-party government is preferable if only because it allows for more serious internal self-criticism after election defeats. On such issues, his characterization of democracy is a relatively conventional elaboration of liberal pluralist principles. Despite his quest for intellectual and political simplicity, it remains arguable that, on their own, such principles may not guarantee the survival of liberal democracy. Issues of representation, size, nature of electorates and so on all have a bearing upon whether citizens would consider themselves to be members of a legitimate democracy. In practice, a pluralist system of checks and balances may be so restrictive as to prevent a duly elected government from carrying out its policies. With the power of government and business to manipulate 'public opinion' there may be little pressure at all upon those in office to change their policies.

Perhaps more important, within Popper's theory of democracy may be discerned a tension between elitism and participation. Because it is assumed that the mass of people cannot govern, Popper reduces democracy to a theory of competing elites (Petras 1966: 9). Yet, democracy is also likened to a community of scientists in which all engage in critical and free debate on important public issues and no one is prevented from participating. Popper provides no means whereby the two approaches may be linked, other than by the unpredictable impact of public opinion or periodic elections. For these reasons, Popper's procedural arguments lie within the tradition of realist and revisionist democratic theory that gives priority to competitive elites and argues for democracy as a method for choosing governments.

Popper's significant departure from realist democratic theory lies in his recognition that control over government is not all there is to creating a democratic state and society. His solution, however, is not to encourage widespread political participation, but to require that the state protect democracy in two ways. First, since democracies must always be open to ideas protection must be given to minorities, except those 'who violate law, and especially ... those who incite others to the violent overthrow of the democracy'; Popper therefore requires that a 'consistent democratic constitution should exclude only one type of change in the legal system, namely a change which would endanger its democratic character' (*OSE II*: 161). Second, because Popper is concerned to avoid the misuse of political power and economic power, he exhorts democratic states to engage in social and economic reforms. He maintains that institutions must be constructed to protect the economically weak against the economically strong (*OSE II*: 125; Popper 1972:14). To safeguard freedom, Popper (*OSE II*: 125) demands 'that unrestrained *capitalism* give way to an *economic interventionism*'. He (*OSE II*: 182) considers that systematic interference with the trade cycle is both possible and defensible. In Popper's view (*OSE II*: 126), 'political power is the key to economic protection'. He argues that unless political power is exercised in a democratic fashion then one runs the risk of losing both political and economic freedom (*OSE II*: 127). He adds that state interests 'must not be lightly invoked to defend measures which may endanger the most precious of all forms of freedom, namely, intellectual freedom' (*OSE I*: 131).

Popper is convinced that economic and social reform are not only possible, but are necessary ingredients of a democratic order. Indeed, he suggests that democratic planning is essential: 'Only by planning, step by step, for institutions to safeguard freedom, especially freedom from exploitation, can we hope to achieve a better world' (*OSE II*: 143). Although such strategies create greater possibilities for increased state power and bureaucracy, these may be diminished by strengthening democratic institutions and by following the principles of piecemeal social engineering (*OSE II*: 193–4). The latter policy is not as restrictive as it is commonly thought (*OSE I*: 285; Popper and Eccles 1974: 109), but it does rule out the nationalization and socialization of the entire private industry of a country. Popper (1972: 13) argues that 'this is not a remedy for all social evils, but rather . . . a threat to the freedom of the individual'. It must be countered, however, that whether such policies are liberating or oppressive depends upon empirical assessment of how they would expand or constrict the core freedoms of individual autonomy and self-development.

A separate point in favour of piecemeal social engineering is thought to be its scientific character. Popper considers it methodologically superior to holistic and revolutionary programmes, in part because piecemeal social engineers accept the limitations of their knowledge. He (*PH*: 85) regards piecemeal social experiments as the basis of all social knowledge, both pre-scientific and scientific. Such knowledge is being developed all the time for practical rather than scientific purposes. For example, the grocer who opens a new shop or a person who joins a theatre queue are each gaining experimental knowledge which may be useful in the future (*PH*: 86 and *OSE I*: 162). The mistakes made in such endeavours are the essential means whereby progress occurs (*PH*: 87). Popper (*PH*: 86–7) generalizes from this insight to suggest that there is no reason why we should not be more systematic and critical in our social experiments. This is the means whereby the scientific method of trial and error is brought into the study of society and politics (*PH*: 87).[8]

By reformulating key questions about democracy, Popper side-steps some of the more usual difficulties of universalist democratic theory.[9] By requiring state action to remedy certain kinds of social and economic problems, Popper offers more of policy substance than the usual realist and proceduralist forms of democratic theory. In addition, his goal is to avoid or minimize the violent conflict that he sees inevitably arising from arguments over 'the good society'. Popper claims that whereas we may not be able to agree on abstract universal values, the shape of an ideal society or the ultimate good of people, we can generally reach agreement on concrete social and economic evils such as poverty and disease. It must be said, however, that Popper has not abandoned universal values. He has just not developed them or their justification in great detail.

A major difficulty is that Popper's policy recommendations are so general and lacking in detail for application to specific contexts that one cannot easily depend upon them for practical guidance. What counts as suffering, or how ought we to measure poverty, for example? Popper, nonetheless, would reject the idea that there could be some precise universal (essential) definition for such subjects. Given the establishment of the institutions he recommends, democratic societies could possibly rely upon democratic debate and negotiation to determine the criteria. The next issue would become that of deciding upon the appropriate means for alleviating suffering. Even here, Popper's theory provides a relevant principle by requiring that those who suffer have a say in how their suffering may be alleviated, or, at a minimum, be able to vote against governments that have attempted the task and failed.

Depending upon one's perception of the main characteristics of a society or period of history, the question of scale is open to debate. What may appear initially to have been an extensive piecemeal social policy may turn out to have more substantial or holistic implications. We may see the institutions of slavery, private property, or apartheid as simply the key focus of political transformation. Nonetheless, if changing these institutions inaugurates a radically new social system, we may be justified in calling the process holist (Freeman 1975: 23). It is not impossible to institute such changes, as Popper (OSE II: 141) acknowledges when he claims that most of Marx's programmes 'have been put into practice' in liberal democracies, but without revolution.

A major advantage of Popper's commitment to non-violence, public criticism and freedom of speech is that it allows us to retain a critical perspective upon all kinds of governments. The theory's minimal proceduralism and gradualism, for example, may accommodate democratic aspirations in less developed or developing countries without subscribing to wholesale westernization and modernization. Popper's substantive policy proposals reject the radicalism of laissez-faire economics and offer the social benefits of gradualism, stability and security. Their negative utilitarianism encourages governments to ameliorate the worst aspects of individualism and capitalism, and allows a legitimate role for state intervention in society and economy. By combining an ethical proceduralism with a requirement for state-initiated reform, Popper's theory advances somewhat beyond the usual forms of democratic elitism and revisionism.

Liberalism, Conservatism and Social Democracy

Popper's social and political thought comprises elements which may be designated liberal, social democratic and conservative. With its respect for individual freedom, and its emphasis upon the power of ideas in promoting progress, critical rationalism lies primarily within the mainstream of the liberal tradition. Nevertheless, a combination of liberal and conservative assumptions are discernible in his conception of human nature, which sets out both an optimistic view of human potential and a largely pessimistic account of human needs. The social vision, however, is the liberal rationalist one of an open society in which the values of freedom, reason, toleration and non-violence prevail. In Popper's theory of history, ideas are the levers of historical progress, and his fallibilist epistemology suggests the scientific and political methods for achieving liberal values. For Popper, critical rational thought, of both a more formal epistemic kind and as a set of ethical values or attitudes, comprise part of a political programme. Central among these is the liberal demand for personal moral responsibility. Popper also offers specific institutional guidelines for building and maintaining democracy, and advocates policies such as piecemeal social engineering, oriented towards protecting individuals from the ravages of the market. The latter programme, however, which is predicated upon the goal of minimizing human suffering, reflects more a residual social democratic concern for social justice.

Possibly, Popper's most distinctive contribution to the liberal tradition resides in the content he gives to its theory of history. By drawing attention to the persuasive power of epistemologies, he gives a fresh perspective upon the history of ideas as social forces. Although Popper displays shrewd insights into the link between ideas and social change, these do not constitute a coherent theory of political development. The analysis suffers from its neglect of the social and economic context in which particular ideas may gain currency.

Popper's emphasis upon human beings as rational creatures rejects any broad developmental conception of self-fulfilment based upon the range of human faculties. The fear of emotional subjectivity has led to an undue emphasis upon rational means for its control. Popper's isolated comments to the contrary do not indicate a weakening of his more usual antipathy towards emotional expression (see *CR*: 357; 1972: 13; *OK*: 12). Such an approach tends to forget that instrumental rationality, for example, can become a powerful form of bondage. For a liberal philosopher, however, the guiding values of liberty, rationality, toleration and non-violence of the open society are relatively undeveloped.

Popper's conservatism is most evident in his political realism and his uncritical attitude towards contemporary liberal democracies. Underlying his stress upon the need for creative and revolutionary thought there is the fear that this will bring social disorder. Hence, such intellectual processes need to be contained within firm traditions whose overthrow cannot be countenanced except to establish a democracy. Popper's political project may justifiably be seen as attempting to provide more suitable traditions or controls upon human thought and action. There remains in Popper's social and political thought, however, an unavoidable conflict between his liberal rationalist values and his perception of the perverse and intractable nature of individuals. His conception of the open society and the programmes for reaching it reflects such contradictions. Certainly, his ethical universalism and cosmopolitanism differentiate him from most conservatives, and this is presented as a weakness by one critic. Minogue (1995a: 83) takes Popper to task for the 'thin texture of his moral understanding' and his abstract notion of tradition which limits the effectiveness of his moral demands.

In supplying reasons for his benign view of liberal democracies, Popper reveals more of his political conservatism. He considers that the achievements of the 'free world' need to be brought to public awareness, because 'we have become unduly sceptical about ourselves' (*CR*: 372). Countries like Great Britain, according to Popper, have been far too ready to accept criticism from their opponents. In order to consolidate our democratic achievements, therefore, we are urged to suspend our critical faculties. But without the pressure of such criticisms Popper is confined to a naive understanding of modern society and a correspondingly ambiguous and ineffectual political programme. Nonetheless, for authoritarian polities with few basic freedoms of speech and assembly, equality of political rights or rudimentary representative institutions, Popper's political vision serves a positive function. The open society operates as a powerful regulative ideal that allows both political critique and indicates the basic requirements for democratic, institutional reform.

Given many of the features outlined above, Popper's critics have usually designated his social and political theory as liberal. Several have even suggested that Popper's work constitutes the most 'formidable' defence of liberalism and democracy since J. S. Mill.[10] Although such claims are given credibility by Popper, who later described himself as an 'old-fashioned liberal', he shares little with the classical liberals, apart from a general respect for freedom. Shearmur (1996: 132) has drawn out these tensions to argue that Popper's advocacy of social engineering conflicts radically with his Kantian commitment to treat individuals as ends in themselves. Partly for this reason, Shearmur argues that Popper's political thought ought to be closer to that of Hayek, with its greater respect for the role of the market.

As an interpretative problem, as opposed to one of ideal coherence, such an argument turns upon which value is given highest priority in Popper's work. Although he makes a number of definitive or categorical moral claims, it is not always clear which one, or even if any, has priority over another. At least one common strategy seems to be that of subordinating epistemic values of rationality to those of freedom and democracy. For example, it is evident that there would always be cases where violent individuals, for example, ought not to be treated as ends in themselves. It is also conceivable that the misery and suffering engendered by 'mass poverty' may be so great that the Kantian principle *demands* social engineering (Popper 1992: ix). To fail to undertake such strategies when they were technically and politically possible, and leave people in their impoverished circumstances, would render empty the principle of treating people as 'ends in themselves'.

If my interpretation above is correct, then Popper's work does not sit as easily within the liberal tradition as I and others have previously argued (e.g. Ryan 1985; Stokes 1995a). Many of his public and private arguments on the role of the state and the market locate him closer to European social democracy. Indeed, Popper (*OSE II*: 238) is explicit that rationalism requires 'planning for freedom and for its control by reason'. Shearmur (1996: 36) reports that as late as 1974, Popper recommended a system where the state ought to take a controlling share (51 per cent) of all public companies. If one wanted to claim Popper for liberalism it would be that of a social liberalism concerned to protect and enhance freedom by selective use of state intervention. It would also have to be a social liberalism stripped of any 'organic' metaphors and that placed a low priority on expressivism. As Shearmur acknowledges, in many respects Popper's political thought resists straightforward categorization.

Whatever its classification, Popper's social and political theory is the necessary complement and precondition to his epistemology. Together, the political theory and the epistemology constitute critical rationalism. It extends the principles of scientific method to politics and social science, and suggests practical measures for combating the political evils he has discerned. As such, it provides the social foundation for epistemology and a more sophisticated conception of rationality. Popper's epistemology and methodology emerge from his political concern to encourage the growth of a free and rational way of life. If there is an underlying coherence or unity to Popper's work, it is to be found in his social and political thought. Critical rationalism also develops a more sophisticated understanding of the role of dogma in both epistemology and politics. It explains why, in certain circumstances, dogma is unavoidable and even morally responsible. The next chapter explains how political values also set limits for Popper's philosophy of social science.

Philosophy and Methodology of Social Science

Popper's philosophy and methodology of social science grow out of his critique of historicism and are a programmatic extension of his political philosophy of freedom and reason. His methodological proposals are based largely upon his understanding of the distinctive political threat that social science poses for the conduct of critical reason. This chapter demonstrates how Popper's political values, namely freedom of the individual, democracy and a concern to alleviate human suffering, underpin his methodological arguments. The focus here is primarily upon his early substantive arguments for a 'unity of method' between natural science and social science. It will be argued that, despite his unifying intention, Popper provides good reasons for treating the two sciences differently. The chapter also examines his rudimentary ethical theory.

Background: Historicist Doctrines of Method

The social sciences never held the same attraction for Popper as natural science (*UQ*: 121). Nonetheless, he considered that social research had great practical urgency and that philosophers 'should not be content to interpret the world but should help to change it' (*CR*: 337). He believed that the best he could do was to tackle serious social problems 'armed with the weapons of a *critic of methods*' (*CR*: 337). Popper wanted to draw attention to the problems arising from historicist versions of scientific method that had become prominent in European politics and political thought. He thought that historicist methods not only yielded poor scientific results, but that they also provided support for political theories that encouraged individuals to return to pre-scientific, dogmatic and irrational modes of thought and action. His practical concern was for the human consequences of these theories, such as the suffering and loss of life under communism and fascism.

Popper constructs the doctrine of historicism from a diverse range of notions, both popular and academic, about the evolution of history and the role of scientific method in its interpretation. Although he extended his critique to include Plato, Hegel, Comte, J. S. Mill and Mannheim, the principal contemporary enemy was Marxism (*OSE II*: 81; Popper 1974b: 1172–3). As we saw in the previous chapter, Popper was most concerned with that form of historicism which has *historical prediction* as its principal aim (*PH*: 3).[1] He considers that anti-naturalistic and pro-naturalistic historicism share vital misconceptions about the nature of their subject-matter and their view of the method of physics.

At their time of publication Popper's polemics against historicism provided sharp and systematic critiques of key problems in politics and philosophy of social science. Although his attack on the political ramifications of historicism was innovative, one pervasive weakness is that it glosses over important differences among those he regards as influential historicists. He also attributes to them positions regarding holism, essentialism, laws and trends, which few would have defended.[2] The methodological doctrines were probably held only among the popularizers of thinkers such as Marx and Mill. Popper aimed not only to criticize intellectually flawed and politically dangerous conceptions of social science, but also to propose a methodological alternative.

The Problem of the Unity of Method

Over the length of his career, Popper (e.g. *PH*: 130; *OSE I*: 286; 1976a; *CR*: 336–46) constantly argued for a unity of scientific method between the natural and the social sciences. By this, he meant that 'all theoretical or generalizing sciences make use of the same method, whether they are natural sciences or social sciences' (*PH*: 130). Popper explored not only the 'logic' of scientific method, but also closely related topics such as the goals of science, the objects of enquiry, the nature of scientific explanation and the epistemic values that guided scientific research. He readily acknowledges that there are differences between the natural and social sciences, but argues that they are less significant than the similarities (*PH*: 130). There are also a number of discrete shifts in emphasis between his early and his later philosophies of science and social science which will be considered in chapters 6 and 7.

Goals of Science: Explanations and Consequences

According to Popper (*LScD*: 49), the choice of methods depends upon our aims. The broad aim of science was 'that of ever discovering new, deeper, and more general problems, and of subjecting our ever tentative answers to ever renewed and ever more rigorous tests' (*LScD*: 281). His methodological rules also set important subsidiary aims for scientists, such as 'we are not to abandon the search for universal laws and for a coherent theoretical system, nor ever give up our attempts to explain causally any kind of event that we can describe' (*LScD*: 61).

For Popper, practical problems were a 'spur' and 'bridle' to the theories of both natural and social science (*PH*: 56). Nevertheless, whereas natural science *may* contribute to the solution of industrial or agricultural problems, for social science the solution of practical problems is mandatory. If social science were not to concern itself with urgent practical problems, it would risk becoming 'barren scholasticism', 'mysticism' or 'irrationalism' (*OSE II*: 222). In social science, therefore, Popper supplements the epistemic aims of explanation and prediction with the non-epistemic, political goals of solving urgent social problems.

Popper's contribution here is to require social science '*to trace the unintended social repercussions of intentional human actions*' (*CR*: 342; *OSE II*: 95). Popper considers those actions that proceed according to intention to be unproblematic, except for the need to explain why there were no unintended consequences (*OSE II*: 96). The term 'unintended consequences' does not refer simply to those actions 'not *consciously* intended', but to consequences 'which may violate *all* the interests of the social agent, whether conscious or unconscious' (*PH*: 158). We must seek causal explanations of how our best laid plans may be disrupted and lead to unwanted outcomes. Social science therefore serves the modest practical and ethical purpose of 'helping us to understand even the more remote consequences of possible actions, and thus of helping us to choose our actions more wisely' (*CR*: 343). As a 'negative' guide to social intervention, one of its most characteristic functions is to '*point out what cannot be achieved*' (*PH*: 61). This requirement resembles Popper's central methodological recommendation for natural science that scientific theories ought to be falsifiable and put in the form of prohibitions (*LScD*: 69).

Unlike natural science, the ultimate goal of social science is practical success, which is to be tempered by the moral requirement of assessing unintended consequences upon human beings.[3] Although Popper denies that this practical orientation entails pragmatism (*PH*: 56), his avowed goals for social research mark out a crucial difference between the methods of natural and social science. For natural science, success or otherwise in practical experimental testing is a means to the pursuit of truth without regard to practical consequences. In social science, however, the test of successful practice is whether or not it contributes to human well-being, such as the alleviation of suffering. The search for truth, or true explanations, is only one of the goals of social science and must be complemented by a wider social ethic.

Objects of Enquiry: Theoretical Problems and Concrete Individuals

Popper argues that the subject-matter of all science is essentially the same. The object of enquiry is 'a generally accepted problem-situation' (*LScD*: 13), comprising an ordered system of both general theories and singular statements. The important point, however, is the theoretical character of all our knowledge, even those statements that purport to describe the discrete facts about our experience. Contrary to those early positivists who regard the subject-matter of science as consisting of concrete objects, Popper (*PH*: 135) considers it to comprise abstract or theoretical entities. This understanding of how facts are always theory-impregnated constitutes Popper's anti-empiricism. Theoretical models in any science are the means for conceptualizing some problem that is always prior to the organization of data. In both natural and social science, Popper (*PH*: 135–6) warns against mistaking our theoretical models or hypotheses for concrete things. In social science, we must be aware that most of the objects of our enquiry, such as 'war' or 'army', are not concrete things, but '*theoretical* constructions'. For Popper the concrete objects are the individuals, men and women, who comprise an army or who are killed in a war.

Popper also attacks the politically dangerous tendency towards methodological holism, a doctrine that advocates that society and history be explained solely in terms of 'wholes' or collectives. Instead, Popper requires all models of social theory to be constructed and analysed '*in terms of individuals*, their attitudes, expectations, relations, etc.' (*PH*: 136). His alternative doctrine, 'methodological individualism', is 'that all social phenomena, and especially the functioning of all social institutions, should always be understood as resulting from the decisions, actions, attitudes, etc., of human individuals, and that we should never be satisfied by an explanation in terms of so-called "collectives" (states, nations, races, etc.)' (*OSE II*: 98). Popper's methodological individualism is not just an ontological theory, but also an epistemological, empirical and ethical doctrine. The doctrine of methodological individualism has generated an extensive secondary literature, but the discussion here will only draw out a few of the more salient issues relevant to the question of the 'unity of method'.

The ontological claim is that what really exists are not societies, or governments, for example, but the individuals that comprise them. Social phenomena, therefore, are abstract objects that have no existence separate from their constituent individuals. If this thesis amounts to the point that individuals are the basic elements of society, then there is little difficulty in granting them ontological priority. Although individuals like the fictional Robinson Crusoe, for example, may exist for a time, physically outside of society, there could be no society without individuals. Lukes (1970: 78) calls this doctrine 'Truistic Social Atomism', and argues that it only requires an assessment of ontological priority, not the denial of ontological status to other larger constituents of society. Nor does it entail any particular methodological thesis.

Popper objects to the scientific use of the term 'whole' or 'totality' to mean *all* the properties of a thing and all its constituent relations. Nevertheless, he does grant a qualified 'scientific status' to the use of the word 'whole' where it means 'certain special properties . . . of the thing in question, namely those which make it appear an organized structure rather than a "mere heap"' (*PH*: 76). In other contexts, however, Popper (1976a: 103) seems to recognize the existence of certain kinds of social object such as 'social institutions'. Thus, social entities larger than the individual have an ontological reality, which must be considered in attempts at social explanation.

Popper's methodological individualism, however, implies an epistemological claim that we can only know about social entities through our knowledge of individuals. This argument appears to be based upon the notion that individuals are observable in a concrete way where social entities such as classes and societies, because of their theoretical status, are not. Popper's (*CR*: 341) distinction between a 'crowd' and the 'middle class' does not demonstrate that only individuals are observable. Obviously, small social units such as a crowd may, under certain circumstances, be directly observable, both for the participants and the observers. But even these are not pristine empirical objects: our attention is directed towards them by some theoretical framework or assumptions that extend beyond their existence as a collection of individuals. Such theoretical assumptions may be more or less complex, but theoretical all the same. Larger social entities such as classes or strata *are* also more or less observable and much more dependent upon complex theoretical assumptions. But this is little different from natural science, which also operates with unobservables. The force of gravity, for example, is only 'observable' in its effects. Such phenomena are regarded as no less real or concrete in natural science, and there seems no reason why the same judgements could not be reached about unobservable social entities. On the other hand, while particular individuals may be observable, many of their important characteristics, such as their intentions, hopes or fears, are not.

The core of methodological individualism lies in its prescription 'that the "behaviour" and the "actions" of collectives, such as states or social groups, must be reduced to the behaviour and the actions of human individuals' (*OSE II*: 91). This methodological precept is based upon an empirical assumption that individuals are the major causal agents in social processes and, further, that social laws or theories can be explained by, or reduced to, laws concerning the interaction of individuals. As indicated earlier, there is no methodological or epistemological reason to select individuals as the prime causal influences before empirical research is done. On this issue there is probably as much evidence to the contrary, that there are social processes that, once set in motion, are largely independent of individual decision, and that causally determine individual behaviour. Such social phenomena as riots or mass poverty may have been initiated by either intended or unintended individual or collective decision, physical accident or natural disaster, or a combination of any of these factors. It is the task of social science to delineate these causal threads and allocate causal priority. Clarifying the place of individuals affected in a social process is a commendable demand, but one that does not entail any prior judgement upon their causal agency. In fact, seeking out the individual's role in a social process may simply underline his or her lack of causal significance in the face of overwhelming social or political forces.

The political character of Popper's social science methodology is most evident in the ethical implications of methodological individualism. Popper's aim is to prevent the real, concrete individual from being sacrificed for an abstract conception such as the greater good of the community. By stressing the importance of individual over institutional obligations, methodological individualism contributes to the freedom of the individual. In addition to protecting the individual from oppressive 'totalitarian' collectives, Popper aims to enhance personal moral responsibility. His empirical project is in the service of this ethic of responsibility: 'We need studies,' he writes, 'based on methodological individualism, of the social institutions through which ideas may spread and captivate individuals, of the way in which new traditions may be created, and of the way in which traditions work and break down' (*PH*: 149).

Popper's requirement that we construct explanation in terms of individuals is designed to enable individuals to see the unintended consequences of their actions and so recover and exercise their individual responsibility for social events. As Quinton (1976a: 27) points out, however, there is no reason why the common good should not be valued in terms of its 'contribution to the welfare of its individual members'. In such a situation, moral obligations to the wider community are not anathema. Since moral values presuppose social relations such as cooperative practices that may protect the individual and further freedom, there may be good reasons for pursuing ethical collectivism and holistic explanation.

On Popper's account, the objects of social science must be both concrete and abstract. While social research can only begin from theoretical constructions or models, their essential constituents are concrete social atoms or individuals, who must in turn be protected and their individual responsibility enhanced. Social science is also explicitly oriented towards urgent practical problems of both a 'public' and a 'private' character (*PH*: 59). What gives the models of social science their significance is not simply any theoretical coherence they may have, or necessarily their truth, but their possible role in clarifying practical, social and political problems for individuals. Popper's demand that social analysis be in terms of individuals signifies a qualitative difference in his conception of the subject-matter of natural and social science. No similar stricture would be applied to natural science such that its analyses be couched in terms of atoms, leptons or quarks. Nor does Popper require that we protect them from larger natural forces or improve the conditions of their existence.

As we have seen, however, there are good reasons for accepting that both individuals and certain kinds of larger social entity are ontologically real, that we can have knowledge about both individuals and social entities, and that neither social research nor social explanation should focus a priori on either level. Popper's focus on the individual arises from his political or moral preferences. But there are no purely logical, epistemological, methodological or empirical reasons why social theories or explanations should not be solved in terms of whichever level – physical, social, institutional or individual – seems appropriate. Our analysis also suggests that even on political and moral grounds Popper's methodological doctrine may not achieve its goals.

Logic of Scientific Method

Popper's third argument for a unity of method is based upon the alleged common logic of scientific procedure and explanation. In its most general form, scientific method is that of trial and error in which scientists propose a tentative solution – a theory – to their problem and offer this for systematic criticism among their community. Criticism may be attempted by searching out contradictions within the logical structure of the theory, and by means of practical testing. This hypothetico-deductive (H-D) method, Popper (*PH*: 131) explains, 'always consists in offering deductive causal explanations, and in testing them (by way of predictions)'. Yet, his discussions of social science demonstrate a number of key differences with regard to the character and the role of 'points of view' in social explanation, the use of 'situational logic', and in the role of practical experimentation or 'testing' of social theories. These differences may be attributed to Popper's implicit recognition of the inherent ethico-political character of social science.

Social and historical explanation – laws and 'points of view'

Popper (*PH*: 122) claims that scientific problems usually arise from the need for scientific explanation of both 'an individual or singular specific event, and the explanation of some regularity or law'. Because of his initial determinism, Popper made causal explanation a priority in his early work.[4] He argues that, depending upon the problem, we may choose to focus on explanation, prediction or testing. If we know of the existence of a universal law we take it for granted and concentrate either upon technological functions, or search out the initial conditions that partially cause an event. This formulation allows Popper to distinguish between the generalizing or *theoretical sciences* such as sociology, economic theory or political theory, and the *historical sciences* such as political or economic history. In Popper's view (*PH*: 144–5), history is only interested in the causal explanation of singular events in which the relevant universal laws are usually trivial. History aims, therefore, both to describe the uniqueness of an event and show how it may also be typical (*PH*: 146).

Both history and social science depend upon the availability of universal sociological laws. For Popper, the most obvious examples of sociological laws are those of modern economic theory such as those behind the theories of international trade or the trade cycle. To build sound social institutions we require knowledge of such social regularities (*OSE I*: 67). Formulated as prohibitions, sociological laws impose limitations on what is attainable by social technology, and are open to falsification (*PH*: 62–3). Like the laws of natural science, these sociological laws provide the basis for causal explanation along the lines of the H-D model. One difficulty here is that whether or not such 'natural' sociological laws exist, most of Popper's examples are deficient (Ackermann 1976: 171; Donagan 1966: 144; O'Hear 1980: 168). What he offers as laws turn out to be either (a) statements of tendencies or statistical regularities, in which case the latter are not causal while the former do not fit the ideal deductive-nomological model of explanation; (b) universal statements which are obviously false or uncorroborated; (c) analytic statements or tautologies, in which case they are unfalsifiable; or (d) examples of natural scientific laws. To claim that the suggested examples are simply hypotheses in need of further elaboration is insufficient defence. Until such laws can be shown to exist, Popper's argument that history and sociology rely on a unity of method based upon a covering law model of explanation is incomplete.

Popper (*PH*: 150; *OSE II*: 260) argues that in conceiving of any scientific problem we begin from a particular 'point of view' that includes, among other things, value-judgements. Here, he (1976a: 97) distinguishes between two kinds of value and interest, namely those that are 'purely scientific', such as 'truth', 'fruitfulness, explanatory power, simplicity, and precision', and 'extra-scientific' values (i.e. moral and political), such as freedom or equality. He claims (1976a: 97) that, although it is impossible to eliminate values from science, we must struggle to 'separate extra-scientific valuations from *questions of truth*'.

Because of history's lack of interest in universal laws, it needs some other means for focusing its attention. For Popper (*PH*: 150), this focus is achieved by consciously adopting a *'preconceived selective point of view'* that serves to organize the facts to be considered. This historical interpretation usually cannot be formulated as a testable hypothesis, but may be selected, as one would a scientific theory, for its fertility. The main point, however, is to be conscious and critical of one's point of view. 'In every other respect,' Popper (*OSE II*: 268) concludes, 'the interpretation must speak for itself; and its merits will be its fertility, its ability to elucidate the facts of history, as well as its topical interest, its ability to elucidate the problems of the day.'

A 'point of view' is also essential to social science if one is to fulfil the practical tasks outlined above and address the most urgent social problems. Yet, as Popper suggests, what we understand as a problem is the result of reflection from a particular standpoint, influenced by our values, interests and previous experience. He supplies a practical guide to making such decisions by advocating 'negative utilitarianism' (*OSE II*: 235, 284–5; *CR*: 345). The task for social science therefore becomes that of choosing the most urgent social problems, searching out their origins and solutions.

What counts as an 'urgent problem' or a 'concrete evil', however, is not always self-evident. Furthermore, the 'point of view' one adopts for social research will be guided by quite different considerations to those that would be relevant to natural science. A 'passion for truth' may well be a safe motivation for natural science, but in social science such a passion must be tempered by self-conscious ethical judgement. The problems of social science do not arise primarily from the pursuit of 'scientific' values, such as those of the explanatory power of a theory. They arise from political judgements based upon values of an 'extra-scientific' kind, such as freedom of the individual, or the relief of suffering. Although both natural and social scientists will need to distinguish between scientific and extra-scientific values, social scientists will also need a strong capacity to distinguish *and* choose between different extra-scientific values.

Popper's social science methodology expressly requires greater consideration of political problems and values than methodology in natural science. Since one's conception of a problem will vary with one's values, interests and experience, this may become a source of interpretative conflict requiring moral judgement by the social scientist. This inherent moral and practical character of social problems would, however, require a more heightened ethical awareness among social scientists than among natural scientists.

Situational logic

Interpretative skills of another kind are relevant for that part of Popper's methodology of social science which goes under the various names of the 'zero method', 'situational logic' or 'rationality principle'. Having chosen one's values, developed a point of view and selected a problem, the historian and social scientist are exhorted to make a 'detailed analysis of the *logic of situations*' (*PH*: 149). This kind of analysis aims to capture what he regards as the most important difference between natural and social science, namely the feature of human rationality. Because human beings are purposive and therefore rational, Popper suggests that social situations are just as amenable as physical events to explanation by means of the H-D model:

> By this [zero method] I mean the method of constructing a model on the assumption of complete rationality (and perhaps also on the assumption of the possession of complete information) on the part of all the individuals concerned, and of estimating the deviation of the actual behaviour of people from the model behaviour, using the latter as a kind of zero coordinate. (*PH*: 141)

Situational logic establishes an optimum model of human rationality by which we may explain both typical forms of human behaviour and deviations from it in any given social or institutional situation. Once the optimum rationality has been ascertained, it operates as a kind of covering law that enables explanation to be put into the H-D form (*PH*: 117–18). One could then generate hypotheses in the form of predictions about how people would behave, or retrodictions about how they would have behaved. Failing predictive success, one would attempt to explain why they deviated from the ideal model.

Yet, by proposing that we assume the 'trivial general law that sane persons as a rule act more or less rationally', Popper (*OSE II*: 265) is making a prior, empirical assumption about human nature.

No matter what the particular character of a situation, it is assumed that human beings will generally act appropriately to it by seeking particular goals or solving problems. Popper (1985) later clarifies his formulation by pointing out that situational analysis requires the assumption of a kind of animating law he designates the 'rationality principle'. This quasi-empirical, but unfalsifiable universal social law asserts the 'almost empty principle' that the various agents involved 'act *adequately, or appropriately*', according to the implicit 'logic' of the situation (Popper 1985: 359). What constitutes this actual logic in a problem situation, however, is another but more crucial empirical question. Nonetheless, Popper's methodological thesis here indicates a significant departure from that prescribed for natural science. The central assumption about individual rationality in social life has empirical content, however limited it may appear to be, and this assumption is unfalsifiable. Whatever their plausibility for social science, such an assumption would be unacceptable for natural science. Perhaps the only parallel would be his early metaphysical determinism.

Popper also takes issue with arguments about the centrality of the search for meaning and understanding in social science and their relative lack of importance in natural science. His later discussion of understanding in the humanities is also relevant to social science. Initially, Popper (*OK*: 183) appears to concede that 'we can understand men and their actions and products while we cannot understand "nature" – solar systems, molecules, or elementary particles'. Nevertheless, in pursuit of methodological unity he denies that there is any sharp distinction and suggests that 'understanding' is also one of the aims of natural science. Even if we agree with Popper (*OK*: 184) that, in some cosmological sense, understanding is central to both social and natural science, and that natural scientists too must seek to 'understand' a scientific problem, we may still note the significant distinction to which Popper alludes in the quotation above. At the level of experimental practice, a natural scientist is primarily searching for explanations based upon causes or regularities, and is not seeking to understand meanings. That is, the goal of natural science methodology is *not* to interpret the meanings that natural objects have for themselves, or for other objects. Such a task is, however, virtually unavoidable for social scientists and it poses problems for Popper's methodology.

Social scientists usually have to undertake two methodological tasks: the search for causes and regularities in social life and the interpretation and understanding of meanings that humans give for their behaviour. It is arguable that situational analysis contributes primarily to the first of these tasks. For example, situational analysis can be used to generate hypotheses about regularities that can be empirically tested, but it does not provide a straightforward means for dealing with the second task of understanding meaning. One may observe empirical regularities in social behaviour, make predictions, confirm or falsify them and so explain *how* individuals behave, without understanding *why* human beings were acting in a particular way. Accordingly, further interpretative work on meaning and understanding would be needed to discover whether a particular person was acting for the reason they gave, or because of some other causal pressure, or even a combination of both. There is a rough similarity here to Popper's early methodology of natural science, however, in the sense that the isolation of regularities does not provide a complete causal explanation, and more empirical investigation is needed.

As is widely acknowledged, the task of interpretation is not unproblematic. Essentially, social science is subject to the constraints of the hermeneutic circle and these constraints are also applicable to situational analysis. In brief, what is a rational action for an individual or group depends upon their own interpretation of rationality, one that may be radically different from the perspective of an outside scientific observer. Investigators will always have to take care that they do not impose their preconceptions of rationality upon their objects of study. Social scientists therefore require qualities of ethical and rational self-reflection of a different order from those demanded of natural scientists.

Experimentation: piecemeal social engineering

In natural science, once we have decided upon our theory or point of view, Popper's recommendation is that we criticize our theories by making bold conjectures, experimentally testing them ruthlessly and searching for mistakes. In many respects, this will necessitate challenging a scientific world-view and risking a revolution in our accepted ways of scientific thinking. Within social science, however, we are urged to be more cautious and seek a balance between taking risks and watching carefully for mistakes. For this reason, social science requires a social technology *'whose results can be tested by piecemeal social engineering'* (*OSE II*: 222). Since errors in social science and social technology have more direct human consequences, some adaptation of the natural science method is necessary. Risk-taking must therefore be minimized and this is to be achieved by ensuring that any practical social experiments are small scale. Because its more limited 'trials' allow for a better assessment of 'errors' and consequences, the piecemeal method is more compatible with the tenets of scientific rationality and is also morally superior.

Popper (1976b: 291) readily acknowledges that his reformist 'social theory' of piecemeal social engineering involves a departure from the preferred revolutionary method of natural science. This minimal modification can be justified with reference to the idea that dealing with the empirical objects of social science requires some moral consciousness of, or responsibility for, their well-being in a way not thought necessary for the objects of natural science. Work in the field of environmental ethics, however, which requires ethical considerations to be applied not only to sentient but also to non-sentient creatures, has challenged such a distinction (e.g. Birch and Cobb 1981; Ehrenfeld 1981). As will be seen in chapter 7, some variation of the piecemeal method may be applicable even in natural science.

Objectivity and Dialogue

A prime epistemic value in Popper's philosophy of natural and social science is 'objectivity', which provides a countervailing form of control against the prejudice inherent in subjective knowledge or feelings of conviction. Popper (*PH*: 155) rejects the view he attributes to the sociologists of knowledge that objectivity depends upon one's personal psychological attitude and therefore that it is not attainable. He accepts that, despite our efforts, we hold all kinds of prejudice, but he argues that this simply requires us to seek other means for becoming objective.

In his earliest writings, Popper (*LScD*: 44) proposes that intersubjective testability is the quality that marks out objectivity. Scientists maintain objectivity by constructing their theories in a falsifiable and deductive form so that they are in principle testable, and then by repeatedly testing them in experimental practice. Thus, objectivity not only has logical and practical dimensions, it also has individual and social ones. Popper revises his concept of objectivity to incorporate social and political values. Objectivity encompasses guidelines on how to approach the whole process of scientific endeavour, from the construction of theories to the making of decisions about their experimental and practical falsification or confirmation. He points out that 'inter-subjective *testing* is merely a very important aspect of the more general idea of inter-subjective *criticism*, or in other words, of the idea of mutual rational control by critical discussion' (*LScD*: 44, fn. *1).

The social core of objectivity resides in the 'public character of scientific method' (*OSE II*: 218). Only if scientific theories, experiments and their results are made public can the scientific community continue its tradition of free critical discussion. Critical dialogue is ultimately governed by widespread recognition of the importance of experience as the arbiter. Popper (*OSE II*: 218) does not include '"private" aesthetic or religious experience' and explains that 'an experience is "public" if everybody who takes the trouble can repeat it'. In summary, objectivity depends upon cooperation, public communication and mutual criticism among scientists; it has nothing to do with an individual's impartiality. Popper echoes Weber's (1949: 60) dictum that an *'attitude of moral indifference* has no connection with *scientific* "objectivity"'. He noted later (1976a: 95) that objectivity 'depends, in part, upon a number of social and political circumstances which make . . . criticism possible'. He makes explicit the link between scientific method and other values:

> Our motives and even our purely scientific ideals, including the ideal of a disinterested search for truth, are deeply anchored in extra-scientific and, in part, in religious evaluations. Thus the 'objective' or 'value-free' scientist is hardly the ideal scientist. Without passion we can achieve nothing – certainly not in pure science. The phrase 'the passion for truth' is no mere metaphor. (1976a: 97)

Since values and epistemic passions are the product of social and political circumstances it is to such an arena that Popper looks for their management.

Central to the maintenance of objectivity are the institutions of the open society and democracy that promote particular ideas such as the critical tradition, social values such as toleration of free discussion, and practices such as publications and conferences (1976a: 96). Such institutions, including those of the state, impose the necessary 'mental discipline' and values of critical thought upon the individual researcher (*PH*: 155–6). The major problem of social science, as Popper (*OSE II*: 221) sees it, is its failure to attain this publicity of method.

Since the main ethical goal of Popper's conception of social science is to encourage greater individual moral responsibility, a more radical step is possible. If we were to pursue logically Popper's concern about harmful impacts upon individuals, then academic social science would also have to promote 'intersubjectivity' and public discussion at another level, namely between the observers and the observed. That is, a morally responsible social science would encourage dialogue between the social experimenters and the subjects of even small-scale 'experiments'. If we are interested in the actual or possible unintended consequences of our social experiments, then part of our task would be to hear the views of those who may have experienced their direct consequences.

Such an ethic would mean extending participation by the observed to their making effective decisions about the content of knowledge accumulated, and even the technical uses to which it may be put. Where the results of social enquiry have the potential to affect the lives of those under investigation, it would not be unreasonable to involve 'the observed' in key decisions about the process. In such cases, social scientists would have to accept the possibility of refusals to undergo investigation, or to circumscribe their enquiries, or suppress public dissemination of any knowledge that had been accumulated. Such decisions could be defensible in terms of impacts upon individuals or groups, and the alleviation of avoidable suffering. This kind of problem is clearly evident in the disciplines of archaeology and anthropology, and their relationship with indigenous peoples in various countries. Indeed, there are now codes of professional ethics designed to cover these concerns.[5]

Criticism of social theories and their resultant social policies is not simply the province of social scientists, but also that of those whose lives may be altered by them. This is at least one part of Popper's rationale for the conduct of piecemeal social engineering and the establishment of democratic institutions. It is not, however, a Popperian requirement or even a possibility for natural science that scientists engage in a dialogue with the object of their enquiry, except perhaps in a metaphorical sense.

Metaphysics and Method: Essentialism and Realism

A recurring theme throughout Popper's work on social science is his opposition to methodological essentialism. By this he means the founding of our basic scientific premises upon the intuition and definition of the universal essence of an object of study (*PH*: 27–8).

He rejects intuitive understanding as the special method of social science (*PH*: 138).[6] He (*OSE II*: 12) also argues that basing science upon the definition of a term or concept leaves us with the problem of infinite regress and does not establish either the truth or certainty of a statement. In his view (*OSE II*: 17–18; *UQ*: 17–31), it is impossible to provide entirely unambiguous definitions of all the terms we use and this inevitably leads to empty controversies about words, which Popper considers to be characteristic of linguistic philosophy.

In *The Poverty of Historicism*, Popper claims that he draws his alternative to essentialism from the practice of modern science, which he sees proceeding by means of methodological nominalism as opposed to realism. Scientists do not enquire into the essence of atoms or light but ask *how* a piece of matter behaves. For this procedure, words are only nominal and '*useful instruments of description*' (*PH*: 29). In Popper's account, scientists accept that precision does not depend upon the precision of scientific language and that their terms remain necessarily vague and undefined. Methodological nominalism in natural and social science demands that we not only describe, but also explain events in terms of regularities and laws (*OSE I*: 32). As Popper (*UQ*: 20) acknowledges, he only later recognized that his methodological nominalism was compatible with metaphysical and methodological realism. Yet, his methodological nominalism would appear to preclude a realist approach that searched for deeper levels of reality (Wettersten 1992: 175).

The problem here is that both Popper's anti-essentialism and the pragmatic orientation of his social science methodology give it a profoundly anti-realist and even instrumentalist character. Popper argues against essentialism because he claims it relies upon intuitionist methods and meaningless definitional dispute. He also criticizes essentialism for encouraging us to think of scientific models as something that lie behind 'changing observable events, as a kind of permanent ghost or essence' (*PH*: 136). Yet, such an account, deprived of intuitionism and definitional requirements, closely resembles Popper's metaphysical realism, which requires that scientists search deeper into reality behind phenomena or appearances. Indeed, Popper (*RAS*: 80–1) writes that he had believed in 'metaphysical realism' and that it was implicit in his first book. Nonetheless, this kind of realism is not evident in his early philosophy of social science. Nor is it prominent in his later contributions to the positivist dispute.[7]

Given the evidence for Popper's anti-realism, it appears that another one of his general methodological rules for social science differs from that advocated for natural science. One could be a methodological realist in natural science but not in social science. Popper later modified his critique of essentialism in natural science (*CR*: 103–5), to argue that he shared the essentialist goal of finding true theories or descriptions of the world. As his own arguments indicate, however, it is simply not the case that searching out deeper layers of *physical* reality requires a belief in 'ultimate' or final explanation, or prematurely ending enquiry. Although probing the deeper layers of *social* reality may confront other difficulties of interpretation, it is not clear why such a task necessarily entails either intuitionism or definitional controversy, or the search for ultimate explanations. Accordingly, there seem to be few reasons why a Popperian methodology of social science ought not to be as realist as that for natural science (Shearmur 1996: 124–5). Popper's antipathy towards essentialism also comes close to a rejection of all philosophies concerned with clarification of concepts, whether the issues are those of definition or not (O'Hear 1980: 8).

It is difficult to explain why Popper remains an anti-realist in social science. One possible reason is the ontological priority he gives to individuals as the primary constituents of social reality and the corresponding lack of interest in social 'wholes'. Furthermore, to penetrate into the deeper layers of individual reality would be to recognize the importance of psychological explanation and give credence to psychological or psychoanalytic methods and techniques that Popper thought unscientific. Popper's rejection of research into social wholes would also tend to rule out investigating the deeper layers of social reality. To do so would risk giving legitimacy to vulgar Marxist methods that gave priority to studies of the material economic base of society and which undermined the role and significance of ideas and arguments. In addition, Popper's preferred method of situational analysis does not require sophisticated realist assumptions, apart from the reality of individuals. Here we may note how an ethico-political value limits the extension of natural scientific methodology to social science.

Critical Dualism

With the higher priority Popper gives to the solution of practical problems in social science, he advocates both a more refined moral responsibility among social scientists and the avoidance of moral relativism. Popper sketches the nature of values and how we may choose them. He begins by criticizing the problematic approaches of naive monism, naive naturalism and naive conventionalism, allegedly characteristic of the closed society. He also opposes the relativistic doctrines of monism, moral futurism and moral intuitionism. He finds expressionist or emotive theories 'trivial, uninformative and useless' (*UQ*: 62, fn. 65a). Unlike his logical positivist forebears, Popper (*OSE I*: 234) does not accept that norms or ethics are meaningless. Accordingly, his ethical theory seeks to avoid historical relativism and retain some element of rationality. He argues for the doctrine of 'critical dualism', which is somewhat similar to the traditional dichotomy between, or autonomy of, facts and values. Rather than the term 'value', he uses, at different times, 'norms', 'decisions', 'proposals' and 'standards'. Although his political commitment to an open society entails advocating a diversity of aims, opinions and values, Popper denies that the selection of values is purely arbitrary.

The concept of a normative, as distinct from a natural, law reminds individuals that they are morally responsible beings and that their morality is their own creation. Although Popper implies that we create our moral world, he obscures the issue when he denies that norms have their historical origin in human creativity. Critical dualism, he writes (*OSE I*: 61), 'has nothing to do with the obviously untenable historical assertion that norms in the first place were *consciously* made or introduced by man, instead of having been found by him to be simply there'. To say that norms are 'man-made', means merely that human beings 'can judge and alter them' (*OSE I*: 64). And yet Popper (*OSE I*: 66) also suggests that all ethics begin with religion.

Popper considers that questions of historical origin are irrelevant for his argument, since all he wishes to propose is that moral norms can be made or changed, that we are 'responsible' for them and that their selection is not an arbitrary matter. The central point appears to be that norms can be, variously, discovered, created, modified and chosen. We can, Popper (*OSE I*: 61) claims, only attempt to improve our present norms in comparison with 'some standard norms which we have decided are worthy of being realized'. More important, such standards are not to be found in nature, which consists of facts and regularities, and which can be neither moral nor immoral. On this view, the spheres of facts and of values are autonomous; values cannot be reduced to facts. For these reasons, Popper appears to subscribe to a form of moral realism (Waldron 1985: 107).[8]

Popper's argument on the logical dichotomy between facts and values partly relies upon distinguishing between the different levels of rationality to be found in the two fields. Where deciding upon facts is amenable to the highest form of rationality, namely scientific method, choosing between values appears to be a somewhat less than fully rational enterprise. Yet, the latter procedure must contain some elements of rationality otherwise it may relapse into an irrational subjectivism, in which ethics are regarded simply as the expression of emotional preferences. Nevertheless, to admit that selecting values is a fully rational and objective process would be to suggest that ethics may be discoverable as facts of social reality.

One of the problems with critical dualism is its pre-Popperian and crude empiricist conception of 'the facts'. While we may agree that the world exists independently of our perception or knowledge of it, this does not warrant the conclusion that the facts which constitute our knowledge are pristine or uninterpreted entities. As Popper and others argue, all 'facts' are theory-impregnated. Facts are selected according to some preconceived theoretical position and also according to the values or norms of accepted scientific practice. All our factual statements are human creations and are therefore embedded in a range of theoretical and value positions.[9] Any scientific analysis is necessarily a holistic enterprise in which it is difficult to disentangle clearly the low-level factual descriptions such as observational statements from more sophisticated general theories and concepts. Such theories are underdetermined by the world. That is, empirical experience is only one factor which determines the validity of a theory (Thomas 1979: 126). Similarly, the holistic character of scientific theories prevents any sharp distinction being made between facts and those values that influence the acceptability of a scientific theory (Thomas 1979: 127). These comments lead us to consider the complementary question of how we may choose or change our values and norms.

Although values may help us to choose our theories and facts, it may still be argued that facts do not, or ought not to, contribute to the selection of values. Popper (*OSE I*: 62) tells us, however, that moral decisions do 'pertain' to facts. All this is intended to mean is that there are a number of 'attitudes' which may be adopted towards any particular social fact such as slavery or poverty. One can, for example, approve or disapprove, or decide to act to change the fact, or alternatively refrain from action. As suggested above, however, we are not always free to adopt just *any* attitude or value towards a set of facts. We have usually adopted a particular value stance towards whatever theory we select to work with, even before we come to choose our facts (Taylor 1973: 161). Part of the work of social science is to reflect upon those prior values and attitudes.

If Popper is to avoid recourse to emotivist and intuitionist arguments he needs to argue that moral positions are capable of rational support. Thus he would need to show that it is possible for one to give objective reasons for one's ethics and attitudes (or policy) towards particular facts. Such cognitivist objectivism, however, implies naturalistic consequences which Popper would wish to avoid. His own arguments for particular ethics, such as those for rationality, indicate the ambivalence in his meta-ethical theory and reveal at least three separate and conflicting approaches which are naturalist, subjectivist and objectivist.

A disguised naturalistic argument is discernible in Popper's initial advocacy of critical rationalism, where he stresses that 'neither logical argument nor experience can establish the rationalist attitude' (*OSE II*: 230). One either practises rationality or one does not. This decision is virtually unconscious and in one sense a natural and empirical practice. One must, however, know that one is practising the rationalist attitude in order to reflect upon it afterwards. This accords with a broader argument that values derive from our factual efforts at surviving, creating and being frustrated in our endeavours. They may also be grounded in the necessary conditions for maintaining human life (Berleant 1973: 27). The objective facts of our social existence may be observable and open to rational and scientific discovery.

Naturalism is evident in Popper's later work, where he claims that values originate from two sources, namely biology and culture. Values, like problems, were created with the emergence of life and not just with consciousness. This allows Popper (*UQ*: 194) to argue that there are two kinds of value: 'values created by life, by unconscious problems, and values created by the human mind, on the basis of previous solutions, in the attempt to solve problems which may be better or less well understood.' Values are inextricably linked with problems. In one sense values are 'facts' of life, and the higher values are merely complex variations upon them, necessary for the maintenance of human social life. Thus Popper (*UQ*: 194) claims that there can be 'objective values, even without consciousness'. On this revised view, it appears as if we 'discover' the unconscious values of human existence and then 'invent' our higher, more social values. Among the difficulties with this approach is that of determining which are the fundamental problems of human or animal life.

Contrary to Popper's original thesis, therefore, certain normative standards may be found in nature, even if it is our evolutionary *human* nature. Whatever Popper's initial doubts about the grounds for commending rationalism, it is clearly a moral good, if only because it fulfils some essential social and human need (Taylor 1973: 161). One of the facts of human nature is that human beings are inherently rational or at least have such a capacity. Since this is virtually a condition of social life it must be considered a moral good. Such an argument is implicit in Popper's own preference for rationality, and thus we may see that morality 'pertains to facts' in a very direct, if not logical fashion. This naturalism provides the basis for an objectivist theory of ethics.

A second foundation for values may be discerned which is strongly subjectivist, if not fideist. Popper (*OSE I*: 66) suggests that Christian ethics may be accepted because of one's 'conviction that it is the right decision to take'. Similarly, he argues for the rationalist attitude because of an 'irrational *faith in reason*' (*OSE II*: 231). On this view, therefore, particular values may be adopted out of an 'irrational' and subjective preference, or intuition of their innate goodness. Such comments return Popper to the discredited subjectivist doctrine of ethical emotivism.

The third approach, however, is more objective in the Popperian sense, in that it allows for the use of rational argument and discussion in making moral decisions (*OSE II*: 232). Similar to choosing a scientific norm, we choose from among the competing moral alternatives according to our assessment of their possible consequences. The difference is that in moral affairs we confront the consequences with our conscience (*OSE II*: 233). The appeal to conscience, however, begs the question, for our conscience may be ordered according to some conception of human or social needs and priorities, or it may be impaired and incoherent. When Popper allows the relevance of *imagined* consequences to value decisions, he also cannot reject the influence of *actual* practical consequences and the possible tenability of moral futurism. With the passage of history some norms will be rendered irrelevant or inappropriate, and new values will be required. This possibility is to be found in Popper's own admission that, in certain political circumstances, peaceful action may be self-defeating and violence may be necessary.

Popper compares the regulative idea of truth with the idea of absolute moral standards. He also suggests that, just as we can make progress towards truth, so too can we make progress in the realm of standards or values (*OSE II*: 386). As Shearmur (1996: 93) notes, however, Popper does not establish any criteria of moral progress or any absolute moral standards. At the level of substantive ethics, therefore, moral validity may be established in a similar way to other theoretical claims, namely by subjecting them to intersubjective critical scrutiny (Shearmur 1996: 107). That is, the procedure for selecting values is similar to those that Popper would use for selecting norms or theories in science where one would apply criteria of coherence, for example, and assess consequences. There remains the difficulty that one still has to make a personal commitment or decision to accept the result of critical procedures, and there may be some who reject both the procedure and its outcomes.

It is difficult to escape the conclusion that, on Popper's arguments, not only can moral decision-making be a rational process, but it is also logically and practically dependent upon the careful assessment of various kinds of facts. Just as the history and practice of science is of prime importance in devising epistemic norms for scientific method, so also are social and historical experiences central in recognizing, devising and changing social ethics. In this respect, Popper is not a thoroughgoing Kantian.[10] The remaining difficulty, however, is that of deciding which meta-values are to guide the study of the human agents and their values. These questions will be considered further in chapter 8.

A Political Philosophy of Social Science

This chapter has argued that there are significant asymmetries between Popper's methodological recommendations for natural and social science. For virtually every key methodological precept, Popper proposes some extra rule for which there is no direct equivalent required for the conduct of natural science. These rules are not simply marginal amendments to a basic methodological core. They are essentially moral or ethical in character, and mark out a radically different intellectual and political enterprise. From this perspective, much of Popper's work on social science methodology has the character of an ethical treatise.

Where Popper explicitly acknowledges that social science requires different methods, as in the case of 'situational analysis' and experiment by 'piecemeal social engineering', he either ignores or understates their significance. In the case of 'situational analysis', for example, he does not acknowledge that both the empirical and methodological assumptions of the 'rationality principle' mark out a major difference between social and natural science. Nor does he see that interpretative skills and reflexivity are not just techniques but are inherent in the enterprise of good social science. In social science, Popper's conception of objectivity requires debate and dialogue, not only between governments and their citizens, but also between social scientists and those who are the objects of their enquiry. Although Popper advocates methodological realism for natural science, his anti-essentialism fosters a distinct anti-realism in social science.

The rationale for a number of these methodological differences can be traced in part to Popper's understanding of social science as a more politically dangerous project than natural science. Whereas he constantly stresses the intellectual promise and spiritual adventure of natural science, he just as often draws attention to the possible perils of social science. In addition to the human costs it could incur, the wrong kind of social science (e.g. historicism) could threaten and undermine the institutional conditions for rational thought and the practice of natural science. For these reasons, social science has to be a more thoroughgoing moral project. At every level, social scientists are required to exercise not only a moral consciousness regarding the goals and objects of their enquiry, but also an individual moral responsibility for the conduct and consequences of their work.

We must understand Popper's philosophy of social science in the wider context of a political philosophy that aims to encourage human beings to acknowledge their own personal moral responsibility for social and political life. In many respects, Popper's ethical project is highly commendable. By analysing social problems in terms of individuals, for example, we are reminded that we must consider the impact of our social theories and plans upon human beings and not become preoccupied with theoretical abstraction for its own sake. This general moral requirement for social science is arguably Popper's most distinctive achievement. Yet, the centrality of values raises the further problem of how we may defend one set of values or moral responsibilities, and reject another. On this problem, Popper's analysis is not entirely coherent. Key policy questions also remain unanswered. How may we encourage the kinds of sophisticated criticism and dissent that his methodology of social science requires? As we shall see in the next chapter, however, Popper does develop and defend the metaphysical underpinnings of his theory of freedom.

6

Metaphysics and Freedom

Although much attention has been given to Popper's epistemology and political theory, the political significance of his metaphysics has generally been neglected. This chapter offers a critical account of Popper's later metaphysics and demonstrates how the idea of freedom is central to his philosophy. We shall review Popper's arguments for realism, indeterminism, the world 3 of objective knowledge and his theory of mind. It will be argued that, while the resulting ontology has important implications for his epistemology and methodology, Popper has not entirely succeeded in establishing his argument for freedom.

The Problem of Freedom

From the 1950s, Popper's conceptions of epistemology, rationality and the metaphysical assumptions underlying them were tailored to take account of the problem of freedom. Only in discussing the significance of his *Postscript* to *The Logic of Scientific Discovery* did he indicate his underlying problem. 'It was not intended to discuss human freedom and human free will,' Popper remarked, 'even though these were really the problems that stood behind it' (*OU*: xix). Given his advocacy of moral, political and intellectual responsibility, he wanted to show that human freedom or agency is not a delusion. Popper's arguments here do not constitute a normative theory of freedom such as may be found in the works of political philosophers, but an ontology. That is, he tries to establish what the world must be like for individual freedom, individual choice and creative thought to be possible. If he is successful, then normative demands for intellectual and moral responsibility can be made upon individuals. The question for Popper is no longer 'How may we best comprehend the world?', but rather 'How may we best comprehend the world such that it allows for the exercise of human freedom?' Certain ways of understanding the world, such as determinism, are ruled out because they appear to preclude the possibility of human freedom.

Since these questions are metaphysical ones, deciding them requires a primarily philosophical method. According to Popper's original falsifiability criterion of demarcation, however, philosophy was a metaphysical (that is, non-empirical) and thereby irrational enterprise. Nevertheless, he came to the view that while philosophical statements may not be testable empirically, they could still be discussed and criticized, and so become rational.[1] Consequently, Popper not only accepted the necessity of metaphysical thought, but also formulated his own substantive metaphysics. His arguments on the topics of realism, indeterminism, propensities, world 3, mind and self, constitute a distinct metaphysical phase in his thought, in which epistemological and methodological problems take a secondary place. Thus Popper takes up the problem of cosmology which is: *'the problem of understanding the world – including ourselves, and our knowledge, as part of the world'* (*LScD*: 15; *QTSP*: 1).

Realism and Instrumentalism

The problem of freedom plays a key role within Popper's cosmology and in his account of the political role of science. It provides one reason for supporting realism and rejecting instrumentalism in science. Where 'critical science' is essential for promoting freedom and maintaining democracy, the uncritical adoration of science may lead to oppression. For Popper, science's main claim to social benefit derives from its utility in making us aware of our human condition and how we may transcend the beliefs and dogmas of our social group.

As the epitome of human creativity, science is 'an adventure of the human spirit', one that is the result of 'that most human of all human endeavours – to liberate ourselves' (*RAS*: 259). Critical science is politically instrumental in promoting liberal democratic values, to such an extent that, in Popper's view, democracy could not survive without science (*RAS*: 260). Yet, science as an emancipatory force was threatened by new superstitions generated by its very achievements. Those who had abandoned its critical core endowed it with unchallengeable authority. More serious was the tendency to regard science merely as an instrument for mastery of the physical world. Popper recognizes that control over nature is easily turned towards the task of controlling human beings and may become another form of bondage (*RAS*: 260). Such problems press him to criticize instrumentalism and defend realism.

Popper's realism is a metaphysical conjecture about the nature of the world and our ways of knowing it.[2] It proposes that there exists a real physical world independent of us that can be known by our senses and discovered by science (*UQ*: 151; *QTSP*: 2). He rejects the idealist notion that the world is merely our dream and that all our knowledge is subjective. For a realist, a scientific theory is a description of or conjecture about the structure of the world, and not just an instrument for prediction. As Popper indicates, however, his arguments against idealism, subjectivism and instrumentalism, and in defence of realism, are 'partly rational, partly *ad hominem*, and partly even ethical' (*QTSP*: 2). His reasons for supporting realism are cosmological, epistemological, methodological and moral.

Popper's conjecture that there exists a real world, of a particular structure that is accurately described by our theories, is cosmological on a number of levels. To accept an instrumentalist conception of scientific theories is to accept them as mere 'gadgets', with the implication that science is no more than 'an activity of gadget-making – glorified plumbing' (*RAS*: 122). For Popper, instrumentalism strips science of its status as a spiritual and rational adventure dedicated to the growth of knowledge. Realism is necessary for a cosmology in which a central part of the human project is to attempt to understand and explain the world in rational terms. If we do not accept realism we cannot have an adequate science nor the enlightenment and emancipation it promises.

Realism provides the metaphysical underpinning for Popper's epistemology and methodology. It provides a kind of premise or set of limits for what is epistemologically or methodologically possible (Popper 1974b: 966). An epistemology that sets itself the task of discovering true explanations can hardly do without a conception of objective reality that is the equivalent of ultimate truth, against which one can judge the adequacy of one's explanation. For Popper, an epistemology that aims for truth, that is, 'correspondence to the facts', or 'correspondence to reality', must be based upon metaphysical realism (*OK*: 42). He also claims that realism is essential for an epistemology that stresses the uncertain and fallible nature of our knowledge. Popper requires realism and a theory of truth in order to avoid the pitfalls of relativism and scepticism. By proposing that there exists an external world and that it has a particular character, Popper's realism also assumes methodological significance.[3] Realism is vital for methodology because it suggests support for the modified essentialism evident in his claim that we 'seek to probe deeper and deeper into the structure of our world' and so make real discoveries (*RAS*: 137).

Popper employs two distinct conceptions of realism. The weaker and less contentious version, which proposes simply that the world exists independent of our knowledge of it, may be called 'common sense realism'.[4] The strong, metaphysical conception, based primarily upon analysis of science, embraces these and a number of other related propositions. The argument that our knowledge, including scientific theories, accurately describes reality, that entities depicted by science are real, and, further, that scientific knowledge grows and progressively approaches the truth, may be designated 'critical' or 'conjectural' (Worrall 1982: 202, 229) or even 'convergent realism' (Putnam 1982: 198–200). These latter doctrines seek to take account of the major problem confronting realists, which is to explain the fact that theories change or become superseded. While our theories are always attempts to describe accurately the structure of the world, they may be improved upon; all our knowledge is fallible and conjectural. There is little anti-realist or instrumentalist quarrel with common sense realism. The main criticism is directed against the larger doctrine that includes correspondence theories of truth and notions of progress towards the truth.

Popper's arguments for realism rely heavily upon revealing the alleged epistemological and methodological weakness of the instrumentalist alternative. For example, he criticizes what he sees as the instrumentalist distinction between '"*observational terms*" . . . and "*theoretical terms*"', on the grounds that all terms are to some degree theoretical (*CR*: 119). For Popper, instrumentalism is also radically flawed because it does not involve the attempt to falsify theories and has no criterion of scientific progress (*CR*: 112). Instrumentalists, however, do test their theories severely with the aim of discovering how comprehensive they are (O'Hear 1980: 93; Worrall 1982: 205). Severe tests that reveal the empirical limitations of a theory may result in its rejection. The criteria of greater predictive power and wider application are also criteria of scientific progress. Popper argues that because there is no recourse to truth or falsity, an instrumentalist may be tempted to rescue any theory threatened by contradictions. As Worrall (1982: 208) points out, however, the requirements of simplicity and unity would constrain instrumentalists from making such *ad hoc* responses. Popperian fallibilism, therefore, is also compatible with a critical instrumentalism that seeks more comprehensive theories and discards those that are found wanting because of their failure to survive testing.

The problem with Popper's critique of instrumentalism in science is that it often misses its target. Instrumentalism and instrumentalists can take account of most of the attributes that Popper requires in a scientific theory and the scientific attitude. Instrumentalists such as John Dewey (e.g. 1980), for example, were also thoroughgoing fallibilists. Nor do instrumentalists have to accept that the success of science is miraculous. As the 'realist' Popper, the 'instrumentalist' Dewey and the 'anti-realist' van Fraassen have noted, science is a biological phenomenon, an instrument in our struggle for survival. Any scientific theory is therefore subject to strong competition, and for van Fraassen (1980: 219) its success can be attributed to its having '*in fact* latched on to actual regularities of nature'. Such success does not require the metaphysical baggage associated with a theory of truth; all that is needed is a notion of 'empirical adequacy'.[5]

Historical studies of science and philosophy offer a few insights into the complexity of these questions. Gardner (1983), for example, has argued that in practice scientists adopted realistic or instrumentalist assumptions according to the stage of development of a theory. Scientific judgement upon whether a given theory is true or only an instrument for prediction has often changed, as new evidence is gathered concerning its predictive power. According to Worrall (1982: 230–1), leading instrumentalists such as Duhem and Poincaré both succumbed to a form of 'creeping realism'. That is, both conceded that certain kinds of well-established laws had empirical content. In effect, the observational or theoretical status of scientific statements shifted according to the historical practice of science. At one level, therefore, instrumentalists are not prevented from offering a rough portrait of aspects of the world. Regarding the distinction between *theories* and the specific *entities* to which they may refer, Hacking (1983: 71) argues that, historically, '*The vast majority of experimental physicists are realists about entities but not about theories.*'[6] Such accounts provide further reasons for thinking that one cannot easily distinguish between sophisticated forms of realism and instrumentalism.[7] The key problem of knowing precisely where a theory impinges upon or describes reality is problematic for both realists and instrumentalists.

O'Hear (1985: 459–60) correctly points out the affinities between 'critical realism' and the anti-realist's 'constructive empiricism'. Popper's notion of 'corroboration', meaning a theory's survival of tests, is analogous to van Fraassen's notion of 'empirical adequacy', meaning 'theories which make testable predictions that survive testing'. Where realists, 'anti-realists' and instrumentalists, to a greater or lesser degree, may construe theories literally, realism and truth are not required to explain the success of science. Following Wachbroit (1986: 363), we may suggest that scientific progress consists in providing better reasons for a theory, and these may be of various kinds. For example, since the predictive power of a theory is a criterion of success, it is also a criterion of progress, by which we judge the claims of our current theories. For the working scientist, metaphysical questions recede before more important practical issues that concern the comparative worth of a theory, and this may be determined according to its empirical adequacy, predictive power or problem-solving ability. Popper himself need look no further than his own philosophy to find an alternative notion of progress based upon the capacity of a theory to solve more problems than its rivals.[8]

Within the idea of convergence and growth of knowledge in Popper's work is a concept of truth that is more than a regulative ideal. This is evident in his adoption of Tarski's correspondence theory of truth (*CR*: 215–50). The central impediment to metaphysical realism remains that there is no way of ascertaining the truth or falsity of statements about reality that are independent of our theoretical frameworks. Furthermore, fallibilism is also incompatible with a strong metaphysical realism that posits a correspondence theory of truth or verisimilitude (Almeder 1987: 93). Popper's philosophy would gain much in coherence if he limited his realism to the more limited common sense variety similar to that found in his earliest work. Such a stance would still take account of the fact that all our knowledge, including scientific theories, consists of fallible, social constructions whose fate is decided according to evolving, socially agreed-upon rules.

Popper's most forceful arguments for realism are explicitly ethical and political (*QTSP*: xviii). He claims that realism provides the necessary ontological foundations for rationality and also for the recognition and alleviation of suffering. In Popper's view, one cannot engage in rational discussion unless one presupposes an external reality *and* the real problems associated with it. The process of emancipation through knowledge depends upon the existence of a real world of a particular kind in which there exist genuine intellectual and human problems. Realism is of ethical significance in other ways. 'As it entails the existence of other minds,' Popper (1974b: 966) writes, 'it is also of the utmost importance for ethics (which is of no interest if we regard the suffering of other people as merely apparent), and altogether for any sane outlook on human life.'

Idealism, for Popper, leads to the conclusion that all our knowledge is subjective illusion. This in turn entails that there is no secure way of knowing whether people are really suffering or whether we are imagining it. Accordingly, there is no basis for invoking the ethical imperative that we should attempt to alleviate suffering. He argues that similar problems beset non-realist approaches to the problems of time and change. If our sense of time is merely illusory, there is little point in trying to plan for a future time that cannot be experienced in some common way. If we are to understand the world in any morally responsible way or to act with any political effect, then, on Popper's account, realism is a necessary working assumption.

Nonetheless, Popper's 'ethical realism' does not provide the guarantees he would prefer. Just as all scientific facts or entities are theory laden, so too there are no unmediated accounts of pain or suffering. This is not to say that certain kinds of suffering or inhumanity are not easily recognizable or demanding of moral action. Rather, Popper's realism provides no greater surety than instrumentalism that we shall interpret more clearly what we see as pain and suffering or that we act to alleviate them. The pragmatic or instrumentalist problem-solving approach does not require strong realist assumptions of the kind that Popper advocates and is no less ethically responsible because of it.

As we saw with Popper's methodology of social science, the search for truth is subsidiary but, where possible, complementary to wider social goals. Instead of understanding our social theories purely as a quest for truth, we may more usefully view them as attempts to solve particular problems. On the arguments from the history of science above, such an approach need not deny the existence of real objects such as individuals and groups. It merely suggests that our social theories about them serve practical political purposes. Furthermore, we may agree with Popper's claim that instrumentalism may lead to the use of science as an instrument for the mastery of nature and the control of human beings. But there is nothing inherent in realism that prevents such a possibility from occurring. Indeed, the relentless and indiscriminate pursuit of truth may have consequences that lead to human oppression.

Popper advocates metaphysical realism for both philosophical and ethico-political reasons. It is important to see that his main problem was to reconcile an ethical concern for freedom with the avoidance of scepticism and relativism. Close scrutiny of Popper's arguments, however, demonstrates that his strong realism with its correspondence theory of truth and theory of verisimilitude cannot be sustained (see chapter 7). Since he cannot operationalize either of these theories, he cannot avoid a tendency towards scepticism and relativism. The only defensible role that the notion of truth can play is that of a regulative ideal with no stronger claim upon us than the moral one of encouraging us to be as careful, accurate and critical of our knowledge as we can. Anything more than a common sense, critical realism about the nature of the world does not help Popper's emancipatory project and presents more difficulties than are necessary. In most practical matters of scientific theory, fact and experimentation, Popper's critical realism is little different from that of a sophisticated instrumentalism.

Indeterminism and Determinism

Although the concept of freedom was fundamental to Popper's social and political thought, its relationship to assumptions in his early epistemology remained unresolved. The major difficulty had been that the scientific indeterminism of *The Logic of Scientific Discovery* was founded upon an implicit ontological determinism. By the late 1940s, Popper's views had firmed sufficiently for him to launch an assault upon all forms of determinism.

Popper requires an argument for indeterminism for ethical and political reasons as much as for scientific ones. A major problem was that determinism in nature implied a determinism in society. Popper characterizes physical determinism as a 'nightmare because it asserts that the whole world with everything in it is a huge automaton, and that we are nothing but little cogwheels, or at best sub-automata, within it' (*OK*: 222). In such a world, human action, scientific creativity and moral responsibility count for nothing, for all is physically predetermined. The discussion of indeterminism therefore arises from Popper's concern with the issues of freedom and free will. The major arguments appear in *The Open Universe* (*OU*: xxi–xxii): 'This book is then a kind of prolegomenon to the question of human freedom and creativity, and makes room for it physically and cosmologically in a way that does not depend on verbal analyses.' Herein also lie the origins of his later arguments for a world 3 of objective knowledge, and the reality of the self and its mind.

Popper attempts to refute key theses of scientific and metaphysical determinism and then establish the case for scientific and metaphysical indeterminism. He seeks first to show that scientific indeterminism refutes metaphysical determinism and draws heavily upon arguments about 'predictability'. The aim is to demonstrate that if our knowledge is part of reality then discovering any indeterminacy in it will imply some indeterminacy in the rest of the world. Second, he makes a more positive argument for metaphysical indeterminism based upon the evidence of testable scientific theory, in particular his propensity interpretation of quantum mechanics and the concept of emergence. This is warranted on the grounds that if our fundamental scientific theories are indeterministic, as quantum theory seems to demonstrate, then metaphysical determinism is shown to be false (Miller 1995: 136).

Popper speculates that determinism may have arisen from the religious stress upon divine omnipotence and omniscience. *Scientific* determinism modifies this view by replacing God with the idea of nature and substituting natural law for divine law (*OU*: 5). Popper (*OU*: 6) explains that 'scientific' determinism is underpinned by the notion that 'every future event can in principle be rationally calculated in advance, if only we know the laws of nature, and the present or past state of the world'. He describes the *metaphysical* or ontological doctrine as one that holds that 'all events in this world are fixed, or unalterable, or predetermined' (*OU*: 8). The main distinction is that the metaphysical doctrine makes no claims about our knowledge of the predetermined events.

Scientific determinism and indeterminism

Popper argues that the common sense view that events are caused does not necessarily lead to determinism because the notion of a cause is quantitative and any predictions based upon it are always imprecise. A determinist would have to account for such imprecision. For the determinist, the world is essentially the same as a clock in which all the parts are linked and whose movements are all predictable in precise fashion. With improved knowledge it is alleged that even a diffuse and apparently chaotic system, such as a cloud, may eventually come to be seen as a clock. Popper (*OU*: 19), however, points out the converse, that with improved knowledge, even the mechanism of a clock will come to look like a cloud of molecules. Even the *prima facie* deterministic theories of classical physics fail to provide a basis for 'scientific determinism'. Thus, the arguments for scientific determinism are considered inconclusive. For Popper, common sense suggests that there exist both clouds and clocks, that predetermination and predictability are matters of degree, and that the latter will vary between the higher and lower organisms. These observations, and the intuition that there exists free will and free human creativity, intimate support for the relatively weaker indeterminist doctrine that 'there exists *at least one* event that is not predetermined, or predictable' (*OU*: 28).

Popper's arguments for scientific indeterminism are based upon five major themes: the intuitive argument for undetermined human creativity, the approximate character of human knowledge, the asymmetry between past and future, the impossibility of self-prediction and the possibility of human rationality. On the first topic, Popper (*OU*: 41) claims, 'the creation of a new work, such as Mozart's G minor symphony, cannot be predicted, in all its details, by a physicist, or physiologist, who studies in detail Mozart's body – especially his brain – and his physical environment.' Such intuitions press Popper to point out a second argument that whatever the strength of a scientific theory, it still only provides an approximate or partial view of the world. Scientific knowledge is essentially incomplete; it is a human creation and not given to us by the facts of the world. Newton's apparently deterministic laws of inertia and gravity, for example, are therefore only approximately true. Where theories are superseded by others of higher universality they must still only be regarded as approximations.

Popper's (*OU*: 55) third argument for indeterminism derives from the trivial claim that whatever our changing knowledge, the actual events of the historical past are unchangeable and the future remains open. His fourth argument is an extension of his polemic against historicism that maintains the impossibility of predictors predicting the results of their own future predictions (*OU*: 62–77). Finally, Popper argues that if determinism is true, then our opinions would also be fully determined. If we had unlimited power to predict the future, there would be no place for rational argument. If scientific determinism is true, we cannot know or rationally discuss it (*OU*: 82–5). The imperfect nature of our knowledge allows for both rationality and freedom.

Popper's main argument against determinism focuses upon the epistemological problem of 'predictability'. For this reason it has attracted much criticism. Essentially, Popper confuses a special type of predictability with determinism. Events and actions may well be predictable, as well as 'free and responsible', without being determined (Clark 1995: 152). The main difficulty is that even if Popper's arguments about prediction – namely the impossibility of a person or machine predicting its own future states of knowledge – are correct, they are irrelevant. At best, they would be relevant in countering the idea of a Laplacean 'World Formula' (Feigl and Meehl 1974: 521–3) that enabled the precise prediction of the future of all human and non-human history as well as retrodictions or reconstructions of the past.

Even if we conceded that metaphysical determinism depended upon some kind of 'knowability' of the world, then this would not require detailed or precise 'knowability' or 'predictability'. One can make certain kinds of general predictions with confidence, but without knowing the precise details of individual events or cases (Weatherford 1991: 157). Conversely, the universe could well be a deterministic one, but, because our attempts at measurement disturb the system in unpredictable ways, it could still be, in principle, unpredictable. The more significant point, however, remains that one cannot refute a metaphysical doctrine with an epistemological one (Earman 1986: 7–8).

It must also be said that Popper's critique takes little account of more sophisticated theories of physical determinism. Because he uses the Laplacean model of physical and scientific determinism he misses key arguments. For example, even if we were to accept that physical determinism were true, this would not provide automatic support for determinism in society and culture. Weatherford (1991: 202) comments: 'Conglomerates of particles do not wear on their sleeve, so to speak, their intellectual, social, or moral significance. Many facts about the world are not directly translatable into statements about physical particles.' Whatever the apparent determinism of the physical world, there is no necessary 'nightmare' for the social world and human moral responsibility and creativity remain possible.

*Metaphysical determinism and indeterminism: propensities
and emergence*

Popper bases his major argument for metaphysical indeterminism upon a physical interpretation of probability called propensity theory.[9] In response to deficiencies in his earlier frequency theory of probability and also to problems in quantum mechanics, he proposed and refined his propensity theory of probability during the years after 1953.[10] Popper considers that this concept denotes 'perhaps the most significant change in my views since 1934' (*RAS*: 282). Far from his original determinist position, in which probabilistic explanation was a weaker form of explanation that could be superseded by causal explanation, causal explanation is now regarded as 'at least partly replaced by probabilistic explanation' (*SB*: 25). In addition, Popper introduces the concept of *emergence* to account for events, such as the beginning of life on earth, that could not have been predicted beforehand.

Propensities may be understood as *'physical realities'* or, more precisely, as 'measures of dispositions' (*UQ*: 154; see also *RAS*: 358). Popper (1957: 70) claims that these measures, represented in statistical laws, describe the 'objective relational properties of the physical world'. Physical propensities are 'real' in that they are able not only to influence experimental results but can also 'interfere' or 'interact' with one another (Popper 1959: 28). Popper considered there to be 'an analogy between the idea of propensities and that of forces – especially fields of forces' (1959: 30).

The idea of propensity introduces a realist view of causality into the understanding of both probabilistic and deterministic laws. If propensities are akin to forces or fields of forces then, for Popper (1957: 69), these 'abstract relational facts' can be regarded as causes. In his words (1967: 39), 'a propensity might be . . . intuitively understood, as a generalization of a "causal" relation, however we may interpret "causality"'.

> Propensities are, like forces, 'occult' entities. They are something like (a) indeterministic (or not fully reliable) 'causes' of certain occurrences and (b) causes (of an almost-deterministic character) determining frequencies if the situation – for example, the experimental arrangements which gives rise to the propensity – repeats itself. (Popper 1974b: 1130)

This represents a substantial shift away from his early view of causation that interpreted it purely in terms of logical necessity.

Propensities can, however, be analogous to Newtonian forces (Popper 1959: 27; *RAS*: 397). Where the probability of an event occurring is equal to 1, a propensity operates as a classical deterministic cause. If it is less than 1, then it becomes a 'disposition' or tendency to produce a particular effect 'not always but in a proportion of cases if the situation repeats itself' (Popper 1974b: 1130). If propensities are regarded as measures of physical forces or of tendencies, then they do not tell us primarily about regularities, but about the forces or conditions that produce a regularity.

The utility of propensity theory lies in the fact that it is concerned with the properties of an unobservable physical reality. It is only the more superficial effects of this reality that we can observe and that make it possible to test a theory (Popper 1959: 31). Popper conjectures that there are hidden structural (and also indeterminate) properties of the world that we can only know in an incomplete way. The notion of propensity therefore introduces the idea that many laws describe tendencies that may or may not manifest themselves. This means that the logic of the H-D model of causal explanation is inapplicable in many cases of scientific explanation, for one could no longer assert a strict symmetry between explanation and prediction.

In the first published versions of the propensity theory, the causal mechanisms that produce a propensity are located in its set of generating conditions which are the experimental arrangements (Popper 1959: 34, 35; *RAS*: 70–1; *OU*: 105). Probabilities are measures of propensities that are generated by experimental conditions and that change with them. Popper regards propensities as dispositional properties somewhat like potentialities. He (1959: 38; 1967: 38) stresses that propensities are only relative to a particular specification in experiments. It is not only the individual structure of penny, photon or die that contribute to a propensity, but the *whole* experimental arrangement.

In 1977 Popper began to use the more general term 'situation' to indicate that propensities exist relative to both experimental *and* natural environments, that is, to closed and open systems. He extended the idea of the 'situational dependence' of probability based on propensities beyond physics to problems in biological evolution and the question of emergence (*SB*: 27). He argues for the existence of such events as 'creative' or 'emergent' evolution in which 'new things and events occur, with unexpected and indeed unpredictable properties' (*SB*: 22). Such events have a zero propensity which means that there are no possibilities of them occurring (*AWP*: 13).

For example, the probability or propensity for any atom to become part of a living organism 'has always been and still is indistinguishable from zero' (*SB*: 28).

Similarly, we are unable to predict the properties of living organisms such as those of a new species. Although we may be able to give a sketchy explanation of the origin of a new species after the event, we would not have been able to predict all its future properties because of its emergent, that is, unique character. Popper denies that complete knowledge of the 'pre-existing possibilities or potentialities' would have allowed us to predict the properties of a new entity or structure beforehand. This is because newly emergent entities, such as the creation of life or consciousness, introduce new propensities into their immediate neighbourhood that affect prevailing propensities and create '*new fields of propensities*, as a new star creates a new field of gravitation' (*SB*: 30). For Popper, the existence of propensities and emergence provides evidence for indeterminism.

Popper's account means that for events such as the origin of life or the emergence of consciousness, we cannot give a precise scientific explanation along either the original H-D model or its probabilistic variation. He considers that the world comprises both universal laws and law-like probabilistic propensities. Whereas the former are considered invariant, the latter 'do change, depending upon the changing situation' (*SB*: 25). The invariant laws, however, are not sufficiently comprehensive or powerful 'to prevent the emergence of new law-like properties' (*SB*: 25). As O'Hear (1980: 136–7; 1985: 465) notes, however, it is not clear just how weaker propensities could overthrow the stronger ones: 'If there were two competing forces in a given situation, surely the stronger would always win.'

Popper's 'scientific' arguments for propensities confront significant difficulties about the kind of reasons and evidence that are to count for and against his theory. Just as Newtonian physics appeared to give credence to determinism, so quantum theory and quantum mechanics seem to support metaphysical indeterminism (Weatherford 1991: 8–9). Both scientific theories, however, depend upon historical judgement based upon the scientific consensus at a particular point in time. Although the ruling consensus may offer support for a metaphysical position, this can only be considered provisional and remains open to challenge. Science can only supplement metaphysical arguments; it cannot be decisive in refuting them.

In review we can say that the rejection of the scientific or epistemological doctrine of determinism does not entail in any simple way the rejection of the metaphysical doctrine. Nor does the scientific evidence of indeterminism, as demonstrated by quantum theory, prove to be decisive. Weatherford (1991: x) argues that quantum mechanics complicates the issue of moral responsibility: 'For if quantum mechanics did establish the existence of importantly undetermined events they would have the moral character of roulette wheels rather than the much-sought-for human agency.' A further difficulty is that with the concept of emergence Popper has introduced the idea of a propensity equal to zero. As we have seen above, Popper indicates that there is no possibility for such events to occur. In these cases there is no propensity and therefore no probability that the event will occur. Miller (1995: 146) points out that 'this looks very much like saying that new possibilities can come about only if something impossible happens first'. Yet, Popper does not want to say that events such as the emergence of life were impossible. Miller (1995: 146) concludes: 'We must recognize not only that zero propensity does not imply impossibility, but that there exist all the time possibilities whose propensity to occur is strictly zero. ... Such events have no propensity to occur, but they may occur nonetheless – by accident, as it were.' On this interpretation, Popper's world comprises not only propensities of varying strengths, but also many chance events, or accidents, for which there were no objective propensities for them to occur. This refinement, however, reintroduces a greater role for pure chance. Such a metaphysical outcome was something that Popper's propensity theory had intended to limit.

Popper's theories of propensity and emergence offer a promising metaphysical research programme that suggests the possibility of different kinds of explanation in both natural and social sciences. Nevertheless, Popper recognizes that his arguments for indeterminacy in the physical world were insufficient foundation for a theory of freedom (1973b: 20; *OU*: 114; *OK*: 226–7). 'For what we want to understand', he stresses (1973b: 24; *OU*: 126), 'is not only how we may act *unpredictably and in a chancelike fashion*, but how we can act *deliberately and rationally*.' This sets the parameters for another ontological project.

The World 3 of Objective Knowledge

Popper's task becomes that of developing a broader theory of human agency that shows first how human beings come to an awareness of their ideas, and then how they formulate and manipulate them.[11] He also wants to show how ideas exist independently from the physical world and yet influence that world. This is a problem if the physical world is closed and nothing non-physical can affect it (Popper 1974b: 1073). He argues against this view stating: 'what we want is to understand how such non-physical things as *purposes, deliberations, plans, decisions, theories, intentions* and *values*, can play a part in bringing about physical changes in the physical world' (*OK*: 229). A theory of freedom requires at least the 'causal openness' of the physical world to the world of ideas. Popper therefore proposes that reality comprises three ontologically distinct worlds. World 1 denotes the world of physical objects and states, 'the world of physics, of rocks, and trees and physical fields of forces' (1973b: 20). World 2 refers to subjective psychological consciousness, 'the world of feelings of fear and of hope, of dispositions to act, and of all kinds of subjective experiences' (1973b: 20). World 3 describes the world of the products of the human mind, or of *'ideas in the objective sense'* (*OK*: 154).

Based upon insights drawn from Plato, Bolzano and Frege, Popper's conception of world 3 gives ontological substance to his long-held epistemological distinction between objective and subjective knowledge. In showing how theories can be viewed separate from their originators, Popper supplies an ontological basis for inter-subjectivity and criticism. The concept of world 3 therefore extends the notion of knowledge that is public and available for all to judge. In terms of Popper's cosmology, it also portrays the process of self-transcendence and thereby liberation. By articulating our scientific theories and self-conceptions we place them in another 'world' so that we can criticize and improve them. In this way we can avoid the pitfalls of subjective knowledge. Ultimately, the world 3 of objective knowledge is justified on political grounds because it aims to show how philosophies, theories and values operate as forms of control upon subjective feelings and the actions or behaviour arising from them.

Popper's main arguments for the existence of the three worlds, however, do not extend much beyond assertions about the interaction between them. World 3 strongly interacts with the physical world when objects such as buildings, bombs or airfields are constructed in accordance with world 3 plans and with theories that are often highly abstract (Popper 1973b: 21). The argument for the existence of world 2 is an extension of the preceding example, based upon the point that 'we must normally grasp or understand a world 3 theory before we can use it to act upon world 1' (Popper 1973b: 21). Such understanding is a thought process whose operation is distinct from its formulated 'objective' results and thus constitutes a separate world 2. Popper considers that world 3 usually interacts with world 1 through the world 2 of mental activity. As he acknowledges, the strength of this argument depends on world 3: 'If world 3 exists, and if it is at least in part autonomous, and if, further, plans in world 3 do affect world 1, then it seems to me inescapable that there also exists a world 2' (1973b: 21–2). The reality of world 2 therefore depends upon a satisfactory justification of a separate, autonomous world 3 of objective knowledge. But since world 3 is defined in opposition to both world 1 and world 2, there is a circularity in the argument. It appears, therefore, that world 3 is more a working assumption than a conjecture.

World 3 contains *all* the products of the human mind both in the broad cultural sense of 'tools, institutions, and works of art', and also in the logical or intellectual sense of 'problems, theories, and critical arguments' (*UQ*: 187). The more general part of this third world includes our ethical and social values, as well as scientific and artistic standards. It may also incorporate true as well as false theories, myths and factual histories (*SB*: 38). World 3 is portrayed as the human equivalent of a bird's nest or spider's web that is simultaneously the material embodiment of an abstract theory or plan. This feature indicates the first difficulty in conceptualizing world 3, in that it contains both the material objects of world 1, such as books and libraries, as well as their abstract contents. Popper (1974b: 1051) also wants to put into world 3 those unembodied objects, such as problems and theorems, that are yet to be discovered and whose logical and conceptual possibilities have yet to be explored. In this 'shadow world', a number system may be said to be a human invention rather than a discovery: 'But the difference between even and odd numbers, or divisible and prime numbers, is a discovery: these characteristic sets of numbers are there, objectively, once the number system exists, as the (unintended) consequences of constructing the system; and their properties may be discovered' (*SB*: 40). The major point is that the contents of world 3 not only have a real existence but they are also partially *autonomous* from the other worlds. Hence our knowledge does not require a knowing subject.

One problem with Popper's conception is that his argument for the reality of world 3 objects, namely whether they can *interact* with the physical objects of world 1, is not an argument for their autonomy. Autonomy implies some separate sphere of existence that is not reducible to physical entities. To base autonomy upon the actual or potential power of an object to cause something is insufficient, for every object has this capacity (Feyerabend 1974b: 480). There is no need to create a separate world for knowledge unless some argument is made for world 3 powers being something special, perhaps more abstract than those of the physical kind. It is also doubtful whether abstraction itself can be a criterion for the autonomy of world 3. Phenomena such as 'energy' or 'spin' are highly abstract, yet they clearly belong to world 1 (Feyerabend 1974b: 481).[12] Furthermore, although it is a relatively uncontroversial thesis that abstract ideas like reasons may act as causes of human behaviour, neither the arguments for a separate ontological domain, nor those supporting its autonomy, are persuasive (see Sachs 1985; Currie 1989).

Popper's espousal of a world 3 is strongly motivated by the need to present 'objective knowledge' as a form of plastic control over human subjects, their culture, society, politics and theoretical knowledge. To acknowledge the power of objective and autonomously evolving theories and problems is to limit the possibility of subjective contamination of our knowledge. Popper (*UQ*: 186) regards world 3 as real, if not more *real* than 'a social institution, such as a university or a police force'. He identifies the 'innermost nucleus of world 3' as the world of 'problems, theories, and criticism', dominated by 'the values of *objective truth, and of its growth*' (*UQ*: 194–5). Within this world, values and standards, like those in the rules of logic, may become 'exosomatic systems of control' (*OK*: 254). Nevertheless, the control that world 3 exerts over human thought and behaviour is essentially 'plastic' (Popper 1974b: 1058), if only because of the autonomously developing nature of the world 3 problems and their eventual feedback upon individuals (Popper 1974b: 1177).

World 3 is postulated for its ethical and political consequences. This is evident in Popper's claim (*SB*: 123) that 'my emphasis upon the importance of the World 3 of the objective products of the human mind may well lead to increased respect for the subjective minds who are the creators of that World 3'. Given the diverse character of world 3, however, it is not clear how such humanist goals can be achieved. The notion that world 3 can maintain a kind of control over both the evolution of theories and over their proponents is radically impaired by its all-inclusive nature. Since world 3 contains all theories and all their consequences then it contains both true and false theories as well as their logical and illogical implications. The false and the inconsistent theories could well operate to control ideas and action just as effectively as the true and consistent ones.

Although designed as part of an argument for a theory of freedom, the idea of world 3 directly undermines Popper's original intention. If world 3 operates as a form of plastic control over human beings and their knowledge, then the scope for freedom is curtailed. Once a form of knowledge has been invented, then human beings can only operate within the parameters of these controls. If this knowledge is already fully formed by virtue of its logical entailments then the scope for human creativity is further reduced. In many respects, human activity at this level consists solely in uncovering pre-existing results. Far from exercising free and creative judgements in this sphere, human beings appear to be determined.

The three-world ontology appears to demonstrate how theories and social institutions come to have a life of their own and dominate the thoughts and actions of human beings. By attaining independence or autonomy from human agency, however, such ideational forces take on the alienated or reified character noted and criticized by Marx (Chalmers 1985: 81; O'Hear 1980: 198). Contrary to his intention, Popper's world 3 shows how human beings eventually relinquish much of their freedom and creativity. This aspect of Popper's ontology of knowledge also bears a striking resemblance to a number of Foucault's contentious theories, notably those of 'discourse' (e.g. Foucault 1974: 116–17) and 'regimes of truth'. More conventionally, by pointing out the impotence of individuals before these impersonal ideational forces, world 3 also suggests the limitations of methodological individualism and the corresponding utility of methodological holism in social explanation (O'Hear 1980: 198).

The World 2 of Mind and Self

Primarily in *The Self and its Brain*, Popper explores the nature of world 2 processes, how they give rise to world 3 and how they may be differentiated from the purely physical objects of world 1. In so doing, Popper completes his pluralist ontology, draws out his views on human nature and enters the philosophical controversy over the mind–body problem. For the solution of the latter problem he proposes a form of dualism called interactionism. Interactionism supports Popper's long-standing view that we are not simply passive observers of a physical world, but are active interpreters who impose our theories on it. Popper offers his interactionism as an alternative to four major materialist philosophies of mind: radical materialism; panpsychism; epiphenomenalism; and the identity theory. The vitality of his argument lies not so much in his refutation of alternative philosophies of mind, as in his own conjectures on the biological and evolutionary basis for mind and self.[13]

Typically, Popper poses a central philosophical question and proposes that its solution must satisfy a theory of freedom. The problem is identified as that of Descartes and is formulated in the question: 'how can it be that such things as states of mind – volitions, feelings, expectations – influence or control the physical movements of our limbs?' (*OK*: 231). Following Compton, Popper suggests that the solution must explain freedom in a way that does not see it as merely due to chance, but as the result of the interplay between '*something almost random or haphazard*, and *something like a restrictive or selective control*' (*OK*: 232). He declares that such a solution depends upon formulating a 'new theory of evolution, and a new model of the organism' (*OK*: 232).

A purely materialist approach is held to be inadequate because it suggests that human beings are simply machines and thus 'prone to undermine a humanist ethics' (*SB*: 5). Popper argues that it is erroneous to believe that matter is in some sense ultimate and that there is no need to have recourse to explanations beyond material ones (*SB*: 5–6). Although he is a Cartesian dualist, Popper denies that there are two kinds of interacting substance in mind–body processes. He prefers to distinguish '*two kinds of interacting states* (or events), physio-chemical and mental ones' (*OK*: 252). Nonetheless, his dualism is compatible with a substantially revised form of materialism (*OK*: 273). If matter is no longer considered to be a 'substance', but more like a 'process', we may reconceptualize what is real and also what constitutes mind (*SB*: 7).

Popper maintains that something is 'real' if it can produce causal effects, and one of the consequences of the discoveries of modern physics is that real entities may be either concrete or abstract. Physical forces or fields of forces are highly abstract theoretical entities, but nonetheless real in the way in which they interact with more ordinary material objects (*SB*: 9–10). Popper conjectures that the reality of the mind can be conceived in similar terms. Furthermore, it is both the product of material biological evolution as well as the producer of further biological advances (*SB*: 11). Despite its abstract powers, the mind has a material foundation, exemplified most clearly in the evolutionary process. Thus he conjectures that matter can transcend itself, 'by producing mind, purpose, and a world of the products of the human mind' (*SB*: 11).

Contrary to the materialist, reductionist approach, which attempts to explain more abstract entities in terms of their more physical causes, such as elementary particles and physical laws, Popper (*SB*: 19) proposes that there exists both 'upward' and 'downward' causation. That is, where physical events may bring about abstract effects, the reverse is also possible. In this revised ontology 'wholes' may bring causal effects upon their constituent parts. For Popper, this also means that the reductionist programme underlying the materialist theory of mind, one that attempts to reduce mind to brain processes, is probably unable to be completed.

Popper sets out his theory of mind in evolutionary terms. Consciousness is conjectured to have become an emergent property of animals because of the pressure of natural selection (*SB*: 29). The next important evolutionary event was the emergence of the human brain and its mind. Where animals also developed consciousness and brains (and possibly a rudimentary state of mind), they would not, according to Popper (*UQ*: 190; *SB*: 438–9), have had any consciousness of self. With the concept of self, however, Popper divides the mind–body problem into two parts. Whereas the first problem concerns the close relationship between physiological states and states of consciousness, the second considers that more refined form of consciousness, the emergence of self. Here, Popper distinguishes between (a) *mind* as a set of mental processes that have the capacity to organize conscious actions and unconscious bodily movements, as well as abstract thought, and (b) the further product of theorizing, the conscious *self*. Where one is born with a mind containing various innate dispositions such as those to learn language or become a self, the actual consciousness of self is the later fulfilment of such a capacity.

The mind is presented as an active set of processes whose major function is to maintain biological survival. In doing this, it utilizes a number of genetically based inborn and unconscious dispositions as well as more conscious capacities. That is, it exercises such dispositions as curiosity and language to extend the conscious ability to anticipate problems and to theorize. The extension of the material, genetic base may be regarded as a form of self-transcendence, as it creates the basis for more abstract cultural learning in the world 3 of objective knowledge (*SB*: 46). For Popper, mind is never a 'stream of consciousness', but an active problem-solver even when it is simply contemplating (*SB*: 128). It is constantly producing anticipations and theories that it checks against the available data and so generates feedback with which it can adjust its information and action.

Popper (*SB*: 109) notes that we are born with minds but need to develop a self or a personal identity. A self that persists over time is the product of the mind's propensity to theorize and make sense of its surroundings. Its emergence also follows the more general evolutionary pattern and is perhaps best exemplified in the procedures by which children develop their capacities and their identity (*SB*: 49). Although one's self-identity is closely related to bodily self-identity it also relies upon cultural values and ideas. As one creates a sense of self, one also defines one's relationship to others and gains awareness of moral responsibility. In Popper's view (*SB*: 472), 'the self-conscious mind has a personality, something like an ethos or a moral character and . . . this personality is itself partly the product of actions done in the past.'

Popper stresses, however, that there is no part of the brain that corresponds to the self. The evidence appears to show the opposite, in that 'the whole brain must be in high activity to be linked with consciousness – a teaming process of unimaginable complexity' (*SB*: 120). At times, the self may seem like a spectator outside of the brain (*SB*: 487). Where a mind may be understood by analogy with an automatic pilot, the self appears to take on a more human form (*SB*: 120): 'Like a pilot, it observes and takes action at the same time.' The difference between animals and human beings is that the latter have a consciousness of self that Popper considers to be 'anchored' in world 3 and its language (*SB*: 144; *UQ*: 196). Human language, he explains, 'makes it possible for us to be not only subjects, centres of action, but also objects of our own critical thought, of our own critical judgement' (*SB*: 144).

These insights are integrated into a theory of biological evolution in which science is a higher form of evolutionary adaptation. Scientific method is not dissimilar to the trial and error approach observed in the biological process of natural selection. Nevertheless, the emergence of mind and world 3 have a special role to play in tempering the 'more or less violent struggle for life' that characterizes natural selection (*SB*: 209–10). Accordingly, Popper's theory of mind and world 3 exhibits its inescapable political and ethical character. We are encouraged to see science as a part of our evolutionary heritage in which may be found the capacity for the elimination of violence and the promotion of human freedom and creativity.

Here we also see refined the familiar notion of controls that are exercised in a plastic way over the sensuous human being. The mind operates first as an unconscious propensity structure controlling autonomic bodily functions, in accordance with controls supplied by genetic inheritance. As it becomes a self, the mind develops language and a moral capacity that also operates as a cultural control upon relations with others. Finally, there is developed that sophisticated set of controls to be found in philosophy and science that provides means for gauging the accuracy of theories and their attendant actions. This system of interacting controls is essentially an open one because of the indeterminate nature of the material and abstract forces that comprise it. Human beings, however, can be free and creative not just because of indeterminacy, but because they can choose to alter many of the cultural controls in response to both theoretical implications and changes in physical and social environment.

It must be said that Popper's arguments for an interactionist dualism put him on the margins of most recent philosophical debates on the self and mind. With few notable exceptions (e.g. Madell 1988; Penrose 1994), contemporary philosophers have abandoned non-physical conceptions of the mind (Lyons 1995: lxvi; Nagel 1993: 37). The current dominant approach is to attempt, by one means or another, to reduce our knowledge of the mind to those theories that can be explained in physical or materialist terms. Popper's strategy, however, is to rule out any radical materialist explanation and to reject any reduction of mental states to physical ones. This strictly limits the relevance of most scientific work in the area, whether in the fields of neurobiology, cognitive science or psychology.

Possibly for this reason, Popper does not address many of the contemporary arguments on the topic (Dennett 1979: 91). Although, in one place (*SB*: 120), he refers to the 'psycho-physical self' as the 'active programmer' to the brain 'which is a computer', Popper seems unaware of the functionalist literature on artificial intelligence. More surprisingly, he also fails to deal with many of the older arguments against dualism that criticize its reliance upon non-material entities such as the 'ghost in the machine' (O'Hear 1980: 201–2). Nevertheless, Popper's work does complement recent developments in its claim that entities such as the brain, consciousness, mind and self are emergent properties of biological evolution (Lyons 1995: lxvi; Searle 1992).

Although Popper denies that he is offering an ontology (*SB*: 4), it is difficult to avoid the conclusion that his arguments are more metaphysical than empirical. That is, they are generally not testable propositions. In at least two areas, however, Popper appears to be correct. The reductionist programme is more a materialist aspiration that remains a research programme rather than anything like a confirmed theory (see Nagel 1993: 38). In this regard, Popper's anti-reductionism has received support from an unlikely materialist quarter. According to McGinn (1989; 1991), no theory will be able to explain scientifically the causal relationship between the brain and mental states such as consciousness, if only because we do not possess the cognitive powers to understand a complex part of our very nature.

Popper is also correct to argue that 'unobservability' does not prevent us from calling something real and that this allows us to retain some provisional access to a non-material conception of mind and self. Such arguments need not encourage us to be satisfied with causal explanation in terms of spirits, ghosts or gods. On the issue of the non-material self and mind, some equivocal metaphysical support may be gleaned from the recent work of Searle (1992). Similar to Popper, Searle argues that consciousness is an emergent and irreducible property of the brain. Unlike Popper, he wants to say that consciousness is a *physical* or material property. Yet, because of his anti-reductionism, and despite his anti-dualist language, Searle's theory remains within dualism (Nagel 1993: 40).

The main question for this book is whether Popper has succeeded in solving the problem of freedom and creativity that stimulated his original quest. Perhaps the best that could be said for Popper's theory of mind is that it strengthens our ordinary, common sense understanding by introducing new notions of biological emergence and propensity. He has sketched an evolutionary history of the mind as an evolving propensity structure that is always creating new possibilities for itself and other minds. In particular, he indicates the general processes of evolution, learning and feedback by which a mind can produce something like a moral character. Popper's arguments therefore extend his metaphysical conjectures on how human freedom and creativity are possible, but their main virtue lies in rounding out a more systematic ontology.

Metaphysics of Freedom

Concerned to provide an ontological foundation for human freedom, Popper has argued for the existence of an 'open universe' in which material and non-material entities can interact in a creative way. As we have seen, however, there remains scope for intellectual and political 'freedom' without hard-core realism, whether of the metaphysical or the scientific kind. Both realism and instrumentalism can produce oppression, and both may allow for moral responsibility. Partly because of his emphasis upon predictability and physical determinism, Popper also fails to refute determinism or to show that determinism rules out freedom. His positive arguments for the links between indeterminism and freedom are also inconclusive.

Certainly, a theory of human freedom, understood as moral responsibility and intellectual creativity, requires that our ideas have some causal effect upon our actions. Given the existence of true and false ideas in world 3 and the 'controls' it is intended to place upon human thought and action, the role of world 3 in fostering freedom and creativity is at best ambiguous. The notion of a realm of public knowledge, a kind of 'public sphere' in which all types of knowledge claims may be discussed freely, remains essential for rational knowledge and politics. But neither freedom of public discussion nor moral agency requires a separate world 3 for ideas. Except for the most extreme materialism or idealism, there seems to be no necessary link between either materialist or non-materialist theories of mind and the maintenance of a humanist ethic of freedom.

Although Popper's ontology offers a challenging conjecture about the various 'worlds' we inhabit, it does not provide decisive arguments in support of a metaphysical theory of freedom. Popper's discussions do, however, open up larger philosophical and sociological research projects. His theory indicates how certain kinds of freedom are possible but gives little direction as to what path we should take and how we ought to exercise these possibilities. Here, the formulation of a social theory of freedom becomes an important task. We need to know not only how we create oppressive ideologies or discourses and lose control over them, but also how we may regain control of them. Understanding how human minds may gain a propensity for non-violence and other humanist values, or decide to choose to exercise their freedom and creativity, is another important question. Popper also needs to set out what constitutes a satisfactory normative concept of freedom that indicates, for example, whether certain types of freedom have priority over others. These questions return us to Popper's early political theory where only limited answers are given.

From a general philosophical perspective Popper's complex metaphysics forms an elaborate structure. Although the three-world ontology constitutes a bold metaphysical proposal it collapses under the weight of its many claims. Most of what is important to

Popper could be argued for without such an ontology. The arguments for propensities and emergence, however, represent a promising research programme that has serious implications for both his epistemology and methodology of natural and social science. Whether Popper chooses to leave the underlying 'causes' of propensities unexplored and remain at the level of statistical tests, or whether he advocates investigation of their underlying 'generating conditions', he is bound to a diminished formalism. Applying the concepts of propensity, holistic causation and emergence to social processes would appear to have great heuristic value. It would also, however, emphasize further the limitations of Popper's early philosophy of social science.

In refining his ontology Popper is also pressed to revise the character of his epistemology. An epistemology devised for a determinist ontology, and which searches for regularities upon which to secure its explanations, is ill-equipped for an open universe in which innovation, novelty and heterogeneity are the norm rather than the exception. The evolutionary model of the mind offers a schema upon which to base a more general approach to understanding the growth of knowledge. The elucidation of Popper's trial and error approach to problem-solving lays the foundation for an evolutionary epistemology that is the subject of the next chapter.

7

Evolutionary Epistemology

This chapter offers a critical account of Popper's evolutionary epistemology and its application to natural and social science. We shall examine the shift of emphasis from a formalist rationality derived from the methods of physics to a problem-solving rationality based upon theories of evolutionary biology. The chapter also raises questions about Popper's proposals for interpretation and his correspondence theory of truth. It is argued that his adoption of an evolutionary epistemology brings a significant modification of his methodology towards a more general and 'holistic' approach. Furthermore, as the formal epistemic requirements for progress decline in significance, the non-epistemic issues – moral, political and institutional – become more prominent.

Epistemological Problems of an Open Universe

Popper's larger epistemological project was to provide a general theory of rationality that entailed elaborating both a descriptive account of, and normative foundations for, a theory of the rational growth of knowledge. His conception of an open universe, however, creates new epistemological problems. The incompleteness and infinite variety of our knowledge contributes to his view that the universe is 'partly causal, partly probabilistic, and partly open: it is emergent' (Popper 1973b: 26). That is, our universe comprises novel entities and events which are not completely reducible to preceding stages or explained with reference to more 'fundamental' processes such as physio-chemical laws. The material cornerstone of Popper's ontology of the open universe is a new conception of the physical world, in which 'all the properties of the physical world are dispositional, and the real state of a physical system, at any moment, may be conceived as the sum total of its dispositions – or its potentialities, or possibilities, or propensities' (*QTSP*: 159).

The concepts of propensity and emergence provide the foundations for revising Popper's epistemology and methodology, especially with regard to falsifiability and explanation. His arguments on propensities signal the end of his espousal of a strict logic of scientific explanation. Popper now presents deductive causal explanation as a limiting case of probabilistic explanation. The idea of propensity also points to the holistic nature of probabilistic explanation. Since propensities are relational forces which can only be understood in terms of a whole physical system or a total experimental arrangement, they represent a fundamentally different kind of explanation, namely, one that focuses upon processes and relations between phenomena. Individual events cannot be explained solely with reference to their own particular properties, but only in terms of a whole, however that is conceived. It could also be said that the whole (physical system or experimental arrangement) influences the behaviour of the parts in an indeterminate manner.

The epistemology appropriate for these new metaphysical assumptions would have (a) to acknowledge the continuity between human and non-human knowledge, and (b) to provide means for the criticism and growth of *both* kinds of knowledge. That is, it would begin from an ontology that comprehends the place of mind and objective ideas in a world of interacting physical and non-physical propensities. Such an epistemology would also be premised upon a weakening of the boundaries between metaphysics and science, and would presume a more sophisticated understanding of scientific progress. Whereas 'freedom from dogmatism' was a criterion of evaluation for the early epistemology and methodology, Popper's later proposals lie within a commitment to a broader metaphysical conception of freedom. For Popper, the best prospects for taking account of such insights lay in formulating an *evolutionary* epistemology.

There are three main stages in the transformation of Popper's conception of rationality. The first step occurs with his social and political conception of rationality as 'openness to criticism' or the critical attitude, which was documented in chapter 4. The second step, outlined in the next section, is based upon arguments about the rational status of metaphysics and its role in the growth of knowledge. The final step occurs with Popper's recognition of parallels between the growth of human knowledge and biological evolution. It is important to note the significant shift that has occurred here towards a 'naturalistic' form of epistemology.

Science and Metaphysics: Rationality as Criticism

In his later work, Popper revises his understanding of, and prescriptions for, demarcation and rationality. In his *Postscript* he repudiates the possibility of sharp demarcation between science and metaphysics (*RAS*: 159), and extols the virtues of metaphysical speculation for scientific advance (*QTSP*: 210). He still thinks it important to identify falsifiable theories, but he now considers this only one technique within a more comprehensive approach to rationality, conceived loosely as arguability or criticizability. On this view, testability was simply 'a certain kind of arguability: arguability by means of *empirical* arguments, appealing to observation and experiment' (*RAS*: 161).

Although metaphysical theories were empirically unfalsifiable, they could still be rational. Popper concludes that it is impossible to eliminate all 'metaphysical elements' from science (*RAS*: 179). He also argues that there are no routine procedures for either designing new scientific theories or deciding upon their falsification (*RAS*: 189). Whereas scientists could still apply the logical criterion of falsifiability, they could not reject pseudo-scientific theories out of hand. Popper recognizes that metaphysical theories often had a greater influence on science than that of many testable theories. Like Darwinism, they have served as research programmes for science (*RAS*: 193).

By recognizing the centrality of metaphysical ideas for science, Popper alters his approach to scientific methodology. The two previously central stages of determining the falsifiability of a theory, and then attempting its empirical refutation, are relegated to a subsidiary role in the progress of science. 'The third, and perhaps the most important one,' Popper wrote (*QTSP*: 161), 'is the relation between the theory and what may be called the "*metaphysical research programme*".' Such programmes provide a speculative theoretical framework that outlines the problems that a scientific theory was supposed to solve. Rarely discussed, they are more often 'implicit in the theories and in the attitudes and judgements of the scientists' (*QTSP*: 161). The distinguishing features of metaphysical theories lie not in their differential claims to truth, but in the point that they are 'vaguer', 'inferior' and irrefutable (*QTSP*: 199).

Popper's focus changes therefore from demarcating between science and metaphysics to demarcating within metaphysics between those theories that are valuable and those that are not. The problem becomes that of determining the *rationality* of a metaphysical theory. Similar to an empirical theory, a non-empirical one may be considered rational if it is able to be criticized and discussed with reference to its problem situation (*QTSP*: 200; *CR*: 198–9). Popper (*CR*: 200) declares that we may judge the truth or falsity of a philosophical theory, as long as we remember that our solutions can never be final. The main task, however, is to demarcate between critical and uncritical theories.

For Popper, the criterion of demarcation within metaphysics becomes the same as in science. The one method of philosophy and of natural science is 'that of stating one's problem clearly and of examining its various proposed solutions *critically*' (*LScD*: 16). In this process, testing is only part of the method of criticism. Whether a theory is worth investigating or not depends upon 'its capacity to provoke rational criticism, and to inspire attempts to supersede it by something better' (*QTSP*: 211). That is, a theory is rational because it does not foreclose critical discussion directed towards improving it.

Popperian epistemology has become the 'theory of problem-solving, or . . . of the construction, critical discussion, evaluation, and critical testing, of competing conjectural theories' (*OK*: 142). This is both a descriptive and a prescriptive project. Although epistemology must distinguish between different kinds of theories such as logical and mathematical, empirical and scientific, and philosophical and metaphysical theories, their rationality lies in a common approach to problems. According to Popper (*CR*: 199), a theory is only rational if it is an attempt to solve real problems and if it can be examined critically. Rational criticism, however, also entails enquiry into whether the theory is true or false or nearer to the truth than another theory (*RAS*: 24–5).

With this revision, Popper moves well beyond his earliest conceptions of rationality and epistemology. No longer is the empirical scientific method of falsificationism the epitome of rationality. Nor is epistemology confined to studying the growth of scientific knowledge. Scientific method is now simply one element of a more comprehensive epistemology founded upon the idea of problem-solving by trial and error criticism. In this regard, Popper's epistemological

project remains primarily a normative one concerned with prescribing certain general standards of rationality that can be applied
across a range of disciplines. These norms, however, have political
significance. For Popper (*RAS*: 155), rational discussion and critical
thinking are 'the means of breaking out of the prison [of our mind
and culture] – of liberating ourselves'.

The normative recommendations still retain the status of proposals, conjectures or conventions, and the Darwinian theory of evolution, as Popper interprets it, provides grounds for adopting the
method of trial and error criticism. By recognizing the continuities
between the world and our knowledge of it, as well as the continuities between metaphysics and science, Popper opens the way towards a more unified and comprehensive *explanation* of the growth
of knowledge as part of an 'evolutionary' epistemology.

Evolutionary Epistemology

As we saw in chapter 2, the core methodological principles of
Popper's early philosophy were drawn from his analysis of Einstein's
discoveries in theoretical physics. Popper (*PH*: 105–19) had considered Darwinian evolutionary theory to be untestable and, therefore,
unscientific. Only from the 1960s did he publicly address the problems of Darwinism and biological evolution. In his early work he
drew upon what he conceived to be Einstein's method, and not his
substantive theory. With Darwin, however, he is more concerned
with the theory of natural selection and not his method. Popper's
project therefore becomes a more empirical and explanatory one of
showing how science and philosophy are a product of and, in some
respects, continuous with human evolution. In the first phase of his
philosophy, he reconstructed the logic of 'heroic' science as a foundation for epistemology and methodology. In this final phase, he recon-
structs the 'logic' of biological evolution in an attempt to show its
similarities to both his reconstructed logic of philosophical argument
and a revised reconstruction of the logic of science.

Biological evolution as problem-solving

Within the biological process of natural selection Popper (1984: 239)
saw a model of the growth of knowledge comparable to that which
he had devised for science and philosophy. The judgement of conti-

nuity between the lowest and the highest organisms arose from the observation that all knowledge grows by means of problem-solving. The amoeba, lower animals and 'primitive man', for example, proceed largely by inborn instinct towards one major goal, that of survival. The operation of this innate or more subjective knowledge is analogous to that of the objective kind, and 'is part of a highly complex and intricate but (in a healthy organism) astonishingly accurate apparatus of adjustment' (*OK*: 77). An unsuccessful attempt to adjust has the dramatic result of an organism's death or the extinction of a species. The activity of problem-solving by trial and error appears, therefore, to have two types of consequence. First, it provides feedback in which the successful solution of a problem influences the behaviour of an animal and enables it to develop, in a chance-like way, new skills and organs that enable it to survive (*OK*: 113). Second, the process may even give rise to new species (*OK*: 242–4).

Popper acknowledges that among the 'higher' evolutionary forms of human life not all problems are those of survival (*OK*: 244). They may be consciously self-critical in their attempt to solve problems and allow their hypotheses to die instead (*OK*: 248). Nevertheless, Popper regards the growth of human knowledge as bearing a remarkable resemblance to the process of evolution as portrayed in Darwin's theory of natural selection. He refers to the '*natural selection of hypotheses*', in which 'our knowledge consists, at every moment, of those hypotheses which have shown their (comparative) fitness by surviving so far in their struggle for existence; a competitive struggle which eliminates those hypotheses which are unfit' (*OK*: 261). Instead of practical success, however, the goal is to solve problems in such a way that our theories increasingly approach the truth (*OK*: 264). The conscious method of criticism is considered 'to continue the work of natural selection on a nongenetic (exosomatic) level' (*UQ*: 140). Popper represents this process by the schema: $P_1 \rightarrow TT \rightarrow EE \rightarrow P_2$. He explains (*OK*: 119):

That is, we start from some problem P_1, proceed to a tentative solution or tentative theory TT, which may be (partly or wholly) mistaken; in any case it will be subject to error-elimination, EE, which may consist of critical discussion or experimental tests; at any rate, new problems P_2 arise from our own creative activity; and these new problems are not in general intentionally created by us, they emerge autonomously from the field of new relationships which we cannot help bringing into existence with every action, however little we intend to do so.

In all organisms, according to Popper, the growth of knowledge begins not with the inductive collection of observations, but with practical or theoretical problems (*OK*: 259–60). At the most basic level all organisms are born with certain kinds of subjective knowledge in the form of innate expectations. These anticipations constitute rudimentary theories that, when disappointed, create the first problems (*OK*: 258–9). The more important problems, however, are those of a second order contained in the 'objective' products of human endeavour, such as science, philosophy and works of art, which are the results of attempts to solve the original problems. Yet, it is the capacity for, and use of, human language that enables humans to think critically (Popper 1984: 250).

Such conjectures lead to a radical revision of Popper's conception of epistemology: 'The main task of the theory of human knowledge, is to understand it as continuous with animal knowledge; and to understand also its discontinuity – if any – from animal knowledge' (Popper 1974b: 1061). This also sets the objective of determining the nature of these continuities and discontinuities. Here, we must enquire into the adequacy of Popper's descriptions of (a) biological evolution and (b) the growth of human knowledge.

Following Bradie (1986: 403) we may distinguish two main programmes of research into evolutionary epistemology. One programme aims to explain human and animal cognitive mechanisms such as brains, eyes, sensory systems, etc. in terms of biological theories of evolution. The second aims to explain the growth of human knowledge, such as ideas, culture and science, by using models, analogies and metaphors drawn from evolutionary theory. The first programme is *phylogenetic* in that it is largely concerned with the evolution of cognitive capacities and structures in a species. Because the second programme is primarily concerned with the development of knowledge and learning among individuals over their lifetime, it may be regarded as *ontogenetic*. In each case, however, the processes (whether biological or conceptual) are quite different (Bradie 1986: 412). Popper's proposals for an evolutionary epistemology incorporate both types of programme.

A first question therefore concerns the application of cultural analogies and metaphors to the descriptions of biological processes. In the phylogenetic process of biological evolution there are no goals and there is only one problem, that of survival. By referring to 'choice' and 'goal-seeking', Popper imposes inappropriate cultural metaphors upon natural processes. Accordingly, his model becomes less 'evolutionary' and less able to provide independent support for his philosophical arguments. He (*OK*: 145) also claims that theories 'correspond to endosomatic organs'. Bradie (1986: 415) points out that this representation confuses the difference between the 'phylogenetic evolution of biological organs and their ontogenetic development'. Another significant point of contrast between biology and human culture is Popper's (*OK*: 262) use of the phylogenetic model of the 'evolutionary tree', which grows from a common stem into more branches. This evolutionary process is the exact opposite of his model of the growth of human knowledge in which many branches converge upon a single unifying theory (see Bradie 1986: 416). A further complication is his anthropomorphic use of metaphors such as 'trial and error' to describe the process of biological evolution.

According to Bradie (1986: 417), all models of evolutionary epistemology contain three components, namely, a source of variation, a selection mechanism and a mechanism for transmission and retention of information. For Popper, the sources of variation are theories, and the selection mechanism is the capacity for problem-solving. World 2 human beings fulfil the third function by creating theories or artefacts in textual form that are retained in world 3. These are transmitted through various means such as publications and learning by the humans that comprise world 2. Although Popper recognizes that there are differences between biological evolution and the growth of human knowledge, he does not see them as significant. Nor does he think that they provide reasons for treating his arguments as analogies or metaphors.

By comparison to human culture, the process or 'method' by which biological survival occurs is somewhat limited. The ontogenetic process of individual organic survival occurs through the exercise of unconscious genetic cognitive capacities and instinct and, where relevant, behavioural learning. The survival of a species, however, is a phylogenetic process that occurs primarily by means of the blind process of random selection (see also Ruse 1986a: 61–5).[1] Perhaps the most serious disanalogy is that the growth of our non-biological human knowledge is less the result of 'blind' chance than conscious intention and teleology. In science, for example, the method of trial and error is far from being a blind or random process. For Popper, it is primarily a self-conscious process of theory and experiment directed towards seeking the truth. The relevant analogy would not be 'natural selection', but possibly that of 'artificial selection' (Bradie 1986: 432). Even if we substitute the notion of an evolutionary 'problem' for that of 'goal', then there is still only one biological problem and that is the survival of the species. Bradie (1986: 424) points out further difficulties with the analogy:

> The organism contributes to the survival of the lineage by means of its reproductive success which is a measure of its fitness. What corresponds to 'conceptual fitness'? Truth? Darwinian fitness is relational and admits of degrees. Truth does not. Perhaps empirical adequacy is a better analogue. Even so, empirical adequacy or truth is not the only goal of conceptual activity.

In conceptual evolution there are numerous problems and various criteria of 'selection'.

For Popper, human survival is a necessary but not a sufficient goal. Given his political recommendation that we alleviate poverty and unnecessary suffering, Popper's goals are set within a higher framework of values which include human dignity and freedom. In addition, he advocates higher forms of creativity in the fields of art, science and philosophy. Moreover, the 'methods' by which humans pursue their goals of survival are multiple and hardly correspond to the process of 'natural selection'. For example, Popper wants to retain the goal of truth, and conceptual progress is ideally measured by its 'verisimilitude'.

There are also particular evolutionary capacities, such as those for creating 'objective knowledge', for problem-solving and self-reflection, which, when exercised, have no analogy with non-human organisms. That is, the distinctively human exercise of these capacities produces outcomes that are not essential for the physical survival of either individuals or the whole species. In some areas of scientific knowledge their pursuit may even be a threat to human survival. On Popper's claims about the adaptive function of our human cognitive capacities, O'Hear (1989: 127) is right to point out that our ability to search for truth may just as well militate against survival as promote it.[2]

As Popper acknowledges, human life is distinctive in its capacity to create new problems self-consciously. One of those new problems derives from our very biological capacity for knowledge. Humans have the power to change radically the course of human and non-human evolution (for example, by means of large-scale scientific experiments and programmes of genetic adaptation). For non-humans there is no choice in such matters, whereas for humans there is the possibility of choice between alternative courses of action, and these are often essentially moral choices.

Such criticisms demonstrate two main difficulties with Popper's arguments. Contrary to the general thrust of his claims, his version of evolutionary epistemology has more of the character of an analogy than of any theoretical continuity. Second, the revisions to Darwinian theory he proposes are so radical as to constitute a repudiation of Darwinism (see Baigrie 1989: 66 and Ruse 1986a: 64).

Human culture as 'rational' problem-solving

There are numerous parallels or analogies between the biological process of evolution and the growth of cultural forms of knowledge such as science. Popper's account, however, tends to obscure the differences between empirical description and the normative prescription that is necessary for human culture. Where evolutionary biology may suggest certain limits to our capacities for acquiring human knowledge, it cannot provide a satisfactory normative guide to making choices between competing theories and concepts.

Given that humans are reflective and intentional creatures, we do not just want a *descriptive* account of how their knowledge grows; we want to know how to guide their choices. That is, we will want to know what we *ought* to do. Whatever the merits of his specific arguments, by demonstrating epistemological continuity Popper has merely described these processes. What remains important at the level of human culture is whether we can show that any particular form of knowledge arrived at is superior or inferior to any other. Hence, we must return to questions concerning the rationality of our knowledge. Popper also describes the problem-solving process in human knowledge with reference to the normative criteria of rationality.

In Popper's account, rational criticism proceeds in four stages similar to biological problem-solving. The first step is to delineate the problem for which the theory is offered as a solution. This requires analysis of the intellectual context or problem situation – the second step. The next step is to propose a tentative theory or series of theories as a solution to the problem. The key final stage occurs with the attempt to eliminate errors among the competing theories. Proceeding by whatever practical or theoretical means are appropriate, the aim is to isolate and eliminate contradictions within a theory and in its relationship to the problem it was designed to solve. The difficulties raised by the elimination of errors constitute a new problem. Taking account of the multiplicity of tentative solutions and trials, Popper offers a revised schema (see figure 1). The

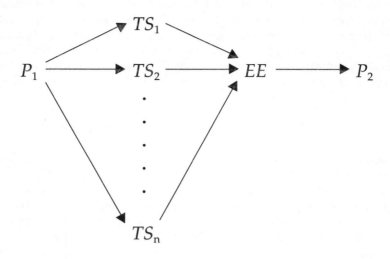

Figure 1 (Source: *OK*: 243)

process of error elimination is a generalized method of falsification. In science we try to refute theories: first, by attempting to isolate logical contradictions within a theory and ascertaining the extent of its falsifiability; and, second, by empirically testing them against the available evidence. In Popper's view, scientific problems are problems of explanation and therefore amenable to the application of deductive logic.

Although metaphysical and philosophical theories are *empirically* irrefutable, they must still be examined critically with the aim of showing them to be true or false. The criteria for confirmation or refutation are broader and bear upon whether the theory has successfully solved the designated philosophical problem as determined by a critical analysis of the problem situation. Where philosophical theories may suggest practical and theoretical problems for further investigation, it is their relationship to their problem situation that is important in their later critical evaluation.

Because science consists of empirical and metaphysical theories that are rarely differentiated clearly, it must proceed from the most general 'philosophical' method of problem-solving to the more logical and empirical methods. Logical form itself is no longer the hallmark of rationality in science. Popper (*CR*: 221) writes: 'it is not the marvellous deductive unfolding of the system which makes a theory rational or empirical but the fact that we can examine it critically.' Accordingly, the method of falsifiability and falsification is only one weapon amongst many in the critical armoury of rational science. Such techniques can only be applied after the less definitive work of ascertaining the nature of the problem situation has been completed. Even deciding upon the falsifiability of a theory and its empirical refutation is essentially an interpretative procedure open to the collective judgement of the community of scientists. The rationality of science or philosophy incorporates philosophical, social and historical dimensions that cannot be conveyed by any simple formula.

Although Popper supplies a variety of familiar precepts for undertaking criticism, when compared to his early epistemology based upon science, the normative criteria for epistemological progress and the accompanying methodological prescriptions are much less specific. For example, with his proposal (*UQ*: 22; *CR*: 184) that the highest form of intellectual creativity and rationality has become the discovery of a new problem, Popper provides a general criterion of progress.[3] Nevertheless, unlike biological evolution, in the sphere of culture (including science), our conceptions of a new problem, or of a trial, an error, success, solution, progress, feedback, and of truth or falsity, are subject to interpretation and thereby contestable. Furthermore, the specific techniques of criticism and results of communal judgement may change over time.

In view of these tendencies towards relativism, Popper's three-world ontology offers a residual notion of objective truth based upon the immutability of logic.[4] Here, the presumed universal applicability of formal analysis, and its alleged independence from actual human thought, suggests the existence of at least one refuge from relativism and irrationalism. Even in his later work Popper (1976a: 98–9; *OK*: 121; *CR*: 64) praises the virtues of deductive logic as the 'theory of rational criticism'. Thus his epistemology still exhibits a residual logicism. Elsewhere in Popper's problem-solving conception of knowledge and rationality, the general criteria proposed allow greater possibility for varying standards of rationality, and the prospect of relativism. If rationality is defined as our way of choosing between theories, and this involves appraising whether a theory has solved its problem better than another theory, then evolutionary epistemology in the cultural sphere encompasses nearly every conceivable method of argument.

Problems of Interpretation and Politics

Given that neither the falsifiability or falsification of theories, nor philosophical problems can be determined without reference to their contexts or problem situations, the less definitive skills of interpretation and judgement are necessary in both science and philosophy. Popper's proposals, however, do not distinguish sufficiently between (a) rationality understood as an ideal norm of human behaviour and against which we can evaluate different kinds of actual behaviour, and (b) rationality as an empirical assumption about human action. There are also grounds for suggesting that Popper's schematic summary of the problem-solving process ought to be amended to take account of the interpretative judgements needed at each stage of deliberation.

By directing us towards problems and problem-solving Popper's epistemology takes a hermeneutic turn (*OK*: 162).[5] This arises from his demand that we first assess our theories or objects of enquiry against a relevant problem situation, that is, in effect, the intellectual context within which we locate a problem (*LScD*: 16). All analysis, whether in philosophy, science or history proper, must appraise the evolution of the relevant problem situation, and will therefore contain some historical and interpretative dimension. Except perhaps for logic and pure mathematics, for Popper, the different fields of knowledge range along a continuum, from the most metaphysical to the more empirical domains. This is regardless of whether the objects of study are natural or human.

Popper proposes a revised version of his method of situational analysis as the common method of interpretation. This takes account of perceptions or meanings that any human actor, philosopher, scientist or historian has of their problem situation or theoretical context. Originally devised for social science, situational analysis distinguishes between 'the situation as the agent saw it, and the situation as it was (both, of course, conjectured)' (*OK*: 179). An observer seeks to evaluate one against the other and thereby locate and account for any misperceptions that could have influenced the theory and action of a philosopher, scientist or other human actor. Delineating the problem situation would demonstrate the constraints and possibilities available to human agents as problem-solvers and so indicate the scope for, or limitations of, their rationality within that situation.

In social scientific explanations of human action this prescription raises two interconnected issues concerning evaluation. It appears that, for Popper, the problem-solving form of instrumental rationality is the epitome of rationality. He (*OK*: 179) makes this assumption clear when he writes: 'we can interpret an action as an attempt to solve a problem.' For this reason, the method would be more applicable to natural science and much of philosophy where the primary task is the self-conscious exploration of problems. These instrumentalist assumptions, however, make the methodology more problematic for explaining and understanding other types of human action. Within Popper's work therefore may be found a bias towards interpreting virtually all forms of human behaviour in instrumental or procedural terms, somewhat akin to the model of rational choice theory.[6]

Those human activities that do not resemble 'problem-solving' are, by definition, either irrational or of a lesser form of rationality. Expressive action exemplified in the production of creative works of art and literature, affective or emotional behaviour, and activities such as meditation and contemplation all have to be reinterpreted either as instrumental, problem-solving behaviour or as somewhat lesser forms of rational action. We need only refer to Weber's famous categorization (1978: 24–6) to demonstrate that rational human action may be of at least four types, namely, instrumental, value-oriented, affective and traditional. In this vein, Minogue (1995b: 237–8) has pointed out that human 'action' may be the expression of an individual's attachment to intrinsic values such as religion, or social duty or routine, and not problem-solving forms of instrumental action.

The second issue concerns an ambiguity evident in the assumptions required by the situational method and what Popper calls the 'rationality principle'. As we saw in chapter 5, he refers to this as a quasi-empirical, universal social law asserting the principle that the various agents involved 'act *adequately*, or *appropriately*' according to the implicit 'logic' of the situation (1985: 359; see also Popper 1976a: 102).[7] Thus, it becomes possible to show how non-instrumentalist behaviour that was not directed towards problem-solving, of the kind mentioned above, may be adequate or appropriate to the situation. Nonetheless, the social scientist observer would still have to take account of their prior preconceptions about adequacy or appropriateness of action in the situation.[8]

The problem situations in natural science are also not quite as straightforward as may be assumed. In practice, the scientific choice of problem is often subject to various complementary intellectual, financial and institutional influences (see Ziman 1987). An evolutionary epistemology of science may need to supply epistemic and ethical guidance on what influences would be legitimate to consider. Within Popper's hermeneutic approach, however, there is no finality, for a theory or interpretation is revisable as new knowledge and evidence become available. Understanding a theory becomes a continuously unfolding project in which public debate is the ultimate arbiter. Furthermore, Popper (1974a: 56–7) does not think that the alien nature of different or competing cultural or scientific perspectives will result in incommensurability or the breakdown of rational communication.

While interpretative skills are needed to delineate the problem, they are also needed to propose a theory or a solution, for deciding whether errors have been eliminated or not, and, finally, to outline the character of the new problem. Whereas formal logic and empirical skills can aid the process in science, they cannot be decisive. Our decisions will have to depend upon interpretative judgements, which will have to consider many factors, including our values, purposes and interests. If there is an interpretative dimension not only at the beginning, but at every stage in the problem-solving process, then the model could indicate it. These comments suggest that it would be possible to refine Popper's schema, $P_1 \to TT \to EE \to P_2$, to take account of these interpretative elements, as shown in figure 2. Despite the perils of an infinite regress, this example merely indicates the more pervasive problem of interpretation in any field of knowledge. It portrays more clearly the actual procedure of the growth of knowledge where disagreements may occur at every stage in the problem-solving process. Such an approach, however, concedes a

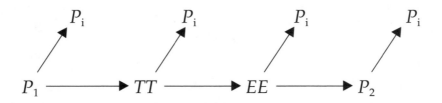

Figure 2 (Source: Stokes 1989: 502)

Note: P_i = a problem of interpretation that is also to be solved according to the original schema.

particular historical and contextual relativism to scientific and philosophical enquiry. Each investigator must assess the work of their predecessors or contemporaries. Which part of the communal culture is chosen for attention depends upon one's point of view and this, in turn, may be revised after assessment of 'data', and dialogue with other members of the community. There is no definitive method or decision procedure available for determining such issues.

Popper's proposal that rationality consists of critical problem-solving presupposes a minimal prior consensus on certain values, ends and interests. Unless the plurality of interpretations is grounded in some shared values – minimally, those pertaining to critical discussion – no agreement on the status of a problem or theory is possible. Epistemology must therefore suggest the social and political preconditions for the successful application of its epistemic norms. A central social and political task becomes that of understanding and overcoming the social and psychological impediments to rational thought as conceived by Popper. By what means, for example, can we encourage 'openness to criticism'? This is not just a matter of method, but of social and possibly psychological reconstruction. Because of his antipathy towards subjectivism and psychology, Popper does not explore such problems. Discovering the biological basis of our natural rationality and formulating an appropriate methodology, however, is only part of the project.

The Problem of Truth: Correspondence and Consensus

One further difficulty for Popper's evolutionary epistemology lies in reconciling his insistence upon the role of critical discussion and argument in deciding upon the adequacy of a theory/interpretation with his attachment to a correspondence theory of truth. Given Popper's claim that he considers all criticism to be criticism of a theory's claim to be true, he requires a theory of objective truth in order to distinguish between pure and applied science, and between the search for knowledge and the search for power (*CR*: 226), and to avoid relativism.

Popper takes his inspiration from Alfred Tarski, who rehabilitated the notion of truth as 'correspondence to the facts'. Tarski's achievement was to overcome certain paradoxes in the concept of truth, such that, in Popper's view, we can now unashamedly speak of theories as being true or false (*OK*: 316).[9] Popper acknowledges that this theory does not provide any rigorous epistemological guidance; it merely reinforces our common sense notion of truth (*OSE II*: 371). That is, Tarski's theory does not provide a criterion of truth and, according to Popper, we must not ask for such a criterion for it is simply unavailable (*OK*: 318). This does not, however, prevent us from having some intuitive idea of truth, and using it as a regulative idea to guide us (*OSE II*: 373). As Habermas (1976b: 217) remarks, Popper wants us to forgo a definable standard of truth, but retain an 'understanding' of what we *mean* by truth, and how we may translate this into rules for testing hypotheses. The critical point is that even in hermeneutics there are standards or criteria for satisfactory interpretations and, further, such formal and informal criteria are implicit in Popper's epistemology (Habermas 1976b: 217–18).

This is the crux of Popper's concept of verisimilitude which 'allows us to speak, without fear of talking nonsense, of *theories which are better or worse approximations to truth*' (*OK*: 335; see also *CR*: 215–50). Although he argues that there cannot be a criterion for the application of this concept either, his attempts to define the concept look remarkably like one. If a theory is judged to have more empirical content, it may be designated as closer to the truth, even though it may be a false theory. Popper considered that his standards for testability and corroboration were the 'proper methodological counterpart to this new metalogical idea' (*CR*: 235). Although he claims that the degree of corroboration cannot be a 'measure' of the verisimilitude of a theory, it can be taken as 'an indication of how its verisimilitude *appears* . . . compared with another theory' (*OK*: 103).

The problem is not just that Popper and others have agreed that the attempt to provide a formal definition of verisimilitude has failed (*RAS*: xxxv).[10] It is that, ultimately, he advocates a consensus theory of truth. Judgement upon the adequacy, meaning, truth or falsity of a theory, is a decision resulting from its critical discussion by a scientific or philosophical community. Such a judgement is made on the basis of assessing the results of formal analysis and, where relevant, by empirical testing, and it may later be revised as the scientific or philosophical consensus changes. Popper explains:

> Although in such discussion we cannot as a rule distinguish (with certainty, or near certainty) between a true theory and a false theory, we can sometimes distinguish between a false theory and one which *may* be true. And we can often say of a particular theory that, in the light of the present state of our critical discussion, it appears to be much better than any other theory submitted; better, that is, from the point of view of our interest in truth; or better in the sense of getting nearer to the truth. (*RAS*: 27)

In scientific practice, therefore, truth is what the prevailing consensus deems it to be.

No invocation of a correspondence theory of truth, however, can overcome the obstacle that to regard the growth of knowledge as a process of problem-solving is to introduce the historical relativism that Popper would usually wish to avoid. Unless we have a satisfactory objective *criterion* of truth (and it is doubtful whether any such criterion can be formulated), then we remain with a consensus theory which utilizes a variety of criteria for theory choice. This does not entail a total relativism in which no secure rational judgements can be made. It merely claims that such judgements will derive from critical discourse upon the best available reasons and that the conclusions reached will change as the interests, ethics, evidence and reasons change.

Epistemology, Science and Politics

It is implicit in Popper's analysis that evolution has an inherent value and that knowledge gained from biological evolution has an epistemic priority among scientific theories. That is, evolutionary biology indicates our human capacities in ways that are superior to, or not offered by, physics or chemistry, for example. To claim that human epistemology is continuous with our evolutionary heritage is to strengthen the appeal of whatever epistemic precepts are thought to be continuous with evolution. The unavoidable dilemma here is that both our scientific description of the facts of evolution and our choice of what features ought to be emulated are coloured by prior philosophical judgement and cultural images, metaphors and assumptions. As we have seen, prescriptions for trial and error, problem-solving and criticism can be defended independent of assumptions about evolution. This is not to say that philosophers cannot learn from scientific accounts of empirical process, but that drawing sensible prescriptions for human action is a complex process.[11] One simply cannot select empirical biological traits and present them as normative prescriptions. Such difficulties beset any naturalistic endeavour, whether in epistemology or ethics.[12]

Whatever Popper's stated claims about his evolutionary epistemology, it has the status of an analogy and in many respects the analogy is not strong. Indeed, the original intuition of discontinuity between cultural and organic forms of knowledge is directly relevant to the methodology of natural science. Although Popper proposes the same problem-solving methodology for both biology and culture, it is important to note at least two main problems. First, because of the need to formulate a 'point of view' based upon values, and the resolution of difference by discussion, there is no direct analogy between the interpretation process in humans and non-humans. This, in turn, indicates that epistemological criteria for selecting scientific theories or interpretations are significantly different from those evident in evolution, where survival is the only criterion of success and where it is misleading to speak of 'progress'.[13] Given Popper's recurring stress upon how our higher critical capacities allow us to eliminate our theories instead of each other (e.g. *OK*: 248; 1973a: 96–7; 1987: 152), the discontinuities between human and non-human evolution are crucial. The normative criteria that constrain and override epistemology and methodology are moral ones.

Nowhere is this more evident than in Popper's late call for moral responsibility among scientists. He notes that 'all science, and indeed all learning, has tended to become potentially applicable' (1994a: 121). Although science may be oriented to the epistemic goal of truth, its practical achievements often result in infringements of other values. Accordingly, he considers that the scientist has a special obligation to 'foresee as far as possible the unintended consequences of his work and to draw attention, from the very beginning, to those which we should strive to avoid' (Popper 1994a: 129). Such strictures have greater methodological consequences than Popper seems to recognize, and may act as a conservative control on scientific work. In effect, they introduce the same practical concern for caution that he regards as necessary for social science. With the requirement for rigorous testing, scientists may well have to decide to desist because of possible or actual impairment of human life or health.[14] Whatever the theoretical merits of our bold conjectures, we may have to refrain from ruthless practical testing and opt for more limited piecemeal experiments. In many cases, it would be more rational, in an ethical sense, to be cautious in experimental practice. The more bold and general the theory, the more restrained the testing may need to be. In natural as well as social science, conservative trials may help avoid unforeseeable and harmful consequences to nature and society. Popper's later metaphysics and his evolutionary epistemology require his epistemological and methodological radicalism to be qualified.

This is only one relatively straightforward example of how human interests and values bear upon scientific work and how they serve to influence the strict application of epistemic norms. By demonstrating the interaction between the three worlds, Popper's evolutionary epistemology shows why scientific rationality cannot be confined to purely epistemic considerations. Awareness of the mutual interaction of Popper's three worlds may alert us to the social and biological consequences of science. The practical consequence is that no scientist ought to seek truth regardless of human cost. Indeed, given Popper's moral concerns, his epistemological prescription could be revised to read: pursue truth and the growth of knowledge to the extent compatible with the advancement of human welfare and the avoidance of suffering. On this account, 'good' knowledge is that which fits both ethical and epistemological criteria. Epistemology is only one part of a broader, holistic conception of rationality that requires us to take account of context.[15]

The moral lesson to be drawn from Popper's work is that, with regard to violence, a certain discontinuity between human and non-human knowledge ought to be maintained. The epistemological project requires the political one implicit in Popper's earlier work, which obliges us not only to search for the social foundations of rationality, but also to establish political institutions for protecting it. In Popper's terms, we must learn to constrain our dogmatic, animal drives and instincts and encourage our higher, critical faculties. Evolutionary epistemology needs to be complemented by substantive knowledge about social and historical change and the formation of democratic cultures.[16] Yet, Popper (1987: 152) thinks that the political goal of so widely disseminating the values of critical reason that we simply eliminate our theories instead of each other is a utopian dream.

Given the importance of choosing problems and the role that 'points of view' and values play in this process, a central question is that of how to argue rationally in support of them. The core values of rationality and criticism are prime examples. These and other issues will be explored in the next chapter with reference to the school of critical theory.

8

Critical Rationalism and Critical Theory

Since the 1950s, a number of philosophers known as critical theorists have engaged in debate with Popper and offered a series of criticisms of critical rationalism. Although the 'positivist dispute' between Theodor Adorno and Popper in the 1960s is the most well known of these critical encounters, problems arising from it have occupied the attention of later critical theorists, such as Jürgen Habermas. This chapter examines Popper's philosophy from within problem situations set by members of the Frankfurt School of critical theory. Such an analysis allows us to assess how well Popper's arguments withstand systematic critique originating from a different standpoint with its origins in Marxism. Reviewing this conflict also illuminates issues central to the argument of this book such as the relationship between politics, epistemology and method, as well as the nature of criticism and critique. Because of the scope and complexity of the debates, this chapter does not provide a comprehensive account of the 'positivist dispute'.[1] The aim here is to indicate the main lines of intellectual engagement. Of particular concern will be Habermas's efforts to supply a coherent, non-dogmatic defence of rationalism. It will be argued that, despite their initial antagonism, there are areas of 'convergence' or 'reconciliation' between critical rationalism and critical theory.[2]

Background

Critical theory is the philosophy and social theory developed by those working within, or closely associated with, the Frankfurt

Institute of Social Research, established in Germany in 1923. Under the threat of National Socialism, the Institute transferred to the USA in 1935, but returned to Frankfurt in 1950. Although critical theory built upon the Marxist critique of political economy, it came to reject key tenets of Marxism, such as its dependence upon the proletariat for revolutionary change and even its reliance on scientific method. Critical theorists still regarded the critique of political economy as important, but they focused more closely upon those forms of commodification, domination and authority exercised through culture and ideology. As a consequence, they became more pre-occupied with intellectual issues of social science and philosophy rather than with political organization and action.

As philosophers, critical theorists shared the Enlightenment view that the exercise of reason could lead to emancipation, but they refused to exempt reason and rationality from their radical critique. Reason was both the subject (i.e. originator) and the object of critique. As social theorists, critical theorists undertook the task of criticism as 'ideology-critique' and proceeded by the method of internal or 'immanent' critique. Originally, their political project aimed to unmask the forms of ideology and reification that contributed to class oppression and inequality. Nonetheless, the early critical theorists thought that changes in capitalism had so reduced the possibility of realizing the bourgeois ideals of freedom and equality that even the power of internal critique had been undermined. They then reframed their critique as a search for the utopian potential within culture (Benhabib 1986: 174).

Politically, the early critical theorists regarded themselves as revolutionaries, not reformists. Yet, because they saw similar rationalizing tendencies at work under fascism, Stalinism and liberal capitalism, such theorists were not only critical of capitalism and fascism, but also of democratic socialism and Marxian communism. Although their critique was often 'negative' in pointing out the distortions of human knowledge and the constraints upon human action, the overall political aim could be termed utopian. In general, critical theorists saw their role as attempting to reveal the unrealized political possibilities for emancipation available in the present, whether or not the social conditions existed for attaining emancipation. Nevertheless, critical theorists often disagreed over where to search for such possibilities and tended towards pessimism in assessing the prospects for their realization.[3]

It would be difficult to argue, however, that the critical theorists provide an external critique of critical rationalism. Both philosophies lie within the Enlightenment tradition and represent different approaches to the problem of emancipation through knowledge. Although both schools owe strong debts to Kant and Weber, critical theory, unlike critical rationalism, also draws upon the heritage of Hegel, Marx and Freud. Both are concerned about the role and influence of ideas and ideology in history; both conceive the acquisition of and reflection upon knowledge as being inherently and instrumentally bound to the realization or suppression of political values. Members of the two traditions are acutely aware that, depending on different assumptions, both substantive knowledge and theories of knowledge can as easily foster freedom as its opposite, oppression. Central to this awareness is a concern to understand and expose the phenomena of illusion, myth, dogma and their political effects, especially those evident in totalitarianism. Nonetheless, the two traditions conceptualize these problems and how to overcome them in different ways.

The Positivist Dispute

During the late 1950s and early 1960s, members of the Frankfurt School made a sustained attack on what they saw as the predominant social science methodologies of positivism and empiricism. Because of his role as a leading philosopher of natural and social science, his critique of Marxism and dialectics, as well as his reformist politics, Popper's writings provided a focus for their criticism. For him, the work of the Frankfurt School represented much of what he rejected in intellectual and political life. Their residual Marxism, their criticisms of liberal democracy, their political pessimism, as well as their convoluted prose and use of terms like 'totality', placed them among the 'enemies of the open society'.

The Frankfurt School's critique of Popper focused upon his alleged positivist epistemology, the application of rationality to choice of moral and political values, as well as issues of politics, history and social theory. The significance of the dispute was therefore not narrowly epistemological or methodological. It indicated differences over larger political issues. For the critical theorists, for example, positivist epistemology and methodology had become instruments of domination. The nature of the methodological dispute itself is not always clear, however, because the antagonists have different meanings for the term 'positivism' and different vocabularies for discussing the issues. Although Popper held a number of views ascribed to positivists, he had a different understanding of positivism as the philosophy of logical positivism or empiricism. He resolutely opposed the positivist philosophy that identified the methods of science with knowledge itself, exaggerated the role of empirical facts in scientific method, and relied upon the methods of verificationism and induction (Ray 1979: 152). Critical theorists make a number of pertinent criticisms of Popper, but they often miss their mark because he is not entirely representative of the positivist tradition they wish to attack. Nonetheless, extensive debate occurred over the following problems: the unity of scientific method; the neutrality of epistemology and scientific method; the correspondence theory of truth; and questions of value and rationality.[4]

The unity of scientific method

Critical theorists took issue with claims that natural and social science shared the same hypothetico-deductive (H-D) method and the same goal of causal explanation to be pursued by attempting to falsify theories (Habermas 1988: 25). In addition, critical theorists argued that positivists construed too narrowly their objects of enquiry. Popper's early injunctions against social holism, for example, would preclude 'society' from becoming an object of study or reform. All of which had the political consequences of unduly limiting the scope of social criticism, and preventing social scientists from seeking radical change in society. On these grounds the critical theorists present the positivist project as primarily a cognitive one that disguises its conservative function of affirming the existing structure of society.

Certainly, Popper held variations of such methodological views. The difficulty is that, although he had proposed a unity of scientific method, by the 1960s he had reconceptualized it as one in which natural and social science, as well as philosophy, proceeded by the method of problem-solving through trial and error and rational criticism. Popper also advocated this method for the tasks of interpretation in both the social sciences and the humanities. Accordingly, the strict logic of the H-D model and falsifiability were only appropriate for certain stages of investigation and, even then, only for select aspects of natural science.

The issue is further complicated by Popper's recognition (1976a: 96–7) that the search for knowledge could be stimulated by both theoretical and practical problems, and that these would depend on one's point of view and one's values. Although the search for truth remained essential for natural science, in social science the instrumental criterion of success was also important. If one adds the requirement of 'moral responsibility' and assessment of social consequences to the practice of natural science, then a more 'holistic' Popperian methodology emerges that adds a significant qualification to the search for truth. Depending on the stage of the enquiry, non-epistemic values may complement and even override epistemic values. The unity of method proposed, and implied, by Popper hardly resembles that evident in his early work and which was the main focus of criticism by critical theorists.

Popper's methodological shifts are evident in his 1961 symposium essay (1976a), and Adorno responds by appearing to assimilate Popper's arguments into his own theoretical and political agenda. He points out that by allowing for the significance of both epistemological and practical problems Popper can also begin from a 'problematic condition of the world'. Although Adorno (1976c: 109) finds little to quarrel with in the problem-solving approach, he (1976a: 41–2; 1976c: 111–12) rejects Popper's scientific stress upon 'solutions' and argues that criticism does not always require confronting theories with factual evidence. Given his account of the nature of rational criticism in metaphysics, Popper could hardly disagree.

Despite these agreements, critical theorists differ with Popper over the subject-matter of social science and the significance of this for method. Since the subject-matter of social science comprises relations of meaning, Habermas (1976a: 140) argues that methodological objectives cannot be limited to the empirical explanation of causal relations. The focus upon causal explanation ignores the importance of social science as an interpretative or hermeneutic project that has the goal of attaining understanding. This goal of understanding ought not to be reinterpreted instrumentally as that of solving a problem. For Habermas (1971: 171), the hermeneutic method of enquiry was also different because of its unavoidable circularity. Knowing subjects (including social scientists) are immersed in, and can only begin from, their own worlds of meaning and interpretation that they attempt to revise and refine in dialogue with others (Habermas 1976a: 134, 152).

For critical theory, the relevant model for social science is that of psychoanalysis, not natural science (Habermas 1974: 9). Social scientists do not and cannot stand outside social facts in the way that natural scientists can distance themselves from the natural world and their place in it as biological beings. This condition also makes the relationship between social theory, evidence and falsifiability much more problematic (Ray 1979: 150). Habermas (1974: 37) argues that in testing hypotheses about political organization, 'all the participants must have the opportunity to know what they are doing – thus they must form a common will discursively'. As was argued in chapter 5, however, Popper's methodology implicitly requires dialogue between observers and the observed.

Both Adorno (1976c: 113–14) and Habermas (1986: 50) commend Popper's advocacy of criticism and self-criticism. Adorno (1976c: 121–2) and Popper (1992: 137–50) also share the view that criticism is part of the process of enlightenment that may lead towards emancipation. One of its tasks is to unmask the ideological claims to truth or illusory appearances of theory, and show how they impede emancipation. Popper's general arguments (1992: 138), and his specific political critiques of historicist methodologies, lie broadly within this enlightenment project. In social science, however, critical theorists generally begin from the notion of society as a 'totality', not from its discrete parts. Just as Popper would repudiate critical theory's apparent reliance upon concepts of 'essence' and 'appearance', he would also reject critical theory's broader meanings of 'totality' and 'emancipation'. For Popper, the call for a 'totalizing' critique, if interpreted literally, would be both impossible to operationalize and politically dangerous if attempted.

On the vexed issue of 'totality' the differences between critical theory and critical rationalism seem incommensurable. Nevertheless, if we use 'totality' simply as a metaphor for larger scale, historical social tendencies, and 'totalizing' as a method that takes account of such phenomena, then a different conclusion may be reached. Given his resort to terms such as 'western civilization' and allowing the search for 'meaning in history', Popper should have fewer objections beyond its misleading terminology. Both critical theorists and critical rationalists accept that social enquiry relies upon asserting general claims, confronting them with specific instances and then refining the generalization in the light of these instances (Ray 1979: 168).

Adorno (1976c: 121) and Habermas (1976a: 141; 1976b: 222) both point to the limitations and harmful social and political effects of unreflective, low-level, empirical sociology of the kind deployed in public opinion research.[5] For Habermas (1986: 51), the problem is not just that Popper gives legitimacy to those forms of social research 'which yield information usable in social technologies'. Habermas wants to defend traditions of research that have as their aim the 'enlightenment' of people about their social situation and the 'pathological' constraints upon them. As Adorno (1976b: 69) argues, social theory cannot just describe society, it must also be transformative or critical of both its concepts *and* the object of its enquiry. Adorno (1976b: 71–2), for example, points to the problem of how those using positivist and empiricist methodology do not just investigate social facts but decide what constitutes a social fact. For Adorno (1976b: 73), this explains the irrelevance of many empirical studies and makes nonsense of their claims to exactitude and value.

Given the evolution of a more sophisticated Popperian philosophy on these topics, and his rejection of social research not oriented to serious practical problems, a number of the criticisms directed against his work are misplaced. Politically, he is not limited to theoretical problems, nor methodologically is he committed only to analysing small-scale social or historical problems. There remain, however, definite limits to the scope of Popper's incipient 'holism'. Given his rejection of utopianism and revolution, he would restrict social criticism to that which could be both understood and contained within liberal democracy. As the critical theorists rightly claim, Popper is confined to providing immanent or internal social criticism. This does not mean that radical criticisms could not be made and acted upon within the limits of liberal or social democracy. Indeed, Habermas (1974: 278) acknowledges that seriously taking up Popper's challenge could be politically unsettling. Within both politics and science, the calls for 'open discussion' and individual and scientific 'moral responsibility' for the consequences of one's work are potentially radical. The relevant criticisms, therefore, would be that he does not extend his political critique far enough. Although he could justifiably claim that he was not a sociologist, Popper often made empirical generalizations on the health of liberal democracies that were uncritical. As Popper (1976b: 291) confirms, his gradualist social theory contrasts with his radical theory of method for natural science.

The critical theorists also claim that Popper does not confront the methodological implications of the hermeneutic circle in *natural* science. Habermas (1976a: 152; 1976b: 203), for example, draws out the implications of Popper's claim that facts are selected by theories. He demonstrates that there is a hermeneutic circularity even in natural science that makes the determination of facts dependent upon interpretation, and thereby the falsifiability and falsification of theories more difficult. On the other hand, Popper's early critique of positivism and empiricism has important ramifications for the scientific status of critical theory. Ray (1979: 165) suggests that if we understand Popper's critique as one that 'leads logically to a hermeneutic circle in which theory and facts are understood dialectically, this favours an interpretation of critical theory as a potentially reliable methodology, that is, as "scientific"'.

Epistemology as social theory

Critical theory's analysis of positivism and critical rationalism, however, cannot be exhausted by a critique of scientific method. Such a strategy would concede too much to the positivist outlook. It would rule out the process of philosophical self-reflection or limit its scope to those procedures sanctioned by the methodology of science. As evident in the work of Habermas (1971: 67–8), critical theory begins from claims that it is not just scientific method that produces legitimate knowledge, and that epistemology cannot be reduced to the philosophy of scientific method. Theorists such as Habermas wish to restore the role of philosophy to the critical analysis of concepts, and recover sociology for understanding the social function of epistemology. For these reasons, Habermas (1972: 43–63) represents epistemology as a form of social theory. This is not the same as claiming that epistemology can be reduced to social theory. The key point is that we cannot understand the nature of claims to knowledge without clarifying their function within social systems. Habermas aims to demonstrate (a) the social function of science, and (b) the guiding role of 'interests' in different forms of knowledge production. In so doing, he clarifies the social and political function of three kinds of knowledge: empirical-analytic knowledge characteristic of natural science, historical-hermeneutic knowledge characteristic of social science and history; and critical reason or reflection, which is the equivalent of a second order critical philosophy.

Critical theorists argue that science and technology are productive forces in the evolution of industrialization, and that science and technology constitute an ideology that legitimates the productive process of industrial society. In this system of production, both science and technology are instruments for extending control over nature and society. Habermas argues that in the twentieth century science and technology have become an ideology that legitimates the priority of purposive-rational or instrumental action. In so doing, it conceals the possibility of other forms of social action, such as communicative action, diminishes the scope for democratic decision-making in the political arena, and increases the power of technocratic elites (Habermas 1971: 104–5). According to Habermas (1971: 111) the ideology of science and technology is more powerful than previous political ideologies because it offers no clear notion of the 'good life' by which existing social conditions may be critically assessed. As Habermas (1971: 114–15) sees it, the ideology of science and technology, as positivistic thinking, has replaced the older 'bourgeois' or liberal ideologies. The problem for critical theory, however, is just as serious. Because scientific thinking itself has become ideology, in the sense of illusion masking oppressive realities, its capacity for engaging in critique of other ideologies is also compromised.

Although Habermas accepts that science and technology function as an ideology of domination, he also thinks that science can be redeemed for critical and emancipatory purposes. This is because science and technology are simply a sub-category of purposive rational action that is indispensable to socio-economic and cultural evolution. Since these are crucial human adaptive capacities used for controlling our environment and facilitating human survival, purposive rational action cannot be abandoned. Science and technology can retain their potential for emancipation, however, only if they do not replace other forms of rational action, such as symbolic interaction or communicative action (Habermas 1971: 118–19). Unrestricted communicative action is needed in order to return technocratic decision-making to the public realm and revive discussion about 'the goals of life activity' (Habermas 1971: 119–20). By such means, public policy may be decided on criteria other than just technical ones.

For Habermas (1971: 52), it is not science itself that legitimates domination, but the instrumental use or exploitation of science through technology. Because of its close connection with industry, administration and the military, science as a social activity is bound by political constraints to pursue particular socially determined purposes and to neglect others. Yet, this function is only possible because the theories and methods of science are available and 'technically utilizable'. Habermas (1971: 99) explains: 'the modern sciences produce knowledge which through its *form* (and not through the subjective intentions of scientists) is technically exploitable knowledge.'[6] Science, understood as both method and scientific theory, is therefore not neutral or value-free.

Habermas complements the sociological critique of science and critical rationalism with a philosophical one based upon the concept of 'interest'. He argues that our different ways of knowing are embedded in interests which may be conceived as the underlying motives, orientations or imperatives which guide our cognitive (knowledge-acquiring) activity. We can only identify 'knowledge constitutive interests' by reflecting philosophically upon problems inherent in the pursuit of the more basic human activities of work, interaction and the preservation of life (Habermas 1972: 196). The term 'interests' does not describe empirical or biological human needs, but is a way of conceptualizing different kinds of 'orientation' towards solving problems that arise from human survival and reproduction. They are universal, that is, 'fundamental characteristics of the human species' – but characteristic of a social system rather than of individuals (Thompson and Held 1982: 7). Habermas argues also that different processes of enquiry serve different interests. He claims further that scientific knowledge is technically utilizable because of the 'interests' of domination and control that lie at the heart of its epistemic structure.

Within natural science the criteria or rules for validity and plausibility of scientific theories are necessarily 'social' since they are formed intersubjectively as the result of reflecting upon the outcomes of action. Science, like labour or interaction, is a form of social action. Further reflection upon these social processes of rule formation demonstrates the existence of particular interests that guide action. From this perspective, Habermas (1972: 308) argues that the empirical-analytical or natural sciences are forms of instrumental action guided by an inherent '*technical* cognitive interest'. This is an interest in objective thought, clearly delineated by specific rules that maintain the progress and growth of knowledge within strict boundaries. Given the imperative of expanding 'feedback monitored action', the cognitive interest (or 'motive') is one of technical control over 'objective processes' (Habermas 1972: 309). Reflection upon cognitive interests has the consequence of making us aware of the attitudes that determine our methodological decisions: 'We become aware ... that empirical-analytical research produces technically utilizable knowledge, but not knowledge which makes possible a hermeneutical elucidation of the self-understanding of acting subjects' (Habermas 1976b: 221). This leads Habermas to criticize Popper for not reflecting upon 'the technical cognitive interests of the empirical sciences' (Habermas 1976b: 199).

The historical-hermeneutic or social sciences are considered to operate in a different fashion. The meaning of the validity of statements and propositions is not bound by the idea of technical control of either the subject or the subject-matter (Habermas 1972: 309).

Such sciences can only operate by comprehending the *meaning* of particular observations of facts. This comprehension cannot be divorced from the social context or tradition of the interpreter, which should itself become more clear as he or she proceeds (Habermas 1972: 310). In this process, self-reflection upon one's tradition and method is central. This is guided by a *'practical* cognitive interest' or orientation towards mutual understanding and possible consensus. Within philosophy and critical social science, even the concept of reason, founded in the process of self-reflection, has an interest in emancipation: 'In self-reflection, knowledge for the sake of knowledge comes to coincide with the interest in autonomy and responsibility. ... Reason is at the same time subject to the interest of reason. We can say that it obeys an *emancipatory cognitive interest*, which aims at the pursuit of reflection' (Habermas 1972: 197–8). Unlike empirical-analytic knowledge, which is a form of purposive-rational action, historical-hermeneutic knowledge and critical reason are forms of communicative or symbolic action.

The central epistemological problem for science is that an interest, such as that of the domination of 'objective processes' in nature and society, becomes incorporated into a method of cognition and then disappears from the awareness of the knowing subjects such as the scientist and research worker (Habermas 1974: 264). Denial of these interests preserves the illusion that pure theory exists and, either explicitly or implicitly, devalues all other forms of science or knowledge as less than rational. One crucial task of intellectual work, therefore, is to bring these universal interests back into consciousness.[7]

Habermas does not devalue knowledge gained by analytic-empirical methods, nor does he entirely reject the Popperian philosophy of natural scientific method. Indeed, Habermas's derivation of the 'technical interest' depends upon a broad agreement with Popper's account (Stockman 1983: 71). Nonetheless, Habermas does criticize the general epistemological illusions (a) that there is only one kind of knowledge, (b) that such knowledge has a priority over other kinds, (c) that it can be conducted without recourse to hermeneutic methods and (d) that it is neutral or value free. Given both its social function and its epistemic structure, scientific methodology is oriented towards technical control and thereby is inherently value-laden. Critical rationalism comes under attack because it colludes in maintaining this illusion of value-freedom with its sharp distinction between facts and values.

For critical theorists, the concept of technical interest is given credence by Popper's stress upon the formal unity of scientific theory and practice.[8] This is evident in the necessary and 'reflexive' connections between hypothesis-formation and testing, and later between problem-formulation and problem-solving. It is further confirmed by Popper's own early metaphorical use of the term 'net' to describe the role of theories (*LScD*: 59): 'Theories are nets cast to catch what we call "the world": to rationalize, to explain, and to master it. We endeavour to make the mesh ever finer and finer.'[9] This image conveys the instrumental imperatives that lie at the heart of scientific method. Science is no mere contemplation; it is purposive-rational action oriented to technical control and mastery of nature. Although Popper criticizes the reduction of science to that of an instrument of control and warns against the misuse and abuse of science, he does not see how deeply implicated science is in instrumental practice. Nor does he appreciate how scientific method allied with technocratic values can reduce rather than expand the scope for democratic decision-making. His view of science therefore remains primarily a normative ideal.

Theories of truth: correspondence and consensus

Critical theorists also contest the Popperian claim that the aim of science is to discover the truth and that better scientific theories are those that correspond to, or come closer to, the truth. For hermeneutic reasons, critical theorists stressed that Popperian method could not provide direct access to the truth or falsity of statements about the 'facts' or observations required for confirmation or falsification of theories in natural science. In social science, however, the critical theorists argue that the search for truth cannot be limited to a search for a theory's correspondence with social reality. For one thing, statements about meaning may also be true or false. For another, since there are structural contradictions within society, social theorists also need to point out the truth or falsity of society itself (Adorno 1976c: 115). Here, Adorno (1976b: 83) appears to identify two different notions of truth: truth as the product of political struggle towards emancipation, and truth as a repudiation of existing society. Within Habermas's work, however, a third notion is evident, namely, a 'consensus theory of truth' that has affinities with Popper's arguments on the subject.

As we saw in the previous chapter, although Popper holds to a regulative ideal of truth manifest in his 'correspondence theory of truth', he describes scientific practice as working by means of 'consensus'. The Popperian concept of objectivity as an intersubjectivity leading to consensus denotes a theory of truth that is proceduralist and that shares a great deal with Habermas's theory. For Habermas, truth may be understood as a validity claim that is the product of discourse and argumentative reasoning about, for example, the results of empirical investigation. Similar to Popper, Habermas (1973: 168) conceives of 'objectivity' as 'intersubjectivity'. In both empirical science and hermeneutics, Habermas (1973: 169), like Popper, considers that 'the truth of propositions is not corroborated by processes happening in the world but by a consensus achieved through argumentative reasoning'. In such a process all claims are open to challenge and discussion.[10]

Habermas's theory, however, proposes the regulative idea of an 'ideal speech situation' that is presupposed in the discourse between members of a communication community, but which is never realized in actual discussion (Habermas 1970). This anticipatory notion of an ideal unconstrained consensus has both political and intellectual elements. Participation in the ideal speech situation is predicated upon the possible absence of internal ideological distortions as constraints upon argument, and upon the absence of external political or institutional constraints. The ideal speech situation requires an equality of power and opportunity to take up dialogue (Habermas 1970: 371).[11] According to Habermas, all speech is oriented towards the idea of truth. Because truth 'can only be analyzed with regard to a consensus achieved in unrestrained and universal discourse', the ideal speech situation offers 'a linguistic conceptualization of . . . the ideas of truth, freedom, and justice' (Habermas 1970: 372). The ideal speech situation is an ideal form of life in which attaining truth requires conditions of freedom and justice. Such a notion gives more content to Habermas's claim (1972: 314) that 'the truth of statements is based on anticipating the realization of the good life'.[12]

Bernstein (1985b: 11) indicates the necessary social foundations of the Habermasian project: 'Non-distorted, reciprocal communication cannot exist unless we realize and institute the material social conditions that are required for mutual communication.' Where the speech community is a restricted one, and the constraints upon discussion are powerful, then the rationality (truth or falsity) of the consensus will be impaired. Similarly for Popper, an adequate or true theory or interpretation is less likely to be produced by a discussion that does not occur in an open society. Such material requirements would also apply to Popper's ideal of the open society. Free and open discussion is hardly possible under the physical and emotional constraints of human suffering, poverty and misery. The fewer constraints and diversions, the closer the discussion is likely to get to the truth. Nonetheless, neither philosopher can supply guarantees for attaining truth.

Here we may observe another fundamental similarity between Popper and Habermas. As far as they represent normative ideals, both their epistemologies demand the construction of a free, equal and democratic society that guarantees openness of critical discussion. Although Habermas (1993: 163–4) rejects interpretations of his concept that represent it as a normative ideal or blueprint for society, elsewhere he implies that ideal presuppositions can be used as a critical standard for evaluating democracies and democratic theory (Habermas 1979: 186–7). Despite the abstract character of such rules, there would appear no reason why they could not have normative force (Ingram 1993: 311).

In practice, both Popper and Habermas hold a proceduralist approach to knowledge claims based upon mutual criticism and the assumption of human fallibility. As Giddens (1985: 114–16) demonstrates, however, a key difference is that Popper provides more epistemological guidance than Habermas on the kinds of argument and critera (e.g. falsifiability, corroboration, etc.) that may indicate the truth or falsity of scientific statements. In so far as both Popper and Habermas maintain a consensus theory of truth, they are both open to similar criticisms. Although both are anti-foundationalists, for example, they are pressed towards certain kinds of foundationalist and universalist claims in order to distinguish their philosophies from relativism and scepticism.[13]

This discussion raises the larger point about the social and political foundations of epistemology. Both Popper and Habermas would agree on the centrality of critical discussion, which is only possible where there are some shared values and beliefs (social and scientific), and both indicate their democratic and non-violent character. Each would agree that in seeking the truth, only 'the force of the better argument' ought to prevail. It is either implicit or explicit in the work of them both (e.g. Habermas 1979: 186–9) that knowledge claims can only be protected by democratic values, practices and institutions. In different ways, each recognizes the importance of basic material conditions of life to the satisfactory resolution of knowledge claims. Where Popper is explicit about the necessary

institutional conditions, Habermas's presuppositions only suggest
the values that could provide a practical model for the determination of truth claims. Essential differences between them appear in
their respective judgements upon the openness of the prevailing
liberal democratic society. They would also differ over the types of
democratic institution that are needed. Where Popper advocates a
'realist' democracy based upon pluralist and representative principles, Habermas advocates a 'deliberative' democracy.

More broadly, it is apparent that where there is a possible incommensurability among competing theories, and where any immediate resolution seems unlikely, it becomes the task of the more social
or non-epistemic values to maintain the scientific activity of discussion and criticism. For these reasons we may conclude, contrary to
Ray (1979: 172), that neither Popper nor Habermas derives political
values from the nature of scientific discourse. By investigating epistemology, each comes to demonstrate how epistemic values emerge
out of fundamental conditions of life, and are inextricably linked
with essential human interests and ethico-political values. Although
each begins from discussions of science and epistemology, both are
driven to examine their place in more fundamental forms of human
interaction. The principles of the 'open society' and the 'rational
society' make possible the systematic pursuit of knowledge and
truth. The question of whether similar rational arguments can be
given for Habermasian norms or Popperian values is the subject of
the next section.

Values and the Defence of Reason

Critical theorists take up the question of whether we can provide
satisfactory grounds for choice of values, and especially the value of
rationality or reason itself. They criticize the positivist and early
Popperian claim that no rational foundation can be given for one's
choice of values, that values and norms cannot be discussed or
selected by rational means. Part of the positivist debate also turns
upon whether there are essential differences between 'facts' and
'values'. These are questions of meta-ethics, the field of enquiry into
the status of ethical claims and the possible criteria that may be used
for selection of substantive ethics or values. This topic extends
beyond the original positivist dispute and takes us into controversies over 'discourse ethics' in the later work of Habermas. It is
arguable that if Habermas succeeds in providing critical theory with

a suitable meta-ethic, he will also have provided a means for over-coming the pivotal incoherence in critical rationalism. In this later development of the positivist dispute the critical theorists include Habermas, and Karl-Otto Apel who influenced critical theory but was never part of the Frankfurt School. The critical rationalists include Popper, as well as Hans Albert, William Bartley and Gerard Radnitzky.

Critical rationalism and values

Critical rationalists have long been aware of the problem of arguing in support of values and the circularity evident in using rational criticism to argue in support of the central norm of rational criticism. Popper's formulation of these problems has also evolved over time, and is open to different interpretations. As we saw in chapter 5, Popper subscribes to the thesis of 'critical dualism' which in most respects is similar to the familiar dichotomy between facts and values. Popper claims that values are discoverable *and* that they can be judged and altered by human beings. Accordingly, he denies that choice of values is arbitrary. In seeking to extend Popper's arguments, Albert (1985: 78, 96) argues that since both epistemology and philosophy of science are normative projects, we can treat ethical statements and systems as 'hypotheses'. The critical rationalist may then seek out and eliminate contradictions and, assuming that 'ought implies can', they may also enquire into whether the principles are capable of realization (Albert 1985: 97–8). Albert (1985: 99–100) indicates that when facts are revised certain values may become incompatible with others, and this becomes a reason for changing or rejecting a value. Because such decisions are subject to rational discussion, criticism and argument, he confirms that they are not irrational or arbitrary.

Regarding the meta-ethical issue of rationality, Popper (*OSE II*: 231) initially claims that the 'rationalist attitude' cannot be established by argument or experience, and whoever adopts it does so because of 'an irrational *faith in reason*'. He also suggests that it is a moral 'decision', similar to the commitment to any value, and which may be assisted by arguments and the assessment of the potential consequences of the decision. It is not, however, 'determined' by them (*OSE II*: 232). He stresses that such decisions remain the responsibility of the individual, hence the accusation of 'fideism' and 'decisionism'. In his early arguments, Popper also does not appear to distinguish between choice of ethics and meta-ethics. In his 1961 'addendum' (*OSE II*: 378–9) and elsewhere (*RAS*: 27–8), however, Popper allows for what Bartley (1987: 211) and others have called 'pancritical' or 'comprehensively critical' rationality. Concerned to reject any kind of justificationism, Popper (*OSE II*: 379) stresses the importance of the principle that 'nothing is exempt from criticism, or should be held to be exempt from criticism – not even this principle of the critical method itself'. Despite Bartley's efforts to defend the principle as a way of both avoiding 'justificationism' and maintaining the coherence of critical rationalism, his arguments have attracted strong criticism from those within and outside of critical rationalism.[14] On the face of it, critical rationalism's defence of criticism is caught between two mutually unacceptable options. Either the defence is based on decision and, because it cannot supply satisfactory reasons, it is therefore *dogmatic*, or it is *circular* in that it is self-applicable or paradoxical because it uses criticism to defend criticism.

Habermas's critique

Habermas's critique (1974: 276) begins with the claim that Popper demarcates too strongly between facts and values and between the processes of knowing and valuing. He argues that by so doing Popper is unable to extend his anti-dogmatism beyond the field of science to problems of value. The further consequence of this is that Popper is unable to defend his project of enlightenment and therefore cannot escape the confines of 'technological rationality'. Given the Popperian conception of knowledge, neither philosophy nor science can fulfil their required 'emancipatory' potential.

Habermas argues that both facts and values are knowable, and he rejects the meta-ethics that either understand or require moral choices to be based upon emotion, faith, pure decision or existential commitment. He claims that, despite elements of rationality in the Popperian proposals for choosing substantive values, critical rationalists do not provide a coherent meta-ethic that supports their moral practice of rational criticism, and that this is therefore 'decisionist'. That is, neither Popper, Albert nor Bartley can, without circularity, provide meta-ethical reasons for why they ought to be rational and critical.

Nonetheless, Habermas contends that, despite their rejection of ultimate foundations, the critical rationalist emphasis on criticism does provide the possibility of rational foundations. In Habermas's view (1990: 7), 'the concept of critical testing . . . becomes the critical rationalist's equivalent for justification'. Since criticism as a procedure is never presuppositionless, he argues that, by holding to the idea of 'irrefutable rules of criticism', critical rationalists allow in a weaker form of Kantian justification (1990: 7). For Habermas (1974: 279), Popper's discussion of methodology presupposes certain prior and secure norms of rationality. Indeed, there is some support for this in Popper's early references (*OSE II*: 377–8) to 'fallibilistic absolutism' that accepts that there are 'absolute mistakes'. It is also supported by his corresponding advocacy of the universalist pancritical rationalist principle that *'nothing is exempt from criticism'*, (*OSE II*: 378) and in his later reference to 'pure deductive logic as an organon of criticism' (Popper 1976a: 98). Habermas aims to elucidate the meaning of the more comprehensive concept of rationality underlying methodological decisions for criticism. He proposes a meta-ethic called a 'discourse ethic' that allows for the rational selection of values.

Discourse ethics

Habermas (1990: 68) begins from the cognitivist assumptions that normative claims have meaning and 'can be treated like truth claims', and that the 'justification' of norms requires argumentative discourse. A discourse ethic that aims at the justification of norms is a higher-level form of communicative action and is also universal. Habermas first enquires into the essential presuppositions for the possibility of intersubjectively valid criticism and argument that are discoverable by philosophical reflection or, more accurately, transcendental deduction (1990: 2). He next gives normative content to these presuppositions and makes explicit the rules of a discourse ethic. Finally, he endeavours to confirm them empirically, as hypotheses, through 'reconstructive science'.

Habermas alluded to the possibility of a transcendental pragmatic analysis in his earlier account of cognitive interests, where he argued that rationality of some kind is a practical constituent of our form of life and essential for social communication. Rationality is present before and during our attempts to reflect upon it and reconstruct it (Habermas 1973: 177). Certain rules of reason or rationality are therefore not open to decision; we are already bound by such rules when we begin to query them. Here, Habermas draws upon

Apel's transcendental-pragmatic arguments against critical rationalism.

Apel's strategy is to show that we must abandon attempts to give a deductive grounding of 'ultimate principles' and instead turn to the unavoidable (universal and necessary) pragmatic presuppositions of argument. Apel (1989: 273–4) accepts that applying the principle of fallibilism to fallibilism leads to a paradox that makes pancritical rationalism untenable. One cannot simply replace the 'principle of philosophical foundations' with the 'principle of criticism', because that too needs to be defended. According to Apel (1989: 282), this defence can only be conducted successfully by transcendental argument. Apel also rejects the claim that the choice of critical rationality can be an arbitrary or irrational decision. One can only make such a choice simply because one has already made a prior pragmatic commitment to reason as a form of life (Apel 1989: 281–2). Habermas (1990: 88) acknowledges his debt to Apel in describing these presuppositions 'as the defining characteristics of the ideal speech situation'. Habermas's project, however, involves elucidating the normative content of those presuppositions and confirming that they have normative validity (1990: 96–7).

The argument for a discourse ethic comprises two main components, namely the principle of universalization and a description of the procedural ethic of discourse itself. Habermas begins from Apel's claim that every communicatively competent actor who takes up a normative argument already presupposes the principle of universalization. Habermas (1990: 63) therefore introduces 'universalization' as a separate moral principle or a rule of argument that is 'designed to take into account the impersonal or general character of valid universal commands'. This 'bridging principle' of universalization, he argues, is an essential component or 'enabling condition' of ethical argument (Habermas 1996: 357). Actors cannot reject this principle without falling into 'performative contradiction'. For Habermas, every valid norm must fulfil the following condition: '*All* affected can accept the consequences and the side effects its *general* observance can be anticipated to have for the satisfaction of *everyone's* interests (and these consequences are preferred to those of known alternative possibilities for regulation)' (1990: 65). The principle aims to exclude as invalid 'any norm that could not meet with the qualified assent of all who are or might be affected by it' (Habermas 1990: 63), and makes consensus possible. It also allows a clear distinction to be made between *evaluative* statements about 'the good life' that are able to be discussed within a concrete historical form of life (1990: 104, 108), and *normative* ones that concern general moral questions about justice. Discourse is not just about individual value preferences, but the 'normative validity of norms of action' (1990: 104).

The discourse ethic itself, however, involves principles of participation and power as Habermas (1990: 66) explains: 'Only those norms can claim to be valid that meet (or could meet) with the approval of all affected in their capacity *as participants in a practical discourse.*' According to Habermas, the discourse ethic stands or falls on two assumptions. The first is that 'normative claims to validity have cognitive meaning and can be treated *like* claims to truth' (1990: 68). The second is that the justification of norms requires real co-operative and intersubjective discourse to occur, not simply individual cogitation. The next step is that of attempting to validate the discourse ethic.

The task of validation is complicated because Habermas (1979: 9) does not want to rely solely on philosophy, nor does he want to base his argument on the usual kinds of empirical-analytical science that produce nomological accounts of observable events. He therefore makes a case for testing his hypotheses in what he terms the 'reconstructive sciences' or 'universal pragmatics'. In this field, theorists seek an empirical reconstruction of the cultural evolution of our moral experience or 'pre-theoretical' knowledge. The aim is to be able to make universal claims that go beyond the assumptions and practices of a particular community or era and therefore avoid contextualism and historicism. Habermas (1990: 15–16) explains:

> Starting primarily from the intuitive knowledge of competent subjects – competent in terms of judgment, action, and language – and secondarily from systematic knowledge handed down by culture, the reconstructive sciences explain the presumably universal bases of rational experience and judgment, as well as of action and linguistic communication.

Habermas wants to reconstruct the fundamental rules of the moral competencies of the human species. In this project, transcendental arguments furnish 'reconstructive hypotheses' for empirical research (Habermas 1990: 16). As in other empirical enquiries, the propositions are not only arguable and testable, but the results of his investigations are also open to contest. The discourse theory therefore is 'dependent upon, *indirect* validation by *other* theories that are consonant with it' (Habermas 1990: 117).

Habermas considers that Lawrence Kohlberg's theory of the development of moral consciousness allows such a validation. In brief, Kohlberg distinguishes six stages of moral development among all humans, of which the highest stage is where knowledge of what is right depends upon an understanding, commitment to, and application of universal ethical principles (Habermas 1990: 124–5). Perhaps the crucial point of Kohlberg's theory for Habermas (1990: 109) is his account of the transition to the 'postconventional' stage of moral consciousness, where 'moral judgment becomes dissociated from the local conventions and historical coloration of a particular form of life'. This highest stage of moral development resembles the type of impartial moral identity and practice required by the discourse ethic. Habermas accepts that, given his arguments about the universal presuppositions of all knowledge claims, such evidence cannot pass for an *independent* corroboration of his normative theory, but argues that this criterion would be too strong. For one thing, no data used to test an empirical theory can be described independently of the language of the theory. For another, he reminds us of the familiar point that two competing theories cannot be evaluated independently of their governing paradigms. Accordingly, he claims that the principle of coherence is all that is necessary (Habermas 1990: 118).

By indicating the performative contradiction that bedevils critical rationalism's limited meta-ethical claims, Habermas and Apel have demonstrated a core problem in Popper's philosophy. In particular, they show that Popper fails to provide a coherent or non-circular ethical theory that unifies both his ethics and his meta-ethics. The reasons given for his meta-ethical stance are not fully consistent with those advocated for ethical action. One may give good reasons that have withstood intersubjective criticism for ethical actions, but adoption of the meta-ethic of critical reason is based either upon a personal 'decision', or it is circular. Yet, because of the priority Popper gives to rational criticism, he remains a universalist and on the indispensable role of criticism, no compromise is possible. He therefore indirectly supplies a foundation or justification, albeit a somewhat paradoxical one. Nonetheless, because of his resolute anti-foundationalism, expressed through his opposition to justification, his ethical project is incoherent, or at best incomplete.

Habermas's and Apel's critique, however, does allow for the possibility of a non-circular and non-dogmatic defence of critical rationalism. The notion of a discourse or communicative ethic offers an attempt to overcome the dilemma that lies at the heart of critical rationalism. It must be said, however, that Habermas's project depends upon such a diverse range of original argument and evidence that it is not easy for non-specialists to assess. His work has received much critical attention and it is difficult to know whether he has been entirely successful in his attempts to establish a coherent meta-ethic.[15] Apel (1992: 128), for one, protests that by adopting fallibilism Habermas has conceded too much to critical rationalism. Criticism has also been directed towards the content of the ethic and its applicability, and questions raised over whether the 'reconstructive sciences' are significantly different from other sciences. Strong doubts have been expressed about the strengths and weaknesses of the kinds of evidence, including Kohlberg's theory, that would serve as confirmations.

It is beyond the scope of this chapter to evaluate the range of claims made from within critical theory or outside it. At a minimum, it can be said that Habermas has laid the foundation for a compelling research project that deploys key elements of the critical rationalist tradition. Although Habermas's project is both universalist and foundationalist, he allows the propositions supporting it to be fallible and thereby arguable and criticizable. Although critical rationalists have debated foundational issues among themselves (e.g. Wettersten 1995), to the best of my knowledge they have not taken up the enlarged debate. As for the question of convergence, it is conceivable that critical rationalists would find the project of 'grounding' rationality – no matter how fallibilist in spirit – so inimical to their overall philosophy that they may be prepared to accept one of the less damaging alternatives of incoherence or the dogma of decision.

Politics, Critique and Reconciliation

The actual and hypothetical debates between critical rationalism and critical theory suggest a number of conclusions. First, they indicate in stark relief a number of central problems of critique and criticism in two competing strands of twentieth-century modernist thought. Second, they suggest a limited convergence or reconciliation between the two that may be attributed to their common search for foundations for knowledge and politics that entail neither relativism nor scepticism. Finally, the debates demonstrate further that epistemology and methodology may be understood as ethico-political projects.

Critique in one or other of its forms is central to critical rationalism and critical theory. Depending on the historical and intellectual context, both traditions of thought proceed by internal and external critique. More important, critical rationalism and critical theory engage not only in the rational reconstruction of the rules and conditions for knowledge, but also in ethico-political criticism that requires social and political change. Regarding the problem of the 'unity of scientific method', Habermas has come to accept the value of the critical rationalist account of empirical-analytical science. Nonetheless, whatever its emancipatory possibilities, the empirical-analytical method of science remains associated with domination because of its inherent technical cognitive interests (see Wilson 1986b). Habermas also considers the method to be problematic if prescribed uncritically for social science. Social science requires a more sophisticated hermeneutics and stronger social criticism than Popper allows. Despite his anti-instrumentalism, Popper's advocacy of the unity between theory and practice (e.g. hypothesis-formation and testing; problems and problem-solving), as well as his rhetorical use of the 'net' metaphor confirms the technical interest of science in control and success.

It is noteworthy that, in different ways, both Popper and Habermas depart from the more abstract tasks of reconstructing philosophical conceptions of rationality to attempt reconstructions of the rationality evident in the evolutionary process. By so doing they both see rationality as a characteristic of the human species and understand evolution as a process of socio-cultural learning as well as a biological one (Habermas 1979: 122). The difference here is that Popper does not recognize that he commences 'transcendental reflection', but prematurely ends the enquiry (Wellmer in Stockman 1983: 51–2). Nonetheless, Popper and Habermas come to similar conclusions about the 'discovery' of values (*AWP*: 50) and the significance of 'problem-solving' (e.g. Habermas 1979: 121). Habermas's earlier search for cognitive interests arose from his reflection upon the socio-cultural reproduction of the human species and problems 'pertaining to the reproduction of human life' (1973: 177–8). Although they draw different conclusions from their research, both Popper and Habermas allow us to see how our epistemologies have origins in our evolutionary attempts at practical problem-solving. Habermas, however, does not accept that problem-solving exhausts the scope of a critical social science. In so far as Habermas's theory refines and extends insights contained in Popper's brief comments on the origin of values and the problems of an evolutionary epistemology, there appears to be some convergence. Yet, both also confront the intractable difficulty of providing an account of 'natural rationality' that does not simply reflect our current cultural conventions (Barnes 1976: 120).

Both critical rationalism and critical theory enable a radical political critique of society. Although the critical theorists allow for internal and external critique, Popper's more limited internal critique of liberal democracy is not as inherently conservative as usually portrayed (see e.g. Habermas 1974: 278). With some reservations, Adorno (1976c: 120) agrees with Popper that the difference between their positions was that 'he believed that we live in the best world which ever existed' and that Adorno did not believe it. Habermas (1976b: 215), however, is less pessimistic than Adorno about the possibility of the positive resolution of social disagreements and contradictions. Indeed, his espousal of 'radical reformism' departs from the totalizing critique of critical theory and shares more with critical rationalism (Habermas 1971: 49). This does not mean that critical rationalists and, later, critical theorists would agree on what constitutes a significant social or political problem. Arguably, infringements upon those values, such as freedom of speech and democracy, that are essential to open communication, would command the attention of both.

Regarding meta-ethics, Popper's (*OSE II*: 225) appeal to the 'rational unity of mankind' offers a rudimentary argument for the kinds of moral universals necessary among human beings.[16] Given such an assumption, it would be difficult to see how he could resist the substance of Habermas's account of the ideal ethico-political values of open communication. For different reasons, neither Popper nor Habermas wants to prescribe for the 'good life' or the 'good society', but each aims to elucidate the political conditions and discursive norms under which such prescriptions may be rationally determined or 'validated'. Indeed, Habermas's espousal of fallibilist epistemology would make a convergence appear virtually complete. For all this, irreconcilable differences remain, including their views on the ultimate justification of rational criticism. Where Popper offers science as the ideal model of open communication and individual moral responsibility, Habermas still presents science, as it currently operates, as a threat to such values. Any such rapprochement would have to rely upon Habermas abandoning a number of key intellectual and political tenets of the earlier generation of critical theory. It would also depend on the uncertain and purely hypothetical possibility of critical rationalists accepting propositions that had previously been prohibited. Following Wilson (1981: 45), therefore, we may tentatively use the term 'reconciliation' rather than 'convergence' to describe the similarities between the later forms of critical rationalism and critical theory. Such reconciliation is not complete and may be described as 'theoretical' (Wilson 1986b: 293).

These issues have both intellectual and political significance. The debates between critical rationalism and Habermasian critical theory provide support for the general argument of this book. Their discussions and proposals for the resolution of knowledge claims are central. In practice, both Popper and Habermas advocate a proceduralist method that may be called a 'consensus theory of truth'. The arguments also indicate, however, the importance of prior or more fundamental social and political values that make possible the search for truth. With their common emphasis upon free and open communication, both the Popperian notion of the 'open society' and the Habermasian 'ideal speech situation' complement each other. It is still important, however, to distinguish key differences. Popper's concept serves as a rough sketch of the values and institutions (existing and ideal) necessary for the growth of knowledge, and which individuals can decide to accept. For Habermas, such values are not open to individual choice in the same way. The values of the ideal speech situation are necessary presuppositions for rational deliberation that belong inherently to the social acts of speech and communication. One's decision consists only in becoming conscious of such pre-existing commitments and reaffirming them.

This account indicates, however, that both Habermas *and* Popper have an understanding of epistemology as 'social theory'. In short, the later forms of critical rationalism and critical theory indicate the inescapable ethico-political foundations of epistemology and methodology. Both traditions of thought recognize that, conceptually and practically, the problems of knowledge and politics are inextricably linked. Since neither accepts that critique is neutral, then ethics and politics are either prior to, or constitutive of, critical rationality. That is, ethics and politics set the context, objectives for, and limits of, rationality, both historically and conceptually. Indeed, Habermas (1996: 358) has claimed that the principles of discourse 'can be operationalized for other kinds of questions' such as for political legislatures or legal discourse.

Neither Popper (*OSE II*: 391) nor Habermas can avoid the point that whatever the intellectual power of argument, eventually, the individual must still make a personal decision and commitment to accept the better argument. It is not obvious that accusations of performative contradiction, for example, would have sufficient power to deter those who insist on recourse to violence rather than argument. Whether in philosophy, natural science or society, arguments are only one force among many in motivating individuals to act. In this respect, Weber's (1970: 127) original portrayal of the dilemma of choice that confronts us all remains pertinent. Despite their insights, neither Popper nor Habermas devotes much attention to the sociological or institutional problems of encouraging freedom of communication and openness of dialogue.

Conclusion

On the argument advanced in this book, Karl Popper's epistemology consists of proposals for rationality which are also norms for social practice. Epistemology sets rules for the rational appraisal of theories, but these are founded in values guiding social interaction and communication. As a social theory, therefore, epistemology is also based on assumptions about actual and possible forms of life. If we understand epistemology in this way, then we also retain an interest in contributing to the expansion of human capacities.

As we have seen, the possibility of rationality also implies the possibility of political emancipation and the creation of a society of autonomous, yet ethically responsible human beings. Investigating the foundations of rationality and epistemology enables us to know more about the conditions governing both cognitive and broader social practices. Natural science can be useful for epistemology, however, only if it is conceived as one social practice among many. To the extent that Popper holds a narrow view of human nature and a limited conception of the good life, his epistemology and theory of rationality are also somewhat deficient. Although Popper's epistemology encompasses a social and political theory, the latter does not supply all the necessary resources for dealing with the problems facing the former. Bold theoretical adventures have practical consequences and not only require courageous individuals, but also a society that encourages innovation and that can sustain the ensuing political strains.

One sociological question raised by this argument is whether an epistemology designed to promote certain political goals limits its deployment for other political purposes. Could Popperian fallibilism and falsificationist method be used effectively for anti-democratic purposes, as for example, under an authoritarian regime? It is conceivable that for highly specialized fields in natural science, Popper's methodology could be practised as a kind of technique. Nonetheless, it is difficult to see how the whole range of questions relevant to the institutional conduct of science could be asked, and how the ruthless criticism required on certain topics would be allowed. Whereas insular communities of scientists could use falsificationist methods which contributed to the growth of scientific knowledge, the broader exercise of fallibilism would be limited by actual and possible threats of political intervention. The history of science and technology in the USSR has provided evidence for such concerns, and similar problems exist to varying degrees in liberal democratic societies (see, e.g., Miller 1996). Nonetheless, it may be possible for free discussion in natural science to establish models for public discourse elsewhere in society. Certainly, without such conditions Popperian social science would be impossible.

A related normative problem is whether an epistemological commitment necessarily entails a particular political commitment. It is arguable that falsificationist principles do not logically require a commitment to democratic values and practices. But to deny the necessity for democracy would be to deprive science of essential resources for criticism, communication and even international cooperation. To advocate criticism in science and deny the freedom of speech which such criticism would require would be somewhat contradictory. Nonetheless, such a stance could be defended by arguing for the curtailment of certain freedoms in the interest of higher values, such as the survival of the wider society itself.

These are precisely the types of problem raised by those who want to 'Islamize' science and who would see Popperian philosophy as promoting democracy as well as a dangerous rationalism (see Huff 1996: 307). While we may concede that social and political interests will always impinge upon the pursuit of science, it is safe to say that there are certain limits beyond which the performance of science will suffer and the growth of knowledge be impeded. Without a culture of democratic fallibilism to induct research workers into the scientific ethos, the foundations of scientific practice are likely to remain weak and the research outcomes poor. Such constraints could impede scientific progress and limit science to Kuhnian 'puzzle-solving' within research paradigms and programmes set by others. Popperian science, understood as a spiritual adventure, would clearly challenge the ruling theological orthodoxies and therefore be unacceptable.

Both Popper and his critics remind us that satisfactory, rational discourse can only occur in an open, democratic society whose members are freely able to participate in key decisions, not only about particular intellectual issues, but also about the political organization of that society. This perhaps indicates a central message to be gleaned from this study. Where there are limits imposed on political freedom, both our conceptions of rationality and cognitive practices are also impoverished. If liberal democracies are to avoid the authoritarian and regressive consequences of technocratic elitism, then they will also need to increase the opportunities for informed involvement in science and politics. Such democracies will also need to avoid relying upon formulaic approaches to knowledge and public policy that diminish the role of participation, deliberation and negotiation.

Notes

Chapter 1 Introduction: Politics, Epistemology and Methodology

1 See, e.g., Boucher (1985), Schochet (1974) and Skinner (1974).
2 See also Harding (1987: 2–3).
3 See, e.g., Burke (1983: ix), Gray (1976: 339), Lessnoff (1980), Magee (1973: 16–17), O'Hear (1980: 1–3), Parekh (1982: 146), Quinton (1976b: 166–7), Ryan (1985) and Williams (1989).
4 Ravetz's work (1984) on ideological commitments in the philosophy of science indicates some of the issues. For feminist critiques, see Harding (1987), Keller (1985) and Martin (1989).
5 For several accounts of how these problems arise, see Krige (1978) and Ryan (1985).

Chapter 2 Popper's Project: Problem and Method

1 Feyerabend (1974b: 497–8) and Holton (1973: 235–7) dispute the accuracy of Einstein as a proto-falsificationist.
2 See Grunbaum (1989) for a criticism of Popper's account of Freud.
3 Popper was selective both in what he drew from Kant and how he interpreted his work.
4 See also Miller's (1994) 'restatements and defence' of Popper's arguments.
5 All italics in the quotations from Popper's works are his own.
6 Hooker (1981) gives an interpretation of Popper as a formalist, which differs somewhat from that given here.
7 For early discussions about relations between philosophy and history of science see Burian (1977), Giere (1973) and Wartofsky (1976). Similar

problems recur in recent debates about naturalist epistemology in Doppelt (1990), Kornblith (1987), Laudan (1990), Leplin (1990) and Rosenberg (1990).

8 Popper's admission of 'metaphysical research programmes' to scientific status would have been more pertinent. See chapter 7.

9 See also Habermas (1972: 68).

Chapter 3   Methodological Falsificationism and its Critics

1 Some advocates of falsificationist methodology take this to be the method of science and wrongly attribute it to Popper. See Lakatos (1974: 95–103, 180–1).

2 Popper (*LScD*: 191–205) concedes that probability statements are impervious to strict falsification, but considers that his methodological rules could be adapted to take account of them. This would, for example, require scientists to decide what kind of statement of statistical frequency would be unlikely and therefore prohibited by a probability hypothesis. See also O'Hear (1980: 124–5).

3 In responding to Quinean arguments, Popper claims that it is often possible to discern which hypothesis or group of hypotheses would be responsible for a refutation (*CR*: 239).

4 In later discussions Popper (*CR*: 248; 1974b: 1193) appears to concede such a 'whiff' of induction.

5 This becomes part of Popper's revised method outlined in chapter 7.

6 Popper (*RAS*: xxvi–xxx) conceded that the case of Copernicus *may* be a counter-example to his theory of science, but cited twenty others in support of his account.

7 According to Kuhn (1977: 320–39), scientists have markedly different interpretations of such epistemic values, and accord them different weights over time and in different disciplines.

8 See essays in Lakatos and Musgrave (1974).

9 For a different view see Forge (1989).

10 There may be no universal model of explanation (Tuchanska 1992: 108). A comprehensive overview of the problem of explanation may be found in Kitcher and Salmon (1989).

11 Contrary to Popper's (1974b: 1078–80) later arguments, the critical attitude cannot just be interpreted in terms of an objective 'policy'.

12 Popper's later admission of metaphysical research programmes to scientific status would appear to be a step along this path.

Chapter 4   The Politics of Critical Rationalism

1 I am indebted to Jeremy Shearmur's (1996) excellent account of Popper's

political thought and his original research into Popper's unpublished correspondence.

2 This section draws upon the account in Stokes (1995a; 1995b). See also Shearmur's (1995) reply.

3 For literature critical of Popper's views, see Bambrough (1967), Giannaras (1996), Klosko (1996), Levinson (1953) and Wild (1974).

4 In response to Acton (1974: 881), Popper (1974b: 1162, 1164) acknowledges limitations in his critique of the ethical theory of Marx and Engels, and concedes that 'morality is always strongly dependent upon the situation'.

5 See the discussion in Stokes (1984).

6 Taylor (1979b: 1) describes expressivism as an Enlightenment 'notion of man' in which human life has 'a unity rather analogous to that of a work of art, where every part . . . only found its proper meaning in relation to all others'.

7 In a letter to the logical positivist philosopher Rudolf Carnap in 1946, Popper (cited in Shearmur 1996: 32) writes that 'freedom cannot be saved without improving redistributive justice, i.e. without increasing economic equality'.

8 Popper's notion of piecemeal social engineering has attracted wide critical scrutiny including Ackermann (1976: 178), Magee (1973: 86), O'Hear (1980) and Parekh (1982).

9 Norman (1993) and Pickel (1989) have provided insightful reviews of problems arising from Popper's strategy.

10 See Gray (1976: 339), Lessnoff (1980: 105) and Quinton (1976b: 148–9).

Chapter 5 Philosophy and Methodology of Social Science

1 Popper's definition differs from the meaning of historicism that refers to schools of thought that stressed the historical uniqueness of cultures. Characterized by cultural relativism and the method of intuitive understanding, this other meaning stressed pluralism rather than totalitarianism (Marcuse 1973: 197). Popper is aware of the distinction and refers to this more recent rendering of the German word 'Historismus' as historism (*PH*: 17; *OSE II*: 208, 214).

2 For criticisms of Popper's analysis and the views he attributes to historicists, see Donagan (1974), Ryan (1970a: 174–5; 1970b: 215–17) and Suchting (1972). In 1957 (*PH*: v–vii) he published a revised attempt at logically refuting the possibility of scientific prediction. Critiques may be found in McLachlan (1980), Shaw (1971) and Urbach (1978).

3 Only late in his writings did Popper (1994a) discuss briefly the moral responsibility of natural scientists and recommend they assess the unintended consequences of their work.

4 With his propensity theory Popper advocated a form of probabilistic explanation that superseded his analyses of causal explanation (*UQ*: 178). This revision does not affect the following critique.

5 Popper briefly discusses professional ethics in McIntyre and Popper (1983) and Popper (1992: 200–2).

6 Popper seems to think that the only method proposed is that of empathetic understanding or re-enactment, and overlooks the more objective procedures associated with the Weberian notion of *verstehen*, and those of hermeneutics.

7 See chapter 8.

8 Waldron claims, however, that Popper's arguments are more compatible with moral scepticism than moral realism.

9 Whereas in natural science those values which indicate whether a theory is better than another are primarily of an epistemic character, in social science there is a larger role for values of a non-epistemic or social kind. The critical literature shows persuasively how such values not only aid in selecting problems, but are also important in choosing the type of explanation needed, and when to stop investigations. See, e.g., Stretton (1969), Taylor (1973) and Thomas (1979).

10 Popper is selective in what he draws from Kant's theory of morality, which is essentially objectivist, universalist and categorical, not a matter of subjective preference (Walker 1978: 151–2).

Chapter 6   Metaphysics and Freedom

1 These arguments will be discussed in chapter 7.

2 Although there is no explicit treatment of the topic in *The Logic of Scientific Discovery*, Popper acknowledges that a 'robust' realism 'permeates' the work (*RAS*: 81).

3 Oddly enough, elsewhere Popper denies that such an assumption has methodological relevance (*OK*: 74).

4 This may be extended to cover a doctrine of 'scientific realism' that accepts that the terms used by scientists to refer to entities such as electrons denote objects that actually exist. See, e.g., Putnam (1987: 4).

5 Forge (1990: 86) reminds us that van Fraassen is an 'anti-realist', not an instrumentalist: 'for him theories . . . can be true or false, theoretical terms are to be interpreted literally and they may even succeed in referring.' See also Churchland and Hooker (1985).

6 For a recent critique of Hacking, see Shapere (1993).

7 See Almeder (1987: 94) and discussions by Horwich (1991), Jones (1991), Leplin (1986), Murphy (1990), and Musgrave (1992).

8 See also Laudan's proposals (1981) along these lines.

9 This section deals largely with issues as they arise in Popper's philosophy and does not canvass the broader literature.

10 A number of critics argue that Popper's interpretation does not overcome the problem of accounting for single case probabilities in the frequency interpretation (e.g. Mellor 1971: 158; O'Hear 1980: 136–7; O'Hear 1985:

465–6), nor is it corroborated by the two slit experiment in quantum mechanics (Clark 1995: 161; O'Hear 1985: 466–8).

11 See also Popper (1994b).

12 On mathematics and logic see also O'Hear (1980: 188–90).

13 A common criticism (Hebb 1980; Jackson 1980; O'Hear 1980: 201–2) is that Popper fails to refute the theories he rejects.

Chapter 7   Evolutionary Epistemology

1 Popper (1987) later proposed that biological evolution may be less blind than usually thought. On 'active Darwinism', see Curtis (1989) and Watkins (1995).

2 See also van Rooijen (1987: 91).

3 This criterion is more general and arguably superior to that offered by Laudan (1981: 145), who argues in quantitative terms that scientific progress can be measured by the increase in 'problem-solving effectiveness'.

4 Such an interpretation is implied by Popper's comments (1984: 253–4) on logic and prime numbers.

5 See also the critiques by Apel (1983), Farr (1983) and King-Farlow and Cooper (1983).

6 See the critique by Green and Shapiro (1994).

7 Popper does not address any of the recent debates about meaning and understanding, which have emanated from anthropology, the history of ideas and the field of hermeneutics itself.

8 See also Popper (1994a: 154–84).

9 For brief critiques of Popper's appropriation of Tarski, see Chalmers (1982: 151–3) and O'Hear (1980: 206).

10 Kuhn (1970: 238) is right to claim that, if successful, such an algorithm would 'eliminate all need for recourse to group values, to judgements made by minds prepared in a particular way'. See also Chalmers (1982: 157–9) and Newton-Smith (1981: 52–70).

11 For a more optimistic 'naturalist realist' perspective, see Hooker (1989).

12 See discussions in Brown (1988), Giere (1989), Kornblith (1987), Laudan (1990) and Siegel (1989). On evolutionary ethics, see Ruse (1986a; 1986b).

13 For a contrary view, see Hahlweg (1991).

14 Conversely, scientists may decide to continue dogmatically testing a theory well after its apparent falsification, for the reason that it may still promise to enhance human well-being or survival.

15 In some respects, Popper's problem-solving approach resembles the pragmatism of John Dewey (1980: 101, 103).

16 See, e.g., Hall (1997).

Chapter 8　Critical Rationalism and Critical Theory

1　See the earlier accounts by Heller (1978), Hohendahl (1985) and Wilson (1986a; 1986b).
2　Elements of similarity, convergence or reconciliation have also been noted by Giddens (1985), Heller (1978), Hesse (1980), Radnitzky (1970), Ray (1979), Shearmur (1996), Thompson (1984/85) and Wilson (1976).
3　For accounts of the intellectual evolution of critical theory, see Benhabib (1986) and Held (1980). A less sympathetic analysis may be found in Kolakowski (1981).
4　See essays in Adorno et al. (1976) and also Frisby (1972; 1974; 1976), Ray (1979) and Wilson (1986a; 1986b).
5　Even on this topic, from a different perspective, Popper (1992: 154) warns against the perils of 'public opinion'.
6　Yet, Habermas (1976b: 208) does not adopt an 'instrumentalist' view of scientific theories.
7　Habermas's concept of interests has attracted much criticism, even from Habermas himself (see Bernstein 1985b: 12–15). See also Keat (1981), McCarthy (1978: ch. 2) and Overend (1978).
8　See Wellmer (1971: 20) and the discussion by Wilson (1976: 210).
9　Note also the aphorism from the German romantic writer Novalis at the beginning of *The Logic of Scientific Discovery* (*LScD*: 11): 'Hypotheses are nets: only he who casts will catch.'
10　Implicit in the idea of objectivity as intersubjectivity is an ideal notion of the public sphere in which events and occasions were 'open to all' (Habermas 1989: 1).
11　See the critical account in Benhabib (1986: 385–7) and Ferrara (1987).
12　Critics (e.g. Benhabib 1986: 286; McCarthy 1978: 303) have taken up the issue of whether Habermas has simply confused the meaning of truth with the methods required for arriving at truth.
13　For criticisms of Habermas's theory, see Benhabib (1986: ch. 8), Geuss (1981: 65–7), McCarthy (1978: 303–10).
14　See Derksen (1980), essays by Post and Watkins in Radnitzky and Bartley (1987) and Settle, Jarvie and Agassi (1974).
15　See, e.g., Benhabib (1990), Benhabib and Dallmayr (1990), Heller (1984/85), Wellmer (1990) and White (1988).
16　Where Shearmur (1996: 101) understands this universalism in terms of basic epistemological capacities, I interpret it in terms of the ethical capacities needed for the growth of knowledge.

References

Ackermann, R. J. 1976. *The Philosophy of Karl Popper*. Amherst, MA: University of Massachusetts Press.

Acton, H. B. 1974. Moral futurism and the ethics of Marxism. In P. A. Schilpp (ed.), 876–88.

Adorno, T. W. 1976a. Introduction. In T. W. Adorno et al., 1–67.

—— 1976b. Sociology and empirical research. In T. W. Adorno et al., 68–86.

—— 1976c. On the logic of the social sciences. In T. W. Adorno et al., 105–22.

Adorno, T. W., Albert, H., Dahrendorf, R., Habermas, J., Pilot, H. and Popper, K. R. 1976 [1969]. *The Positivist Dispute in German Sociology*. Trans. G. Adey and D. Frisby. London: Heinemann.

Albert, H. 1985. *Treatise on Critical Reason*. Trans. M. V. Rorty. Princeton: Princeton University Press.

Almeder, R. 1987. Blind realism. *Erkenntnis* 26: 57–101.

Apel, K-O. 1983. Comments on Farr's paper (II) some critical remarks on Popper's hermeneutics. *Philosophy of the Social Sciences* 13: 183–93.

—— 1989. The transformation of philosophy: Systematic proposals. In K. Baynes et al. (eds), 250–90.

—— 1992. Normatively grounding 'critical theory' through recourse to the lifeworld? A transcendental-pragmatic attempt to think with Habermas against Habermas. In A. Honneth, T. McCarthy, C. Offe and A. Wellmer (eds), *Philosophical Interventions in the Unfinished Project of Enlightenment*, Cambridge, MA: MIT Press, 125–70.

Baigrie, B. 1989. Popper and progress: A reply to Campbell. *Social Epistemology* 3(1): 65–9.

Bambrough, R. (ed.) 1967. *Plato, Popper and Politics*. Cambridge: Heffer.

Barnes, S. B. 1976. Natural rationality: A neglected concept in the social sciences. *Philosophy of the Social Sciences* 6(2): 115–26.

Bartley III, W. W. 1987. Theories of rationality. In G. Radnitzky and W. W. Bartley III (eds), 205–14.

Baynes, K., Bohman, J. and McCarthy, T. (eds) 1989. *After Philosophy: End or Transformation?* Cambridge, MA: MIT Press.

Benhabib, S. 1986. *Critique, Norm, and Utopia*. New York: Columbia University Press.

—— 1990. In the shadow of Aristotle and Hegel: Communicative ethics and current controversies in practical philosophy. In M. Kelly (ed.), *Hermeneutics and Critical Theory in Ethics and Politics*, Cambridge, MA: MIT Press, 1–31.

Benhabib, S. and Dallmayr, F. (eds) 1990. *The Communicative Ethics Debate*. Cambridge, MA: MIT Press.

Berleant, A. 1973. The experience and judgement of values. In E. Laszlo and J. B. Wilbur (eds), *Value Theory in Philosophy and Social Science*, New York: Gordon and Breach, 24–37.

Berlin, I. 1969. *Four Essays on Liberty*. London: Oxford University Press, 118–72.

Bernstein, R. J. (ed.) 1985a. *Habermas and Modernity*. Cambridge: Polity Press.

—— 1985b. Introduction. In R. J. Bernstein (ed.), 1–32.

Birch, C. and Cobb, J. 1981. *The Liberation of Life: From the Cell to the Community*. Cambridge: Cambridge University Press.

Boucher, D. 1985. *Texts in Context*. Dordrecht: Martinus Nijhoff.

Bradie, M. 1986. Assessing evolutionary epistemology. *Biology and Philosophy* 1: 401–59.

Brown, H. I. 1977. *Perception, Theory and Commitment: The New Philosophy of Science*. Chicago: University of Chicago Press.

—— 1988. Normative epistemology and naturalized epistemology. *Inquiry* 31(1): 53–78.

Burian, R. M. 1977. More than a marriage of convenience: On the inextricability of history and philosophy of science. *Philosophy of Science* 44: 1–42.

Burke, T. E. 1983. *The Philosophy of Popper*. Manchester: Manchester University Press.

Caws, P. 1967. Scientific method. In P. Edwards (ed.), *The Encylopedia of Philosophy*, vol. 7, New York: Macmillan, 339–453.

Chalmers, A. F. 1982. *What is this Thing Called Science?* 2nd edn. St Lucia, QLD: University of Queensland Press.

—— 1985. Methodological individualism: An incongruity in Popper's philosophy. In G. Currie and A. Musgrave (eds), 73–87.

Churchland, P. M. and Hooker, C. A. (eds) 1985. *Images of Science*. Chicago: University of Chicago Press.

Clark, P. 1995. Popper on determinism. In A. O'Hear (ed.), 149–62.

Cleveland, T. and Sagal, P. T. 1989. Bold hypotheses: The bolder the better? *Ratio* (new series) II, 1 December, 109–21.

Cohen, R. S., Feyerabend, P. K., and Wartofsky, M. W. (eds) 1976. *Essays in Memory of Imre Lakatos*. Dordrecht: D. Reidel.

Currie, G. 1989. Frege and Popper: Two critics of psychologism. In K. Gavroglu, et al. (eds), 413–30.

Currie, G. and Musgrave, A. (eds) 1985. *Popper and the Human Sciences*. Dordrecht: Martinus Nijhoff.

Curtis, R. C. 1989. Evolutionary epistemology. *Philosophy of the Social Sciences* 19: 95–102.

Dennett, D. C. 1979. Review of *The Self and Its Brain*. *Journal of Philosophy* LXXVI(2): 91–7.

Derksen, A. A. 1980. The failure of comprehensively critical rationalism. *Philosophy of the Social Sciences* 10: 51–66.

Dewey, J. 1980 [1929]. *The Quest for Certainty*. New York: Perigree Books.

Donagan, A. 1966. The Popper-Hempel theory reconsidered. In W. H. Dray (ed.), *Philosophical Analysis and History*, New York: Harper and Row, 127–59.

—— 1974. Popper's examination of historicism. In P. A. Schilpp (ed.), 905–24.

Doppelt, G. 1990. The naturalist conception of methodological standards in science. *Philosophy of Science* 57(1): 1–19.

Earman, J. 1986. *A Primer on Determinism*. Dordrecht: D. Reidel.

Edgley, R. 1973. Reason and violence: A fragment of the ideology of liberal intellectuals. *Radical Philosophy* 4: 18–24.

Ehrenfeld, D. 1981. *The Arrogance of Humanism*. Oxford: Oxford University Press.

Farr, J. 1983. Popper's hermeneutics. *Philosophy of the Social Sciences* 13: 157–76.

Feigl, H. and Meehl, P. E. 1974. The determinism–freedom and body–mind problems. In P. A. Schilpp (ed.), 520–59.

Ferrara, A. 1987. A critique of Habermas's consensus theory of truth. *Philosophy and Social Criticism* 13(1): 39–67.

Feyerabend, P. K. 1974a [1970]. Consolations for the specialist. In I. Lakatos and A. Musgrave (eds), 197–230.

—— 1974b. Review discussion: Popper's *Objective Knowledge*. *Inquiry* 17: 475–507.

—— 1975. *Against Method*. London: New Left Books.

—— 1978. *Science in a Free Society*. London: New Left Books.

—— 1987. *Farewell to Reason*. London: Verso.

Forge, J. 1989. New directions in the theory of explanation. *Metascience* 7(2): 78–89.

—— 1990. Can we dispense with laws in science? *Metascience* 8(2): 86–93.

Foucault, M. 1974. *The Archaeology of Knowledge*. London: Tavistock.

Freeman, M. 1975. Sociology and utopia: Some reflections on the social philosophy of Karl Popper. *British Journal of Sociology* XXVI: 20–34.

Frisby, D. 1972. The Popper–Adorno controversy: The methodological dispute in German sociology. *Philosophy of the Social Sciences* 2(2): 105–19.

—— 1974. The Frankfurt School: Critical theory and positivism. In J. Rex (ed.), *Approaches to Sociology*, London: Routledge and Kegan Paul, 205–29.

—— 1976. Introduction to the English translation. In T. W. Adorno et al., ix–xliv.

Gärdenfors, P. 1980. A pragmatic approach to explanation. *Philosophy of Science* 47: 404–23.

Gardner, M. R. 1983. Realism and instrumentalism in pre-Newtonian astronomy. In J. Earman (ed.), *Testing Scientific Theories: Minnesota Studies in the Philosophy of Science*, vol. X, Minneapolis: University of Minnesota Press, 201–65.

Gavroglu, K., Goudaroulis, Y. and Nicolacopoulos, P. (eds), 1989. *Imre Lakatos and Theories of Scientific Change*. Dordrecht: Kluwer.

Gellner, E. 1976. An ethic of cognition. In R. S. Cohen et al. (eds), 161–77.

Geuss, R. 1981. *The Idea of a Critical Theory: Habermas and the Frankfurt School*. Cambridge: Cambridge University Press.

Giannaras, A. 1996. Plato and K. R. Popper: Toward a critique of Plato's political philosophy. *Philosophy of the Social Sciences* 26(4): 493–508.

Giddens, A. 1985. Reason without revolution? Habermas's *Theorie des kommunikativen Handelns*. In R. J. Bernstein (ed.), 95–121.

Giere, R. N. 1973. History and philosophy of science: Intimate relationship or marriage or relationship of convenience? *British Journal for the Philosophy of Science* 24: 282–97.

—— 1989. Scientific rationality as instrumental rationality. *Studies in the History and Philosophy of Science* 20(3): 377–84.

Gray, J. N. 1976. The liberalism of Karl Popper. *Government and Opposition* 11: 337–55.

Green, D. P. and Shapiro, I. 1994. *Pathologies of Rational Choice Theory*. New Haven: Yale University Press.

Grunbaum, A. 1989. The degeneration of Popper's theory of demarcation. *Epistemologia* 12: 235–60.

Habermas, J. 1970. Towards a theory of communicative competence. *Inquiry* 13: 360–75.

—— 1971 [1968]. *Toward a Rational Society*. Trans. J. J. Shapiro. London: Heinemann.

—— 1972 [1968]. *Knowledge and Human Interests*. Trans. J. J. Shapiro. Boston: Beacon Press.

—— 1973. A postscript to *Knowledge and Human Interests*. *Philosophy of the Social Sciences* 3: 157–89.

—— 1974 [1971]. *Theory and Practice*. Trans. J. Viertel. London: Heinemann.

—— 1976a [1969]. The analytical theory of science and dialectics. In T. W. Adorno et al., 131–62.

—— 1976b [1969]. A positivistically bisected rationalism: A reply to a pamphlet. In T. W. Adorno et al., 198–225.

—— 1979 [1976]. *Communication and the Evolution of Society*. Trans. T. McCarthy. London: Heinemann.

—— 1986. Ideologies and society in the post-war world. In P. Dews (ed.), *Habermas: Autonomy and Solidarity. Interviews with Jürgen Habermas*, London: Verso, 35–56.

—— 1988 [1967]. *On the Logic of the Social Sciences*. Trans. S. W. Nicholsen and J. A. Stark. Cambridge MA: MIT Press.

—— 1989. *The Structural Transformation of the Public Sphere*. Cambridge: Polity Press.

—— 1990 [1983]. *Moral Consciousness and Communicative Action*. Trans. C. Lenhardt and S. W. Nicholsen. Cambridge: Polity Press.

—— 1993. *Justification and Application*. Trans. C. Cronin. Cambridge: Polity Press.

—— 1996. On the cognitive content of morality. *Proceedings of the Aristotelian Society* (new series) XCVI: 335–58.

Hacking, I. 1983. Experimentation and scientific realism. *Philosophical Topics* 13(1): 71–89.

Hahlweg, K. 1991. On the notion of evolutionary progress. *Philosophy of Science* 58(3): 436–51.

Hall, J. 1997. Social foundations of openness. *Philosophy of the Social Sciences* 27(1): 24–38.

Hanson, N. R. 1970. Is there a logic of scientific discovery? In B. A. Brody (ed.), *Readings in the Philosophy of Science*, Englewood Cliffs, NJ: Prentice-Hall, 620–33.

Harding, S. 1987. Introduction: Is there a feminist method? In S. Harding (ed.), *Feminism and Methodology: Social Science Issues*, Milton Keynes: Open University Press, 1–28.

Hebb, D. O. 1980. The view from without. *Philosophy of the Social Sciences* 10(3): 309–15.

Held, D. 1980. *Introduction to Critical Theory: Horkheimer to Habermas*. London: Hutchinson.

Heller, A. 1978. The positivism dispute as a turning point in German post-war theory. *New German Critique* 15: 49–56.

—— 1984/85. The discourse ethics of Habermas: Critique and appraisal. *Thesis Eleven* 10/11: 5–17.

Hempel, C. G. 1965. *Aspects of Scientific Explanation*. New York: The Free Press.

Hesse, M. 1980. *Revolutions and Reconstructions in the Philosophy of Science*. Brighton: Harvester.

Hohendahl, P. U. 1985. *The Dialectic of Enlightenment* revisited: Habermas' critique of the Frankfurt School. *New German Critique* 35: 3–26.

Holton, G. 1973. *Thematic Origins of Scientific Thought: Kepler to Einstein*. Cambridge, MA: Harvard University Press.

Hooker, C. A. 1981. Formalist rationality: the limitations of Popper's theory of reason. *Metaphilosophy* 12(3/4): 247–66.

—— 1989. Evolutionary epistemology and naturalist realism. In K. Hahlweg and C. A. Hooker (eds), *Issues in Evolutionary Epistemology*. Albany, NY: State University of New York Press, 101–37.

Horwich, P. 1991. On the nature and norms of theoretical commitment. *Philosophy of Science* 58(1): 1–14.

Huff, T. E. 1996. Can scientific knowledge be Islamized? *Social Epistemology* 10(3/4): 304–16.

Ingram, D. 1993. The limits and possibilities of communicative action for democratic theory. *Political Theory* 21(2): 294–321.

Jackson, F. 1980. Interactionism revives? *Philosophy of the Social Sciences* 10(3): 316–23.

Jones, R. 1991. Realism about what? *Philosophy of Science* 58(2): 185–202.

Juengst, E. T. 1996. Self-critical federal science? The ethics experiment within the U.S. genome project. *Social Philosophy and Policy* 13(2): 63–95.

Keat, R. 1981. *The Politics of Social Theory: Habermas, Freud and the Critique of Positivism*. Oxford: Blackwell.

Keller, E. F. 1985. *Reflections on Gender and Science*. New Haven: Yale University Press.

King-Farlow, J. and Cooper, W. E. 1983. Comments on Farr's paper (I) Sir Karl Popper: Tributes and adjustments. *Philosophy of the Social Sciences* 13: 177–82.

Kitcher, P. and Salmon, W. C. (eds) 1989. *Scientific Explanation*. Minneapolis: University of Minnesota Press.

Klosko, G. 1996. Popper's Plato: An assessment. *Philosophy of the Social Sciences* 26(4): 509–27.

Kneale, W. C. 1974. The demarcation of science. In P. A. Schilpp (ed.), 205–17.

Kolakowski, L. 1972 [1966]. *Positivist Philosophy: From Hume to the Vienna Circle*. Trans. N. Guterman. Harmondsworth: Penguin.

—— 1981. *Main Currents of Marxism. Volume 3*. Trans. P. S. Falla. Oxford: Oxford University Press.

Kornblith, H. (ed.) 1987. *Naturalizing Epistemology*. Cambridge, MA: MIT Press.

Kraft, V. 1953. *The Vienna Circle: The Origins of Neo-positivism*. Trans. A. Pap. New York: Philosophical Library.

—— 1974. Popper and the Vienna Circle. In P. A. Schilpp (ed.), 185–204.

Krige, J. 1978. Popper's epistemology and the autonomy of science. *Social Studies of Science* 8: 287–307.

Kuhn, T. S. 1970 [1962]. *The Structure of Scientific Revolutions*. 2nd edn. Chicago: University of Chicago Press.

—— 1974 [1970]. Reflections on my critics. In I. Lakatos and A. Musgrave (eds), 231–78.

—— 1977. *The Essential Tension*. Chicago: University of Chicago Press.

Lakatos, I. 1970. History of science and its rational reconstructions. In R. C. Buck and R. S. Cohen (eds), *Boston Studies in the Philosophy of Science, VIII*, Dordrecht: D. Reidel, 91–136.

—— 1974 [1970]. Falsification and the methodology of scientific research programmes. In I. Lakatos and A. Musgrave (eds), 191–6.

Lakatos, I. and Musgrave, A. (eds) 1974 [1970]. *Criticism and the Growth of Knowledge*. Cambridge: Cambridge University Press.

Laudan, L. 1981. A problem-solving approach to scientific progress. In I. Hacking (ed.), *Scientific Revolutions*, Oxford: Oxford University Press, 144–55.

—— 1990. Normative naturalism. *Philosophy of Science* 57(1): 44–59.

Laudan, R. and Laudan, L. 1989. Dominance and the disunity of method: Solving the problems of innovation and consensus. *Philosophy of Science* 56(2): 221–37.

Leplin, J. 1986. Methodological realism and scientific rationality. *Philosophy of Science* 53(1): 31–51.

—— 1990. Renormalizing naturalism. *Philosophy of Science* 57(1): 20–33.

Lessnoff, M. H. 1980. Review article: The political philosophy of Karl Popper. *British Journal of Political Science* 10: 99–120.

Levinson, R. B. 1953. *In Defence of Plato*. Cambridge MA: Harvard University Press.

Lukes, S. 1970 [1968]. Methodological individualism reconsidered. In D. Emmet and A. MacIntyre (eds), *Sociological Theory and Philosophical Analysis*, London: Macmillan, 76–88.

Lyons, W. 1995. Introduction. In W. Lyons (ed.), *Modern Philosophy of Mind*, London: J. M. Dent, xlv–lxviii.

Mackie, J. L. 1980 [1974]. *The Cement of the Universe: A Study of Causation*. Oxford: Clarendon Press.

Madell, G. 1988. *Mind and Materialism*. Edinburgh: Edinburgh University Press.

Magee, B. 1973. *Popper*. London: Fontana / Collins.

Marcuse, H. 1973 [1959]. Karl Popper and the problem of historical laws. *Studies in Critical Philosophy*. Boston: Beacon Press, 193–208.

Martin, J. R. 1989. Ideological critiques and the philosophy of science. *Philosophy of Science* 56(1): 1–22.

Maxwell, N. 1972. A critique of Popper's views on scientific method. *Philosophy of Science* 39: 131–52.

McCarthy, T. 1978. *The Critical Theory of Jürgen Habermas*. London: Hutchinson.

McGinn, C. 1989. Can we solve the mind–body problem? *Mind* 98(391): 349–66.

—— 1991. *The Problem of Consciousness*. Oxford: Blackwell.

McIntyre, N. and Popper, K. 1983. The critical attitude in medicine: The need for a new ethics. *British Medical Journal* 287: 1919–23.

McLachlan, H. V. 1980. Popper, Marxism and the nature of social laws. *British Journal of Sociology* 31: 66–77.

Mellor, D. H. 1971. *The Matter of Chance*. Cambridge: Cambridge University Press.

Mill, J. S. 1962. On liberty. In M. Warnock (ed.), *Utilitarianism*. London: Collins.
Miller, D. 1994. *Critical Rationalism: A Restatement and Defence*. Peru, IL: Open Court.
—— 1995. Propensities and determinism. In A. O'Hear (ed.), 121–47.
Miller, H. I. 1996. When politics drives science: Lysenko, Gore and U.S. biotechnology policy. *Social Philosophy and Policy* 13(2): 96–112.
Minogue, K. 1995a. Politics and morality in the thought of Karl Popper. *Government and Opposition* 30(1): 74–85.
—— 1995b. Does Popper explain historical explanation? In A. O'Hear (ed.), 225–40.
Murphy, N. 1990. Scientific realism and postmodern philosophy of science. *British Journal for the Philosophy of Science* 41: 291–303.
Musgrave, A. 1992. Discussion: Realism about what? *Philosophy of Science* 59(4): 691–7.
Nagel, T. 1993. The mind wins! *New York Review of Books* XL(5): 37–41.
Newton-Smith, W. H. 1981. *The Rationality of Science*. London: Routledge and Kegan Paul.
Nickles, T. 1980. Introductory essay: Scientific discovery and the future of the philosophy of science. In T. Nickles (ed.), *Scientific Discovery, Logic, and Rationality*, Dordrecht: D. Reidel, 1–59.
Nola, R. 1987. The status of Popper's theory of scientific method. *British Journal for the Philosophy of Science* 38: 441–80.
Norman, W. J. 1993. A democratic theory for a democratizing world? A reassessment of Popper's political realism. *Political Studies* 41(2): 252–68.
O'Hear, A. 1980. *Karl Popper*. London: Routledge and Kegan Paul.
—— 1985. Critical notice. *Mind* XCIV(375): 453–71.
—— 1989. Evolution, knowledge, and self-consciousness. *Inquiry* 32(2): 127–50.
O'Hear, A. (ed.) 1995. *Karl Popper: Philosophy and Problems*. Cambridge: Cambridge University Press.
Overend, T. 1978. Enquiry and ideology: Habermas' trichotomous conception of science. *Philosophy of the Social Sciences* 8(1): 1–13.
Papineau, D. 1989. Has Popper been a good thing? In K. Gavroglu et al. (eds), 431–40.
Parekh, B. C. 1982. *Contemporary Political Thinkers*. Oxford: Martin Robertson.
Penrose, R. 1994. *Shadows of the Mind: A Search for the Missing Science of Consciousness*. Oxford: Oxford University Press.
Petras, J. 1966. Popperism: The scarcity of reason. *Science and Society* XXX: 1–10.
Pickel, A. 1989. Never ask who should rule: Karl Popper and political theory. *Canadian Journal of Political Science* 22(1): 83–105.
Polanyi, M. 1958. *Personal Knowledge: Towards a Post-Critical Philosophy*. London: Routledge and Kegan Paul.
—— 1966. *The Tacit Dimension*. New York: Doubleday Anchor.
Popper, K. R. 1948. What can logic do for philosophy? *Proceedings of the Aristotelian Society, Supplementary Volume XXII: Logical Positivism and Ethics*. London: Harrison and Sons, 141–54.
—— 1950. Indeterminism in quantum physics and in classical physics: Part I. *British Journal for the Philosophy of Science* 1(3): 173–95.
—— 1957. The propensity interpretation of the calculus of probability, and the quantum theory. In S. Körner (ed.), *Observation and Interpretation*, New York: Dover, 88–9.

—— 1959. The propensity interpretation of probability. *British Journal for the Philosophy of Science* 10(37): 25–42.

—— 1967. Quantum mechanics without 'The Observer'. In M. Bunge (ed.), *Quantum Theory and Reality: Studies in the Foundations, Methodology, and Philosophy of Science, Volume 2*, Berlin: Springer-Verlag, 7–44.

—— 1969. A pluralist approach to the philosophy of history. In E. Streissler (ed.), *Roads to Freedom: Essays in Honour of Friedrich A. von Hayek*, London: Routledge and Kegan Paul, 181–200.

—— 1972 [1971]. On reason and the open society: A conversation. *Encounter* 38(5): 13–18.

—— 1973a [1971]. Conversation with Karl Popper. In B. Magee, *Modern British Philosophy*, St Albans: Paladin, 88–107.

—— 1973b. Indeterminism is not enough: A philosophical essay. *Encounter* 40(4): 20–6.

—— 1974a [1970]. Normal science and its dangers. In I. Lakatos and A. Musgrave (eds), 51–8.

—— 1974b. Replies to my critics. In P. A. Schilpp (ed.), 961–1197.

—— 1976a [1962]. The logic of the social sciences. In T. W. Adorno et al., 87–104.

—— 1976b [1970]. Reason or revolution? In T. W. Adorno et al., 288–300.

—— 1984. Evolutionary epistemology. In J. W. Pollard (ed.), *Evolutionary Theory: Paths into the Future*. Chichester: Wiley, 239–55.

—— 1985 [1967]. The rationality principle. In D. Miller (ed.), *Popper Selections*, Princeton: Princeton University Press, 357–65.

—— 1987 [1977]. Natural selection and the emergence of mind. In G. Radnitzky and W. W. Bartley III (eds), 139–55.

—— 1988. *The Open Society and its Enemies* revisited. *Economist* 23 April: 23–6.

—— 1992. *In Search of a Better World*. London: Routledge.

—— 1994a [1969]. *The Myth of the Framework*. Ed. M. A. Notturno. London: Routledge.

—— 1994b [1969]. *Knowledge and the Body–Mind Problem*. Ed. M. A. Notturno. London: Routledge.

Popper, K. R. and Eccles, J. 1974. Falsifiability and freedom. In F. Elders (ed.), *Reflexive Water*, London: Souvenir Press, 69–131.

Putnam, H. 1978. *Meaning and the Moral Sciences*. Boston: Routledge and Kegan Paul.

—— 1982. Three kinds of scientific realism. *Philosophical Quarterly* 32(128): 195–200.

—— 1987. *The Many Faces of Realism*. La Salle, IL: Open Court.

Quine, W. V. O. 1963 [1953]. *From a Logical Point of View*. 2nd edn, revised. New York: Harper and Row.

Quinton, A. 1967. Karl Raimund Popper. In P. Edwards (ed.), *The Encyclopedia of Philosophy, vol. 6*, New York: Macmillan, 398–401.

—— 1976a. Social objects. *Proceedings of the Aristotelian Society* 76: 1–27.

—— 1976b. Karl Popper: Politics without essences. In A. de Crespigny and K. Minogue (eds), *Contemporary Political Philosophers*, London: Methuen, 147–67.

Radnitzky, G. 1970. *Contemporary Schools of Metascience*. Göteborg: Scandinavian University Press.

Radnitzky, G. and Bartley III, W. W. (eds) 1987: *Evolutionary Epistemology, Theory of Rationality, and the Sociology of Knowledge*. La Salle, IL: Open Court.

Ravetz, J. R. 1973. *Scientific Knowledge and its Social Problems*. Harmondsworth: Penguin.

—— 1984. Ideological commitments and the philosophy of science. *Radical Philosophy* Summer: 5–12.

Ray, L. J. 1979. Critical theory and positivism: Popper and the Frankfurt School. *Philosophy of the Social Sciences* 9: 149–73.

Reiss, H. 1970. Introduction. *Kant's Political Writings*. Trans. H. B. Nisbet. Cambridge: Cambridge University Press, 1–40.

Rosenberg, A. 1990. Normative naturalism and the role of philosophy. *Philosophy of Science* 57(1): 34–43.

Ruse, M. 1986a. *Taking Darwin Seriously: A Naturalistic Approach to Philosophy*. Oxford: Blackwell.

—— 1986b. Evolutionary ethics: A phoenix arisen. *Zygon* 21(1): 94–112.

Ryan, A. 1970a. *The Philosophy of John Stuart Mill*. London: Macmillan.

—— 1970b. *The Philosophy of the Social Sciences*. London: Macmillan.

—— 1985. Popper and liberalism. In G. Currie and A. Musgrave (eds), 89–104.

Sachs, M. 1985. *The Open Universe*: An argument for indeterminism. *Philosophy of the Social Sciences* 15: 205–10.

Salmon, W. C. 1981. Rational prediction. *British Journal for the Philosophy of Science* 32: 115–25.

Schilpp, P. A. (ed.) 1974. *The Philosophy of Karl Popper*. 2 vols. La Salle, IL: Open Court.

Schochet, G. J. 1974. Quentin Skinner's method. *Political Theory* 2(3): 261–76.

Searle, G. 1992. *The Rediscovery of the Mind*. Cambridge, MA: MIT Press.

Settle, T., Jarvie, I. C. and Agassi, J. 1974. Towards a theory of openness to criticism. *Philosophy of the Social Sciences* 4: 83–90.

Shapere, D. 1993. Discussion: Astronomy and antirealism. *Philosophy of Science* 60(1): 134–50.

Shaw, P. D. 1971. Popper, historicism, and the remaking of society. *Philosophy of the Social Sciences* 1: 299–308.

Shearmur, J. 1995. Epistemology and human nature in Popper's political theory: A reply to Stokes. *Political Studies* 43(1): 124–30.

—— 1996. *The Political Thought of Karl Popper*. London: Routledge.

Siegel, H. 1989. Philosophy of science naturalized? Some problems with Giere's naturalism. *Studies in the History and Philosophy of Science* 20(3): 365–75.

Skinner, Q. 1974. Some problems in the analysis of political thought and action. *Political Theory* 2(3): 272–302.

Stockman, N. 1983. *Antipositivist Theories of the Sciences*. Dordrecht: D. Reidel.

Stokes, G. 1984. Karl Popper's critique of utopianism. *Flinders Journal of History and Politics* 10: 108–17.

——1989. From physics to biology: Rationality in Popper's conception of evolutionary epistemology. In K. Hahlweg and C. A. Hooker (eds), *Issues in Evolutionary Epistemology*, Albany, NY: State University of New York Press, 488–509.

—— 1995a. Politics, epistemology and method: Karl Popper's conception of human nature. *Political Studies* 43(1): 105–23.

—— 1995b. Popper and human nature revisited. *Political Studies* 43(1): 131–5.

Stretton, H. 1969. *The Political Sciences*. London: Routledge and Kegan Paul.

Stump, D. 1992. Naturalized philosophy of science with a plurality of methods. *Philosophy of Science* 59(3): 456–60.

Suchting, W. A. 1972. Marx, Popper, and 'historicism'. *Inquiry* 15: 235–66.

Taylor, C. 1973. Neutrality in political science. In A. Ryan (ed.), *The Philosophy of Social Explanation*, London: Oxford University Press, 139–70.

—— 1979a. What's wrong with negative liberty? In A. Ryan (ed.), *The Idea of Freedom*, Oxford: Oxford University Press, 175–93.

—— 1979b. *Hegel and Modern Society*. Cambridge: Cambridge University Press.

—— 1980. Understanding in human science. *Review of Metaphysics* 34: 25–38.

Thomas, D. 1979. *Naturalism and Social Science: A Post-Empiricist Philosophy of Social Science*. Cambridge: Cambridge University Press.

Thompson, J. 1984/85. Discourse and rationality. *Thesis Eleven* 10/11: 110–26.

Thompson, J. B. and Held, D. 1982. Editors' introduction. In J. B. Thompson and D. Held (eds), *Habermas: Critical Debates*, London: Macmillan, 1–20.

Tianji, J. 1985. Scientific rationality, formal or informal? *British Journal for the Philosophy of Science* 36: 409–23.

Tuchanska, B. 1992. What is explained in science? *Philosophy of Science* 59(1): 102–19.

Urbach, P. 1978. Is any of Popper's arguments against historicism valid? *British Journal for the Philosophy of Science* 29: 117–30.

van Fraassen, B. C. 1980. *The Scientific Image*. Oxford: Clarendon Press.

van Rooijen, J. 1987. Interactionism and evolution: A critique of Popper. *British Journal for the Philosophy of Science* 38: 87–92.

Wachbroit, R. 1986. Progress: Metaphysical and otherwise. *Philosophy of Science* 53(3): 354–71.

Waldron, J. 1985. Making sense of critical dualism. In G. Currie and A. Musgrave (eds), 105–19.

Walker, R. C. S. 1978. *Kant*. London: Routledge and Kegan Paul.

Warnock, G. J. 1960. Review of *The Logic of Scientific Discovery*. *Mind* 69: 99–101.

Wartofsky, M. W. 1976. The relation between philosophy of science and history of science. In R. S. Cohen et al. (eds), 717–37.

Watkins, J. W. N. 1958. Epistemology and politics. *Proceedings of the Aristotelian Society* 58: 79–102.

—— 1974. The unity of Popper's thought. In P. A. Schilpp (ed.), 371–412.

—— 1984. *Science and Scepticism*. Princeton: Princeton University Press.

—— 1995. Popper and Darwinism. In A. O'Hear (ed.), 191–206.

Weatherford, R. 1991. *The Implications of Determinism*. London and New York: Routledge.

Weber, M. 1949. 'Objectivity' in social science and social policy. In M. Weber, *The Methodology of the Social Sciences*, New York: The Free Press, 49–112.

—— 1970. Politics as a vocation. In H. H. Gerth and C. W. Mills (eds), *From Max Weber*, London: Routledge and Kegan Paul, 77–128.

—— 1978. *Economy and Society*. Trans. E. Fischoff et al. Eds G. Roth and C. Wittich. Berkeley: University of California Press.

Wellmer, A. 1971. *Critical Theory of Society*. New York: Herder and Herder.

—— 1990. *The Persistence of Modernity*. Trans. D. Midgley. Cambridge, MA: MIT Press.

Wettersten, J. 1992. *The Roots of Critical Rationalism*. Atlanta, GA: Rodopi.

—— 1995. Styles of rationality. *Philosophy of the Social Sciences* 25(1): 69–98.

White, S. 1988. *The Recent Work of Jürgen Habermas*. Cambridge: Cambridge University Press.

Wild, J. 1974. Popper's interpretation of Plato. In P.A. Schilpp (ed.), 859–75.

Williams, D. E. 1989. *Truth, Hope and Power: The Thought of Karl Popper*. Toronto: University of Toronto Press.

Wilson, H. T. 1976. Science, critique, and criticism: The 'Open Society' revisited. In J. O'Neill (ed.), *On Critical Theory*, New York: Seabury, 205–30.

—— 1981. Response to Ray. *Philosophy of the Social Sciences* 11(1): 45–8.

—— 1986a. Critical theory's critique of social science: Episodes in a changing problematic from Adorno to Habermas, Part I. *History of European Ideas* 7(2): 127–47.

—— 1986b. Critical theory's critique of social science: Episodes in a changing problematic from Adorno to Habermas, Part II. *History of European Ideas* 7(3): 287–302.

Worrall, J. 1982. Scientific realism and scientific change. *Philosophical Quarterly* 32(128): 201–31.

Ziman, J. M. 1987. The problem of 'problem choice'. *Minerva* 25(1–2): 92–106.

Index